THE WORLD'S CLASSICS

330

THE ENGLISH CONSTITUTION

Oxford University Press, Ely House, London W. 1

GLASGOW NEW YORK TORONTO MELBOURNE WELLINGTON
CAPE TOWN SALISBURY IBADAN NAIROBI LUSAKA ADDIS ABABA
BOMBAY CALCUTTA MADRAS KARACHI LAHORE DACCA
KUALA LUMPUR HONG KONG TOKYO

THE
ENGLISH CONSTITUTION

By
WALTER BAGEHOT

With an Introduction by
THE FIRST
EARL OF BALFOUR

LONDON
OXFORD UNIVERSITY PRESS

WALTER BAGEHOT

Born at Langport, Somersetshire, 3 February 1826
Died at Langport, Somersetshire, 24 March 1877

The English Constitution *was first published in* 1867;
a second edition, with an additional chapter, appeared in
1872. *In* The World's Classics *it was first published in*
1928, *and reprinted in* 1929, 1933, 1936, 1942, 1944,
1949, 1952, 1955, 1958, 1961, 1963, *and* 1968

PRINTED IN GREAT BRITAIN

INTRODUCTION

I

CONSTITUTIONAL treatises are not usually regarded as light reading, yet surely he who thinks Bagehot's 'English Constitution' dull must have brought a dull mind to its perusal. The theme no doubt is weighty. But the author has treated it with an easy originality of manner and method which should make it as attractive to readers of this generation as to us who first read it some sixty years ago. Critics of manner may perhaps allege that the style occasionally wants finish; but they must be hard to please if they deny that it is forcible, rapid, high-spirited, and clear,—that it is always spontaneous and never lacks point.

To my thinking the method is as characteristic as the manner, and not less excellent. It is possible to theorize about politics in many different ways and from many different points of view. Constitutions may be traced historically, described legally, compared critically. The writer may be more concerned to tell us what they have been, ought to be, or will be, than to tell us what they are;—and he is often more competent to do so. The field therefore is large, and, unless I mistake him, Bagehot was not by temperament averse to far-reaching generalizations. But in the volume of 1867 he wisely narrowed his main theme to a single question—how in the years round about 1865-6 (years within his own personal experience) was the work of governing

Great Britain actually performed? He did not pedantically eschew illustrative material. But he never wholly lost sight of his main subject and was rarely faithless to his method.

What was that method? It can perhaps best be understood from a judgement which, in one of his essays, he passes on the author of an unsuccessful political biography,[1] namely that he 'did not look *closely and for himself* at real political life'. Bagehot was not infallible. But he *did* practise his own precepts; he *did* look *closely and for himself* at real political life. Hence his ceaseless endeavours to discover how public business was in fact transacted, as distinguished from the way in which its transaction was officially described; hence the contempt with which this master of political writing regarded what he called the 'literary' view of constitutional procedure.

The political life at which he 'looked closely and for himself' was of great interest. At home the generation of statesmen who fought over the first Reform Bill was dead or dying. Grey, Melbourne, Wellington, Peel, Aberdeen had gone. Palmerston died (in office) while Bagehot was writing. Derby and Russell were about to leave the political stage; Disraeli and Gladstone were about to fill it. The Reform Bill of 1867, which began the new era, was passed immediately after the collected essays were first published, and about five years before the Introduction was written which constituted the only change in the edition of 1872.

In foreign affairs the first of the three Bismarckian

[1] Macknight's *Life of Bolingbroke*.

wars which made the German Empire was over; the second took place while he was writing; the third, followed by the change in France from the Imperial to the Republican régime, occurred shortly before the appearance of the second edition.

In the United States the Civil War was finished, and the constitutional disputes following on the murder of Lincoln were fresh in every one's recollection.

It was in this historical setting that Bagehot wrote his essays, and the fact is of some importance. It not only explains the allusions to passing events in Britain with which he enlivens his pages, but explains why almost all his foreign illustrations were drawn from America and not from Europe. In 1866 the only great nation which had experience of free institutions outside Great Britain was America. United Italy was in its infancy. France was under Napoleon III. Austria and Russia were Empires of the continental type; Imperial Germany was in the making. But no one denied that the United States had for nearly three generations flourished exceedingly under free institutions largely of their own devising. It was natural therefore that he should look across the Atlantic if he desired to find a parallel, and perhaps a contrast, to the constitution he had undertaken to discuss.

For purposes of illustration he could not, I suppose, have done better. For the part of the British constitution which most interested him, and on which, as I think, he did his best work, was the one most obscured by 'literary' treatment, and least like anything to be found in the United States. Its real character could best be understood not through a study of its origins, but by comparing and, if need be, contrasting it, with its great contemporary across the sea. This he called the Presidential system; the British practice he described as the Cabinet system; and if his readers desire to understand his conceptions of the latter, they cannot do better than observe where and how the two most obviously differ.

I will venture to offer them a very summary comparison of my own.

Under the Presidential system the effective head of the national administration is elected for a fixed term. He is (practically) irremovable. Even if he is proved to be inefficient, even if he becomes unpopular, even if his policy is unacceptable to the majority of his countrymen, he and his methods must be endured till the moment comes for a new election.

He is aided by Ministers who, however able or distinguished, have no independent political status, have probably had no congressional training, and are by law precluded from obtaining any during their term of office.

Under the Cabinet system everything is different. The head of the administration, commonly called the Prime Minister (though he has no statutory position), is selected for the place on the ground that he is the statesman best qualified to secure the support of a majority in the House of Commons. He retains it only so long as that support is forthcoming. He is the head of his Party. He must be a member of one or other of the two Houses of Parliament; and he must be competent to 'lead' the House to which he belongs. While the Cabinet Ministers of a President are merely his officials, the Prime Minister is *primus inter pares* in a Cabinet of which (according to peace-time practice) every member must, like himself, have had some parliamentary experience, and gained some parliamentary reputation.

The President's powers are defined by the Constitution, and for their exercise (within the law) he is responsible to no man. The Prime Minister and his Cabinet, on the other hand, are restrained by no written constitution; but they are faced by critics and rivals whose position, though entirely unofficial, is as 'constitutional' as their own; they are subject to a perpetual stream of unfriendly questions to which they must make public reply; and they may at any moment be dismissed from power by a hostile vote.

From these points of view the position of a President is far stronger than that of a Prime Minister; for he cannot be expelled from office, and his powers cannot be curtailed. But there is another side to the picture. His prerogatives, though unassailable, are narrowly limited. He commands all the forces of the Republic, but he cannot legislate. He can appoint whom he will to office, but the Senate must approve. If his policy involves the smallest doses either of legislation or taxation (and what large policy does not?) it rests with Congress to supply them;—and Congress may be hostile. He may pursue any foreign policy he pleases, and negotiate what treaties he thinks fit. But after his negotiations have been successfully carried through they will be entirely barren unless two-thirds of the Senate are prepared to agree with him,—and again the Senate may be hostile.

Now the position of a Prime Minister, so much weaker intrinsically than that of a President, is often stronger where co-operation is required, because he belongs essentially to a co-operative system,—a system in which nothing is self-supporting, in which all the working parts are interdependent. He and his Cabinet must co-operate or there would be no Government. His Government and the House of Commons' majority which supports it must co-operate, or the Government must resign. Moreover, these needs are not unilateral; they are mutual. The party majority which refuse to support their leaders not only hamper a policy which (be it good or bad) is that of their Government, but they probably injure their own electoral prospects. Leaders who refuse to work together not only weaken their Cabinet and their Party, but probably do little to strengthen their own political position. An administration whose policy unduly strains the loyalty of any large section of its supporters is obviously making things easy for its opponents.

It would seem, then, that Cabinet Government after the British model is more closely knit than Presidential Government after the American model, —and this not because America is a federal country while Britain is a unitary one, but because the great men who founded the Republic deliberately preferred a system in which the task of conducting national affairs was entrusted to three independent organs of Government, dissimilar in character, chosen at different times, for different periods, with different duties, by electorates differently constructed, each justly claiming to be the choice of the people. There is no constitutional reason why the President, the Senate and the House of Representatives should co-operate to carry out any common policy; and it is easy to imagine cases in which they would be reluctant to do so. If these were to occur when unity and rapidity of national action were required, the country would have to trust to the political genius of its people rather than to the formal machinery provided for it by the constitution.

The weaknesses of the British constitution are of a very different character. Whatever be its faults, it certainly does not suffer from too elaborate a system of checks and balances. The House of Commons need not keep a Government in office a day longer than it likes. But if the majority decide to keep it, evidently they have every inducement to provide the money and pass the laws which the policy of that Government requires. They form part of a co-operative system, they are an element in an interdependent whole; and if we look at that whole from Bagehot's point of view, from the point of view of the business man contemplating the two-Party system, and asking himself how the business of the community can be carried on through so unwieldy a body as the British Parliament, the British form of Cabinet Government seems simple and effective.

In considering a constitution whose changes have

so often been of the silent sort, unmarked either by revolutionary violence or dramatic legislation, we are apt to lose our way for want of chronological landmarks, and our sense of proportion for want of political standards. To my thinking at least, the gradual growth and final establishment of the Cabinet system has been of greater importance than anything in our constitutional history since the Revolution settlement,—greater, for instance, than the series of Reform Bills which began in 1832. It never became a Party watchword; it was never clamoured for by a mob; it has never been recognized by statute; nor can any man tell us exactly when it became fully effective. But now that it is embedded in the very centre of constitutional practice we can see that it involves two or three familiar consequences. The first is that as between the Houses of Parliament the House on which all Governments depend for their existence must be the House which *leads*. The second is that the House which leads, if it is to do its work, must be an organized body, not a mob. The third is that, so far as we know, the only kind of organization natural to a free assembly, and sufficiently flexible to be in touch with public opinion, is organization by Party. The first of these doctrines must obviously affect our views on the House of Lords; the second and third, less obviously, but as I think in a much more important fashion, ought greatly to influence our views on the modern position of the Crown. To these topics I now turn.

II

It might perhaps be thought that after his brilliant analysis of Cabinet Government there was little for Bagehot to say about the British Constitution except by way of epilogue. He had made a resolute effort to penetrate the legal forms and ceremonial trappings which cluster round ancient institutions till he reached the core of our national administration. He had insistently inquired how we—a self-governing community—did in fact govern ourselves; and to all seeming he had found the answer. We govern ourselves through a Cabinet, selected from the legislature, presided over by a Prime Minister, and entirely dependent on a House of Commons which we ourselves have chosen. What more is there to be said? It is true that we have a Second Chamber; but it plays, and in modern times has always played, a secondary part. It is true that we have a Monarchy; but what, under the Cabinet system, can the Monarch have to do but act on the advice of his Ministers, take the supreme part on great ceremonial occasions, and assist works of general beneficence by his sympathy and patronage? Or (to translate these questions into Bagehot's peculiar terminology) since the 'efficient parts' of the constitution work so well, why trouble much about the parts which are predominantly 'dignified'?

To this question Bagehot would, I think, have replied *in the first place* that in the case both of the House of Lords and the Monarchy there are 'efficient' as well as 'dignified' elements to be taken into account. And no doubt he is right. During the

last 140 years or so in which the making of constitutions has greatly occupied the Western World,
the need for a Second Chamber has rarely been
successfully disputed; and the House of Lords,
though not the invention of constitution-makers,
has long and honourably filled that position. It has
never striven for domination. It has never been
corrupt. Its errors, or what we now deem to have
been its errors, were shared by great bodies of en-
lightened contemporary opinion. Its debates have
been distinguished. Quite apart from controversial
politics it has done, and is doing, excellent work in
Private Bill legislation, and (when time permits)
non-party revision of Measures sent up to it from
the House of Commons. It is, I suppose, richer in
eminent specialists than the other House, and it certainly provides them with much fuller opportunities
for expressing their views in Parliamentary debate.[1]

[1] Bagehot, in his chapter on the House of Lords, seems,
I think, to have committed (I admit in very good company) a theoretical error which is not without importance.
He talks as if the creation of Peers by the Crown was the
'remedy' provided by the Constitution for a deadlock
between Lords and Commons. But this is really misleading. When there is a difference of opinion between
the President of the U.S.A. and Congress about a piece
of legislation which the latter has passed and the former
has declined to sanction, the difficulty may be got over
by Congress passing it again with a two-thirds majority.
This really *is* a constitutional remedy; for it solves the
immediate problem, and leaves the constitution unaltered. We cannot say as much for the *ad hoc* creation
of Peers. It is true that on the only occasion on which
the Royal prerogative was thus used or mis-used the
change in the House of Lords was small. Twelve new
Tory Peers were sufficient to sanction what Bagehot in

Whether in addition to these functions it can in these days, with its present constitution, efficiently perform the duties of 'delay and revision' assigned to it by Bagehot is another matter. I do not propose to discuss this subject here, partly because it would take me on to ground more controversial than befits this peaceful preface, partly because the space at my command will be better occupied with the reflections suggested by Bagehot's treatment of the third characteristic element in our Constitution,—I mean the Monarchy.

Here also Bagehot found elements which belonged to the 'efficient' rather than to the 'dignified' parts of our Constitution. He held (most rightly) that, quite apart from forms and ceremonies, a Monarch of experience and capacity, fully informed on public affairs, and in close personal touch with his Ministers, would always be a most valuable element in the body politic. He thought the post of 'Sovereign 'over an intelligent and political people was the post 'which a wise man would choose above any other ' (p. 66). And, since he was certainly a wise man, who, in spite of not infrequent gibes, regarded the English as a 'political and intelligent people', we may assume that he would have been well pleased had

his essay on Bolingbroke called 'a mean peace effected by desertion'. But cases might easily be imagined in which one or two applications of this 'constitutional remedy' under modern conditions would practically destroy the historic Constitution so far as a Second Chamber is concerned. I am not arguing, be it observed, that this operation would necessarily be wrong. That is not my business. I am only observing that it should be called by its right name. It should not be a remedy but a revolution.

Destiny placed him on the throne. With some naïveté he has indicated the sort of speech that on fitting occasions such a King might make to his Ministers. He would address them (it appears) somewhat as follows:

> 'The responsibility of these measures is upon you. Whatever you think best must be done. Whatever you think best shall have my full and effectual support. *But* you will observe that for this reason and that reason what you propose to do is bad; for this reason and that reason what you do not propose is better. I do not oppose, it is my duty not to oppose; but observe that I *warn*' (p. 67).

There is a certain unintended humour in this sketch of an imaginary address by an imaginary Monarch to imaginary Ministers on the problems raised by an imaginary crisis. Its object, however, is clear enough, and no one need criticize its substance. It is at any rate in perfect harmony with Bagehot's view that constitutional Kings, *if* they possess character, ability, and industry, may even in matters of pure policy do very valuable service to the State.

But he was haunted by the 'if'. He argued that no long hereditary line, be it of Kings or be it of peasants, can maintain a steady level of excellence through many generations. In a Royal line there would doubtless be Queen Victorias and Prince Alberts. But there would also be George the Thirds and George the Fourths;—in other words, there would be men of character and industry but little ability; there would also be men of some ability but no character and little industry. Both these varieties, and others that could easily be imagined, must, even at the best, make an occasional appearance. When that happened we should have a 'bad Monarch', and (says Bagehot) while 'the benefits of 'a good monarch are almost invaluable, the evils of 'a bad monarch are almost irreparable' (p. 78).

Presumably this (surely somewhat excessive) estimate of Royal influence refers rather to social than to political affairs, and is therefore scarcely within the compass of a discussion on the Constitution. Let us then turn to politics proper, and consider his views on the Monarchy regarded as representing the 'dignified' side of our institutions. They are easily summarized. He thought it a national necessity, but a necessity born of our national weaknesses. On both these points his opinions were expressed with all his usual vigour. As regards *necessity*, he tells us, for example, that the 'use of the Queen (Victoria) in a dignified capa-'city is incalculable'; that 'without her in England 'the English Government would fail and pass away' (p. 30); and that 'the "efficient" part (*i.e.* the Cabinet 'system) depends upon the "dignified" part for the 'power which the "efficient" part requires but cannot 'itself produce'. As regards the national weaknesses which produced the necessity, he is quite as uncompromising; but his theories here require a commentary which I cannot omit, yet cannot compress into a few paragraphs.

Bagehot, it appears, was profoundly impressed by the inequalities he observed in the mental equipment of different sections of the community. He tells us that 'the lower orders, the middle orders, are 'still, when tried by the standard of the educated

'"ten thousand", narrow-minded, unintelligent,
'incurious'. And, he adds a little farther on, 'a
'philosophy which does not ceaselessly remember,
'which does not continually obtrude, the palpable
'difference of the various parts (of the population)
'will be a theory radically false' (p. 6). This is
certainly not a fault with which his own philosophy can be justly charged. But what was the
moral he drew from these uncomfortable reflections? It was that since the population consists of
educated thousands and unintelligent millions we
must count ourselves fortunate in the possession of
a Constitution which has two aspects, appealing
respectively to the intelligence of the few and the
emotions of the many. For the educated thousands
there is the 'efficient' aspect, the whole system of
Parliaments, Cabinets, Party Government, and the
rest. For the unintelligent millions there is the
'dignified' aspect (described also as 'theatrical',
'mystical', 'religious', or 'semi-religious'), which
delights the eye, stirs the imagination, supplies
motive power to the whole political system, and yet
never strains the intellectual resources of the most
ignorant or the most stupid. It is, of course, bound
up with the Monarchy; indeed to all intents and
purposes it *is* the Monarchy. It provides the disguise which happily prevents the ordinary Englishman from discovering that he is not living under a
Monarchy but under a Republic;—for (says Bagehot) 'it is only a disguised Republic which is suited
'to such a being as the Englishman in such a century
'as the nineteenth'.

Our author indeed does not attempt to conceal

the friendly surprise (flavoured with a little contempt?) with which he regards those of his countrymen (unhappily the vast majority) who are taken
in by this travesty. 'So well is our Government
'concealed,' he says, 'that if you tell a cabman to
'drive to Downing Street he will most likely never
'have heard of it.' But, except in the interest of his
profession, why should the cabman have heard of
it? The implied criticism, of course, is that while
he would certainly know Buckingham Palace where
Queen Victoria was performing her 'dignified'
duties, he knew nothing of Downing Street where
her Cabinet was 'efficiently' carrying on the real
business of Government. But need such ignorance
provoke either surprise or blame? If the cabman
was a strong Party man it is even chances that he
regarded the Cabinet Ministers then meeting in
Downing Street as a danger to their country. If
he was not a strong Party man it may well be that
he regarded them as (for the moment) the successful
competitors in the game of 'ins' and 'outs';—a game
played between opponents who called themselves
by different names, but, so far as he could see, did
very much the same kind of thing in very much the
same kind of way whenever they had the chance.

These are the familiar comments indulged in by
the hostile and the indifferent on each successive
occupant of that historic street. Praise, of course, is
not withheld; but as a rule it is cooler and somewhat
more qualified. In past years, for example, I have
known it taking the form of thanking Heaven that
the 'right people' were in Office, while lamenting
the ill fortune which had prevented them from

making full use of the opportunities provided by a faithful but disillusioned Party.

Now why should the meeting-place of an unconnected succession of administrations, thus criticized, thus observed, and thus defended, differing from each other in opinion and glorying in their differences, arouse patriotic feelings in the ordinary citizen? Patriotism involves conceptions of unity and continuity. The coldest patriot recognizes himself as part (by birth or adoption) of an enduring 'Whole'. He has feelings, however vague, about its past. He entertains, however faintly, hopes and fears about its future. How can the machinery of Cabinet Government either suggest or strengthen sentiments like these, even at their lowest level? It assumes their existence. It cannot perform its duties without them. But are they its natural product? Admittedly it works through Party at every stage—Party Cabinets in Downing Street, Party majorities in the House of Commons, Party majorities in the constituencies. These cannot of themselves give us unity, because they are at once the product and the instrument of partisan separations. They cannot of themselves give us continuity, because partisan majorities have ever proved unstable. They do the Nation's work and on the whole do it well; but is it not at the cost of deepening and hardening national divisions? If therefore Bagehot's cabman sought a shrine symbolic of his country's unity and continuity rather than of its controversies and quarrels, evidently it was to Buckingham Palace that he should have looked rather than to Downing Street.

I am disposed therefore to think that while Bagehot showed admirable skill in penetrating through external forms to administrative realities, he was not equally successful in penetrating through administrative realities to the national qualities which underlie them and make them possible. Indeed he hardly tried. Though the many uncomplimentary things he says about our national incapacities suffice to show that there is a problem to be solved, he made little effort to solve it. He held (as we know) that the vast majority of his fellow countrymen were 'narrow-minded, incurious, unintelligent', moved for the most part rather by the outward shows than the inner verities of their constitution. Yet he would never have denied that throughout their history they had shown themselves eminently fitted for self-government. He thought them individually incapable of comprehending its 'efficient' parts. Yet he would certainly have owned that, collectively, they have given to the world an example of ordered freedom and reasonable statesmanship which nations not of English race or speech have never found it easy to equal. He would have owned that the institutions under which we are now living have neither been copied from an alien model, nor invented by domestic theorists, but are to all appearance the unpremeditated product of our qualities helped by our good fortune. To complete the bundle of paradoxes, his own teaching seems to show that while this country as a whole yields to no other in its corporate sense of unity and continuity, the working parts of its political system are organized (with two exceptions to be mentioned presently) on a Party basis,—in other words, on systematized differences and unresolved discords.

The lines on which a solution of these problems can best be sought has already been indicated, but Bagehot never followed them for any distance. If we would find the true basis of the long-drawn process which has gradually converted medieval monarchy into a modern democracy, the process by which so much has been changed and so little destroyed, we must study temperament and character rather than intellect and theory. This is a truth which those who recommend the wholesale adoption of British institutions in strange lands might remember with advantage. Such an experiment can hardly be without its dangers. Constitutions are easily copied, temperaments are not; and if it should happen that the borrowed constitution and the native temperament fail to correspond, the misfit may have serious results. It matters little what other gifts a people may possess if they are wanting in those which, from this point of view, are of most importance. If, for example, they have no capacity for grading their loyalties as well as for being moved by them; if they have no natural inclination to liberty and no natural respect for law; if they lack good humour and tolerate foul play; if they know not how to compromise or when; if they have not that distrust of extreme conclusions which is sometimes misdescribed as want of logic; if corruption does not repel them; and if their divisions tend to be either too numerous or too profound, the successful working of British institutions may be difficult or impossible. It may indeed be least possible where the arts of Parliamentary persuasion and the dexterities of Party management are brought to their highest perfection.

Should any one be inclined to regard this as an overstatement, let him seriously consider these last qualifications for Cabinet Government. Let him note how difficult it would be to work the system even in the country of its origin, if the House of Commons instead of being organized by division into two main Parties or three, were disorganized by division into (say) half-a-dozen of approximately equal strength. And if this vision of confusion and intrigue fails to move him, let him consider another hypothesis. Let the political parties be reduced to two (admittedly the most convenient number for Cabinet Government), but let the chasm dividing them be so profound that a change of Administration would in fact be a revolution disguised under a constitutional procedure. Does not this illustration, like the first, show how delicate is the political machinery whose smooth working we usually take as a matter of course?

It may perhaps be replied that if a majority of the House of Commons want a revolution they ought to have one; and no doubt if the House of Commons on this point fully represented the settled convictions of the community the reply suffices. But if not? Is there any means of ensuring that in these extreme cases the House of Commons *would* represent the settled will of the community? Is there any ground for expecting that our Cabinet system, admirably fitted to adjust political action to the ordinary oscillations of public opinion, could

deal with these violent situations? Could it long sur-
vive the shocks of revolutionary and counter-revolu-
tionary violence? I know not. The experiment has
never been tried. Our alternating Cabinets, though
belonging to different Parties, have never differed
about the foundations of society. And it is evident
that our whole political machinery pre-supposes a
people so fundamentally at one that they can safely
afford to bicker; and so sure of their own moderation that they are not dangerously disturbed by the
never-ending din of political conflict. May it
always be so.

III

These observations bring us back to the question
whether, apart from character and temperament,
there are within the constitution itself elements able
to mitigate the stresses and strains inseparable from
party warfare.

I think there are two,—the Public Services and
the Crown. Great indeed are the differences
between them. The Public Services are no more
than a wheel in the 'efficient' part of our constitutional machinery. The Crown is typical of the
'dignified' part. The Public Services are (so to
speak) below Party. The Crown is above it. Yet
both of them are, in a very real sense, independent
of it, and both are indispensable.

Of the Public Services generally, and the Civil
Service in particular, I need say little. They do not
control policy; they are not responsible for it.
Belonging to no Party, they are for that very reason
an invaluable element in Party Government. It
is through them, especially through their higher

branches, that the transference of responsibility from one Party or one Minister to another involves no destructive shock to the administrative machine. There may be change of direction, but the curve is smooth. If administrative continuity has (so far) been quite unbroken even by the most abrupt vicissitudes of Party warfare, it is largely to the silent work of the Civil Service that this happy result is due.

Wider horizons open before us when we turn to the second of the non-Party elements in our political system—I mean the Monarchy. British Kingship, like most other parts of our ancient constitution, has a very modern side to it. Our King, in virtue of his descent and of his office, is the living representative of our national history. So far from concealing the popular character of our institutions (as Bagehot supposed) he brings it into prominence. He is not the leader of a party, nor the representative of a class; he is the chief of a nation,—the chief indeed of many nations. He is everybody's King; by which I do not so much mean that he is the ruler of the Empire, as that he is the common possession of every part of it. He is the predestined link uniting all the various communities, whatever be their status, of which the Empire is composed. The autonomous democracies, including among them Great Britain, the mother of them all, each regard him as their constitutional head; and besides this he is the chief of all the diverse races in all the scattered territories, for whose welfare Great Britain, in the course of generations, has made herself responsible.

These no doubt are developments unforeseen by Bagehot, and scarcely realized, even now, by the world at large. They would have greatly changed his view of the Monarchy. He would no longer have treated it as little more than a dignified and venerable survival of an earlier age, shorn of all prerogative that could threaten liberty, and valuable chiefly through its facile appeal to the imagination of the ignorant. He would, I believe, have seen how great a part it is destined to play in the consolidation of Empire; how important is its aid in maintaining moral unity in the face of all the difficulties due to physical separation. He would certainly have noted how impossible this would have been if the twentieth-century Monarchy, like that of the eighteenth, had taken a hand in the Party game; or like that of Bagehot's own day was acting in (what are now) Dominion affairs on the advice of Ministers dependent on British majorities. The Empire in its modern shape is a bold experiment and a very novel one. On its success hangs the assurance of peace, happiness, and prosperity, over no small portion of the world; and when we reflect that without the Crown the experiment could never even have been tried, we cannot doubt that among the transformations which by insensible degrees have converted our most ancient and most venerable institutions to the most modern uses, not the least fortunate and successful has been the transformation of the British Monarchy.

WHITTINGEHAME   BALFOUR.
     November, 1927.

CONTENTS

---

[1] This Introduction first appeared in the second edition of 1872. It has been here transferred to the end of the book because it has the nature rather of an epilogue than of a prologue, and because the removal leaves the reader free (as in the first edition) to open at once on the main theme.

THE
ENGLISH CONSTITUTION

NO. I. THE CABINET

'On all great subjects,' says Mr. Mill, 'much remains to be said,' and of none is this more true than of the English Constitution. The literature which has accumulated upon it is huge. But an observer who looks at the living reality will wonder at the contrast to the paper description. He will see in the life much which is not in the books; and he will not find in the rough practice many refinements of the literary theory.

It was natural—perhaps inevitable—that such an undergrowth of irrelevant ideas should gather round the British Constitution. Language is the tradition of nations; each generation describes what it sees, but it uses words transmitted from the past. When a great entity like the British Constitution has continued in connected outward sameness, but hidden inner change, for many ages, every generation inherits a series of inapt words—of maxims once true, but of which the truth is ceasing or has ceased. As a man's family go on muttering in his maturity incorrect phrases derived from a just observation of his early youth, so, in the full activity of a historical constitution, its subjects repeat phrases true in the time of their fathers, and inculcated by those fathers, but now true no longer. Or, if I may say so, an ancient and ever-altering constitution is like an old man who still wears with attached fondness clothes in the fashion of his youth: what you see of him is the same; what you do not see is wholly altered.

There are two descriptions of the English Constitution which have exercised immense influence, but which are erroneous. First, it is laid down as a principle of the English polity, that in it the legislative, the executive, and the judicial powers, are quite divided—that each is entrusted to a separate person or set of persons—that no one of these can at all interfere with the work of the other. There has been much eloquence expended in explaining how the rough genius of the English people, even in the middle ages, when it was especially rude, carried into life and practice that elaborate division of functions which philosophers had suggested on paper, but which they had hardly hoped to see except on paper.

Secondly, it is insisted that the peculiar excellence of the British Constitution lies in a balanced union of three powers. It is said that the monarchical element, the aristocratic element, and the democratic element, have each a share in the supreme sovereignty, and that the assent of all three is necessary to the action of that sovereignty. Kings, lords, and commons, by this theory, are alleged to be not only the outward form, but the inner moving essence, the vitality of the constitution. A great theory, called the theory of 'Checks and Balances', pervades an immense part of political literature, and much of it is collected from or supported by English experience. Monarchy, it is said, has some faults, some bad tendencies, aristocracy others, democracy, again, others; but England has shown that a government can be constructed in which these evil tendencies exactly check, balance, and destroy one another—in which a good whole is constructed not simply in spite of, but by means of, the counteracting defects of the constituent parts.

Accordingly, it is believed that the principal

characteristics of the English Constitution are in-applicable in countries where the materials for a monarchy or an aristocracy do not exist. That constitution is conceived to be the best imaginable use of the political elements which the great majority of States in modern Europe inherited from the medieval period. It is believed that out of these materials nothing better can be made than the English Constitution; but it is also believed that the essential parts of the English Constitution cannot be made except from these materials. Now these elements are the accidents of a period and a region; they belong only to one or two centuries in human history, and to a few countries. The United States could not have become monarchical, even if the Constitutional Convention had decreed it, even if the component States had ratified it. The mystic reverence, the religious allegiance, which are essen-tial to a true monarchy, are imaginative sentiments that no legislature can manufacture in any people. These semi-filial feelings in government are in-herited just as the true filial feelings in common life. You might as well adopt a father as make a monarchy; the special sentiment belonging to the one is as incapable of voluntary creation as the peculiar affection belonging to the other. If the practical part of the English Constitution could only be made out of a curious accumulation of medieval materials, its interest would be half historical, and its imitability very confined.

No one can approach to an understanding of the English institutions, or of others which, being the growth of many centuries, exercise a wide sway over mixed populations, unless he divide them into two classes. In such constitutions there are two parts (not indeed separable with microscopic accuracy, for the genius of great affairs abhors nicety of division): first, those which excite and preserve the reverence of the population—the *dignified* parts, if I may so call them; and next, the *efficient* parts—those by which it, in fact, works and rules. There are two great objects which every constitution must attain to be successful, which every old and celebrated one must have wonderfully achieved: every constitution must first *gain* authority, and then *use* authority; it must first win the loyalty and confidence of mankind, and then employ that homage in the work of government.

There are indeed practical men who reject the dignified parts of government. They say, we want only to attain results, to do business: a constitution is a collection of political means for political ends, and if you admit that any part of a constitution does no business, or that a simpler machine would equally well what it does, you admit that this part of the constitution, however dignified or awful it may be, is nevertheless in truth useless. And other reasoners, who distrust this bare philosophy, have propounded subtle arguments to prove that these dignified parts of old governments are cardinal components of the essential apparatus, great pivots of substantial utility; and so they manufactured fallacies which the plainer school have well exposed. But both schools are in error. The dignified parts of government are those which bring it force—which attract its motive power. The efficient parts only employ that power. The comely parts of a government *have* need, for they are those upon which its vital strength depends. They may not do anything definite that a simpler polity would not do better; but they are the preliminaries, the needful pre-requisites of *all* work. They raise the army, though they do not win the battle.

Doubtless, if all subjects of the same government

only thought of what was useful to them, and if they all thought the same thing useful, and all thought that same thing could be attained in the same way, the efficient members of a constitution would suffice, and no impressive adjuncts would be needed. But the world in which we live is organized far otherwise.

The most strange fact, though the most certain in nature, is the unequal development of the human race. If we look back to the early ages of mankind, such as we seem in the faint distance to see them— if we call up the image of those dismal tribes in lake villages, or on wretched beaches—scarcely equal to the commonest material needs, cutting down trees slowly and painfully with stone tools, hardly resisting the attacks of huge, fierce animals—without culture, without leisure, without poetry, almost without thought—destitute of morality, with only a sort of magic for religion; and if we compare that imagined life with the actual life of Europe now, we are overwhelmed at the wide contrast—we can scarcely conceive ourselves to be of the same race as those in the far distance. There used to be a notion—not so much widely asserted as deeply implanted, rather pervadingly latent than commonly apparent in political philosophy—that in a little while, perhaps ten years or so, all human beings might, without extraordinary appliances, be brought to the same level. But now, when we see by the painful history of mankind at what point we began, by what slow toil, what favourable circumstances, what accumulated achievements, civilized man has become at all worthy in any degree so to call himself —when we realize the tedium of history and the painfulness of results—our perceptions are sharpened as to the relative steps of our long and gradual progress. We have in a great community like England crowds of people scarcely more civilized than the majority of two thousand years ago; we have others, even more numerous, such as the best people were a thousand years since. The lower orders, the middle orders, are still, when tried by what is the standard of the educated 'ten thousand', narrow-minded, unintelligent, incurious. It is useless to pile up abstract words. Those who doubt should go out into their kitchens. Let an accomplished man try what seems to him most obvious, most certain, most palpable in intellectual matters, upon the housemaid and the footman, and he will find that what he says seems unintelligible, confused, and erroneous—that his audience think him mad and wild when he is speaking what is in his own sphere of thought the dullest platitude of cautious soberness. Great communities are like great mountains—they have in them the primary, secondary, and tertiary strata of human progress; the characteristics of the lower regions resemble the life of old times rather than the present life of the higher regions. And a philosophy which does not ceaselessly remember, which does not continually obtrude, the palpable differences of the various parts, will be a theory radically false, because it has omitted a capital reality—will be a theory essentially misleading, because it will lead men to expect what does not exist, and not to anticipate that which they will find.

Every one knows these plain facts, but by no means every one has traced their political importance. When a state is constituted thus, it is not true that the lower classes will be wholly absorbed in the useful; on the contrary, they do not like anything so poor. No orator ever made an impression by appealing to men as to their plainest physical wants, except when he could allege that those wants were caused by some one's tyranny. But thousands have made the greatest impression by appealing to some vague dream of glory, or empire, or nationality. The ruder sort of men—that is, men at *one* stage of rudeness—will sacrifice all they hope for, all they have, *themselves*, for what is called an idea—for some attraction which seems to transcend reality, which aspires to elevate men by an interest higher, deeper, wider than that of ordinary life. But this order of men are uninterested in the plain, palpable ends of government; they do not prize them; they do not in the least comprehend how they should be attained. It is very natural, therefore, that the most useful parts of the structure of government should by no means be those which excite the most reverence. The elements which excite the most easy reverence will be the *theatrical* elements—those which appeal to the senses, which claim to be embodiments of the greatest human ideas, which boast in some cases of far more than human origin. That which is mystic in its claims; that which is occult in its mode of action; that which is brilliant to the eye; that which is seen vividly for a moment, and then is seen no more; that which is hidden and unhidden; that which is specious, and yet interesting, palpable in its seeming, and yet professing to be more than palpable in its results; this, howsoever its form may change, or however we may define it or describe it, is the sort of thing—the only sort—which yet comes home to the mass of men. So far from the dignified parts of a constitution being necessarily the most useful, they are likely, according to outside presumption, to be the least so; for they are likely to be adjusted to the lowest orders—those likely to care least and judge worst about what *is* useful.

There is another reason which, in an old constitution like that of England, is hardly less important. The most intellectual of men are moved quite as much by the circumstances which they are used to as by their own will. The active voluntary part of a man is very small, and if it were not economized by a sleepy kind of habit, its results would be null. We could not do every day out of our own heads all we have to do. We should accomplish nothing, for all our energies would be frittered away in minor attempts at petty improvement. One man, too, would go off from the known track in one direction, and one in another; so that when a crisis came requiring massed combination, no two men would be near enough to act together. It is the dull traditional habit of mankind that guides most men's actions, and is the steady frame in which each new artist must set the picture that he paints. And all this traditional part of human nature is, *ex vi termini*, most easily impressed and acted on by that which is handed down. Other things being equal, yesterday's institutions are by far the best for to-day; they are the most ready, the most influential, the most easy to get obeyed, the most likely to retain the reverence which they alone inherit, and which every other must win. The most imposing institutions of mankind are the oldest; and yet so changing is the world, so fluctuating are its needs, so apt to lose inward force, though retaining outward strength, are its best instruments, that we must not expect the oldest institutions to be now the most efficient. We must expect what is venerable to acquire influence because of its inherent dignity; but we must not expect it to use that influence so well as new creations apt for the modern world, instinct with its spirit, and fitting closely to its life.

The brief description of the characteristic merit of the English Constitution is, that its dignified parts are very complicated and somewhat imposing, very old and rather venerable; while its efficient part, at least when in great and critical action, is decidedly simple and rather modern. We have made, or rather stumbled on, a constitution which— though full of every species of incidental defect, though of the worst *workmanship* in all out-of-the-way matters of any constitution in the world—yet has two capital merits: it contains a simple efficient part which, on occasion, and when wanted, *can* work more simply and easily, and better, than any instrument of government that has yet been tried; and it contains likewise historical, complex, august, theatrical parts, which it has inherited from a long past—which *take* the multitude—which guide by an insensible but an omnipotent influence the associations of its subjects. Its essence is strong with the strength of modern simplicity; its exterior is august with the Gothic grandeur of a more imposing age. Its simple essence may, *mutatis mutandis*, be transplanted to many very various countries, but its august outside—what most men think it is—is narrowly confined to nations with an analogous history and similar political materials.

The efficient secret of the English Constitution may be described as the close union, the nearly complete fusion, of the executive and legislative powers. No doubt by the traditional theory, as it exists in all the books, the goodness of our constitution consists in the entire separation of the legislative and executive authorities, but in truth its merit consists in their singular approximation. The connecting link is the cabinet. By that new word we mean a committee of the legislative body selected to be the executive body. The legislature has many committees, but this is the greatest. It chooses for this, its main committee, the men in whom it has most confidence. It does not, it is true, choose them directly; but it is nearly omnipotent in choosing them indirectly. A century ago the Crown had a real choice of ministers, though it had no longer a choice in policy. During the long reign of Sir R. Walpole he was obliged not only to manage parliament, but to manage the palace. He was obliged to take care that some court intrigue did not expel him from his place. The nation then selected the English policy, but the Crown chose the English ministers. They were not only in name, as now, but in fact, the Queen's servants. Remnants, important remnants, of this great prerogative still remain. The discriminating favour of William IV made Lord Melbourne head of the Whig party when he was only one of several rivals. At the death of Lord Palmerston it is very likely that the Queen may have the opportunity of freely choosing between two, if not three statesmen. But, as a rule, the nominal prime minister is chosen by the legislature, and the real prime minister for most purposes—the leader of the House of Commons—almost without exception is so. There is nearly always some one man plainly selected by the voice of the predominant party in the predominant house of the legislature to head that party, and consequently to rule the nation. We have in England an elective first magistrate as truly as the Americans have an elective first magistrate. The Queen is only at the head of the dignified part of the constitution. The prime minister is at the head of the efficient part. The Crown is, according to the saying, the 'fountain of honour'; but the Treasury is the spring of business. Nevertheless our first magistrate differs from the American. He is not elected directly by the people; he is elected by the representatives of the people. He is an example of 'double election'. The legislature chosen, in name, to make laws, in fact finds its principal business in making and in keeping an executive.

The leading minister so selected has
his associates, but he only chooses among
circle. The position of most men in
forbids their being invited to the cabinet; the position
of a few men ensures their being invited. Between
the compulsory list whom he must take, and the
impossible list whom he cannot take, a prime
minister's independent choice in the formation of
a cabinet is not very large; it extends rather to the
division of the cabinet offices than to the choice of
cabinet ministers. Parliament and the nation have
pretty well settled who shall have the first places;
but they have not discriminated with the same
accuracy which man shall have which place. The
highest patronage of a prime minister is, of course,
a considerable power, though it is exercised under
close and imperative restrictions—though it is far
less than it seems to be when stated in theory, or
looked at from a distance.

The cabinet, in a word, is a board of control
chosen by the legislature, out of persons whom it
trusts and knows, to rule the nation. The particular
mode in which the English ministers are selected;
the fiction that they are, in any political sense, the
Queen's servants; the rule which limits the choice
of the cabinet to the members of the legislature—
are accidents unessential to its definition—historical
incidents separable from its nature. Its characteristic is that it should be chosen by the legislature out
of persons agreeable to and trusted by the legislature. Naturally these are principally its own
members—but they need not be exclusively so. A
cabinet which included persons not members of the
legislative assembly might still perform all useful
duties. Indeed the Peers, who constitute a large
element in modern cabinets, are members, nowadays, only of a subordinate assembly. The House of

Lords still exercises several useful functions; but the ruling influence—the deciding faculty—has passed to what, using the language of old times, we still call the lower house—to an assembly which, though inferior as a dignified institution, is superior as an efficient institution. A principal advantage of the House of Lords in the present age indeed consists in its thus acting as a *reservoir* of cabinet ministers. Unless the composition of the House of Commons were improved, or unless the rules requiring cabinet ministers to be members of the legislature were relaxed, it would undoubtedly be difficult to find, without the Lords, a sufficient supply of chief ministers. But the detail of the composition of a cabinet, and the precise method of its choice, are not to the purpose now The first and cardinal consideration is the definition of a cabinet. We must not bewilder ourselves with the inseparable accidents until we know the necessary essence. A cabinet is a combining committee—a *hyphen* which joins, a *buckle* which fastens, the legislative part of the state to the executive part of the state. In its origin it belongs to the one, in its functions it belongs to the other.

The most curious point about the cabinet is that so very little is known about it. The meetings are not only secret in theory, but secret in reality. By the present practice, no official minute in all ordinary cases is kept of them. Even a private note is discouraged and disliked. The House of Commons, even in its most inquisitive and turbulent moments, would scarcely permit a note of a cabinet meeting to be read. No minister who respected the fundamental usages of political practice would attempt to read such a note. The committee which unites the law-making power to the law-executing power—which, by virtue of that combination, is, while it lasts and holds together, the most powerful body in the state—is a committee wholly secret. No description of it, at once graphic and authentic, has ever been given. It is said to be sometimes like a rather disorderly board of directors, where many speak and few listen—though no one knows.[1]

But a cabinet, though it is a committee of the legislative assembly, is a committee with a power which no assembly would—unless for historical accidents, and after happy experience—have been persuaded to entrust to any committee. It is a committee which can dissolve the assembly which appointed it; it is a committee with a suspensive veto—a committee with a power of appeal. Though appointed by one parliament, it can appeal if it chooses to the next. Theoretically, indeed, the power to dissolve parliament is entrusted to the sovereign only; and there are vestiges of doubt whether in *all* cases a sovereign is bound to dissolve parliament when the cabinet asks him to do so. But neglecting such small and dubious exceptions, the cabinet which was chosen by one House of Commons has an appeal to the next House of Commons. The chief committee of the legislature has the power of dissolving the predominant part of that legislature—that which at a crisis is the supreme legislature. The English system, therefore, is not an absorption of the executive power by the legislative power; it is a fusion of the two. Either the

---

[1] It is *said* that at the end of the cabinet which agreed to propose a fixed duty on corn, Lord Melbourne put his back to the door, and said, 'Now is it to lower the price of corn, or isn't it? It is not much matter which we say, but mind, we must all say *the same*.' This is the most graphic story of a cabinet I ever heard, but I cannot vouch for its truth. Lord Melbourne's is a character about which men make stories.

cabinet legislates and acts, or else it can dissolve. It is a creature, but it has the power of destroying its creators. It is an executive which can annihilate the legislature, as well as an executive which is the nominee of the legislature. It *was* made, but it *can* unmake; it was derivative in its origin, but it is destructive in its action.

This fusion of the legislative and executive functions may, to those who have not much considered it, seem but a dry and small matter to be the latent essence and effectual secret of the English Constitution; but we can only judge of its real importance by looking at a few of its principal effects, and contrasting it very shortly with its great competitor, which seems likely, unless care be taken, to outstrip it in the progress of the world. That competitor is the Presidential system. The characteristic of it is that the President is elected from the people by one process, and the House of Representatives by another. The independence of the legislative and executive powers is the specific quality of the Presidential Government, just as their fusion and combination is the precise principle of Cabinet Government.

First, compare the two in quiet times. The essence of a civilized age is, that administration requires the continued aid of legislation. One principal and necessary kind of legislation is *taxation*. The expense of civilized government is continually varying. It must vary if the government does its duty. The miscellaneous estimates of the English Government contain an inevitable medley of changing items. Education, prison discipline, art, science, civil contingencies of a hundred kinds, require more money one year and less another. The expense of defence—the naval and military estimates—vary still more as the danger of attack seems more or less imminent, as the means of retarding such danger become more or less costly. If the persons who have to do the work are not the same as those who have to make the laws, there will be a controversy between the two sets of persons. The tax-imposers are sure to quarrel with the tax-requirers. The executive is crippled by not getting the laws it needs, and the legislature is spoiled by having to act without responsibility: the executive becomes unfit for its name since it cannot execute what it decides on; the legislature is demoralized by liberty, by taking decisions of which others (and not itself) will suffer the effects.

In America so much has this difficulty been felt that a semi-connexion has grown up between the legislature and the executive. When the Secretary of the Treasury of the Federal Government wants a tax he consults upon it with the Chairman of the Financial Committee of Congress. He cannot go down to Congress himself and propose what he wants; he can only write a letter and send it. But he tries to get a chairman of the Finance Committee who likes his tax;—through that chairman he tries to persuade the committee to recommend such tax; by that committee he tries to induce the house to adopt that tax. But such a chain of communications is liable to continual interruptions; it may suffice for a single tax on a fortunate occasion, but will scarcely pass a complicated budget—we do not say in a war or a rebellion—we are now comparing the cabinet system and the presidential system in quiet times—but in times of financial difficulty. Two clever men never exactly agreed about a budget. We have by present practice an Indian Chancellor of the Exchequer talking English finance at Calcutta, and an English one talking Indian finance in England. But the figures are never the same, and the views of policy are rarely the same. One most angry controversy has amused the world, and probably others scarcely less interesting are hidden in the copious stores of our Anglo-Indian correspondence.

But relations something like these must subsist between the head of a finance committee in the legislature, and a finance minister in the executive.[1] They are sure to quarrel, and the result is sure to satisfy neither. And when the taxes do not yield as they were expected to yield, who is responsible? Very likely the secretary of the treasury could not persuade the chairman—very likely the chairman could not persuade his committee—very likely the committee could not persuade the assembly. Whom, then, can you punish—whom can you abolish—when your taxes run short? There is nobody save the legislature, a vast miscellaneous body difficult to punish, and the very persons to inflict the punishment.

Nor is the financial part of administration the only one which requires in a civilized age the constant support and accompaniment of facilitating legislation. All administration does so. In England, on a vital occasion, the cabinet can compel legislation by the threat of resignation, and the threat of dissolution; but neither of these can be used in a presidential state. There the legislature cannot be dissolved by the executive government; and it does not heed a resignation, for it has not to find the successor. Accordingly, when a difference of opinion arises, the legislature is forced to fight the executive, and the executive is forced to fight the legislative;

[1] It is worth observing that even during the short existence of the Confederate Government these evils distinctly showed themselves. Almost the last incident at the Richmond Congress was an angry financial correspondence with Jefferson Davis.

and so very likely they contend to the conclusion of their respective terms.[1] There is, indeed, one condition of things in which this description, though still approximately true, is, nevertheless, not exactly true; and that is, when there is nothing to fight about. Before the rebellion in America, owing to the vast distance of other states, and the favourable economical condition of the country, there were very few considerable objects of contention; but if that government had been tried by the English legislation of the last thirty years, the discordant action of the two powers, whose constant co-operation is essential to the best government, would have shown itself much more distinctly.

Nor is this the worst. Cabinet government educates the nation; the presidential does not educate it, and may corrupt it. It has been said that England invented the phrase, 'Her Majesty's Opposition'; that it was the first government which made a criticism of administration as much a part of the polity as administration itself. This critical opposition is the consequence of cabinet government. The great scene of debate, the great engine of popular instruction and political controversy, is the legislative assembly. A speech there by an eminent statesman, a party movement by a great political combination, are the best means yet known for arousing, enlivening, and teaching a people. The cabinet system ensures such debates, for it makes them the means by which statesmen advertise themselves for future and confirm themselves in present governments. It brings forward men eager to speak, and gives them occasions to speak. The

---

[1] I leave this passage to stand as it was written, just after the assassination of Mr. Lincoln, and when every one said Mr. Johnson would be very hostile to the South.

deciding catastrophes of cabinet governments are critical divisions preceded by fine discussions. Everything which is worth saying, everything which ought to be said, most certainly *will* be said. Conscientious men think they ought to persuade others; selfish men think they would like to obtrude themselves. The nation is forced to hear two sides—all the sides, perhaps, of that which most concerns it. And it likes to hear—it is eager to know. Human nature despises long arguments which come to nothing—heavy speeches which precede no motion —abstract disquisitions which leave visible things where they were. But all men heed great results, and a change of government is a great result. It has a hundred ramifications; it runs through society; it gives hope to many, and it takes away hope from many. It is one of those marked events which, by its magnitude and its melodrama, impress men even too much. And debates which have this catastrophe at the end of them—or may so have it—are sure to be listened to, and sure to sink deep into the national mind.

Travellers even in the Northern States of America, the greatest and best of presidential countries, have noticed that the nation was 'not specially addicted to politics'; that they have not a public opinion finished and chastened as that of the English has been finished and chastened. A great many hasty writers have charged this defect on the 'Yankee race', on the Anglo-American character; but English people, if they had no motive to attend to politics, certainly would not attend to politics. At present there is *business* in their attention. They assist at the determining crisis; they assist or help it. Whether the government will go out or remain is determined by the debate, and by the division in parliament. And the opinion out of doors, the secret pervading disposition of society, has a great influence on that division. The nation feels that its judgement is important, and it strives to judge. It succeeds in deciding because the debates and the discussions give it the facts and the arguments. But under a presidential government a nation has, except at the electing moment, no influence; it has not the ballot-box before it; its virtue is gone, and it must wait till its instant of despotism again returns. It is not incited to form an opinion like a nation under a cabinet government; nor is it instructed like such a nation. There are doubtless debates in the legislature, but they are prologues without a play. There is nothing of a catastrophe about them; you cannot turn out the government. The prize of power is not in the gift of the legislature, and no one cares for the legislature. The executive, the great centre of power and place, sticks irremovable; you cannot change it in any event. The teaching apparatus which has educated our public mind, which prepares our resolutions, which shapes our opinions, does not exist. No presidential country needs to form daily, delicate opinions, or is helped in forming them.

It might be thought that the discussions in the press would supply the deficiencies in the constitution; that by a reading people especially, the conduct of their government would be as carefully watched, that their opinions about it would be as consistent, as accurate, as well considered, under a presidential as under a cabinet polity. But the same difficulty oppresses the press which oppresses the legislature. It can *do nothing*. It cannot change the administration; the executive was elected for such and such years, and for such and such years it must last. People wonder that so literary a people as the Americans—a people who read more than

any people who ever lived, who read so many newspapers—should have such bad newspapers. The
papers are not so good as the English, because they
have not the same motive to be good as the English
papers. At a political 'crisis', as we say—that is,
when the fate of an administration is unfixed, when
it depends on a few votes, yet unsettled, upon a
wavering and veering opinion—effective articles in
great journals become of essential moment. *The
Times* has made many ministries. When, as of late,
there has been a long continuance of divided parliaments, of governments which were without 'brute
voting power', and which depended on intellectual
strength, the support of the most influential organ
of English opinion has been of critical moment. If
a Washington newspaper could have turned out
Mr. Lincoln, there would have been good writing
and fine argument in the Washington newspapers.
But the Washington newspapers can no more
remove a president during his term of place than
The Times can remove a lord mayor during his year
of office. Nobody cares for a debate in Congress
which 'comes to nothing', and no one reads long
articles which have no influence on events. The
Americans glance at the heads of news, and through
the paper. They do not enter upon a discussion.
They do not *think* of entering upon a discussion
which would be useless.

After saying that the division of the legislature
and the executive in presidential governments
weakens the legislative power, it may seem a contradiction to say that it also weakens the executive
power. But it is not a contradiction. The division
weakens the whole aggregate force of government—
the entire imperial power; and therefore it weakens
both its halves. The executive is weakened in a very
plain way. In England a strong cabinet can obtain

the concurrence of the legislature in all acts which facilitate its administration; it is itself, so to say, the legislature. But a president may be hampered by the parliament, and is likely to be hampered. The natural tendency of the members of every legislature is to make themselves conspicuous. They wish to gratify an ambition laudable or blameable; they wish to promote the measures they think best for the public welfare; they wish to make their *will* felt in great affairs. All these mixed motives urge them to oppose the executive. They are embodying the purposes of others if they aid; they are advancing their own opinions if they defeat: they are first if they vanquish; they are auxiliaries if they support. The weakness of the American executive used to be the great theme of all critics before the Confederate rebellion. Congress and committees of Congress of course impeded the executive when there was no coercive public sentiment to check and rule them.

But the presidential system not only gives the executive power an antagonist in the legislative power, and so makes it weaker; it also enfeebles it by impairing its intrinsic quality. A cabinet is elected by a legislature; and when that legislature is composed of fit persons, that mode of electing the executive is the very best. It is a case of secondary election, under the only conditions in which secondary election is preferable to primary. Generally speaking, in an electioneering country (I mean in a country full of political life, and used to the manipulation of popular institutions), the election of candidates to elect candidates is a farce. The Electoral College of America is so. It was intended that the deputies when assembled should exercise a real discretion, and by independent choice select the president. But the primary electors take too much interest. They only elect a deputy to vote for

Mr. Lincoln or Mr. Breckenridge, and the deputy only takes a ticket, and drops that ticket in an urn. He never chooses or thinks of choosing. He is but a messenger—a transmitter: the real decision is in those who chose him—who chose him because they knew what he would do.

It is true that the British House of Commons is subject to the same influences. Members are mostly, perhaps, elected because they will vote for a particular ministry, rather than for purely legislative reasons. But—and here is the capital distinction—the functions of the House of Commons are important and *continuous*. It does not, like the Electoral College in the United States, separate when it has elected its ruler; it watches, legislates, seats and unseats ministries, from day to day. Accordingly it is a *real* electoral body. The parliament of 1857, which, more than any other parliament of late years, was a parliament elected to support a particular premier—which was chosen, as Americans might say, upon the 'Palmerston ticket'—before it had been in existence two years, dethroned Lord Palmerston. Though selected in the interest of a particular ministry, it in fact destroyed that ministry.

A *good* parliament, too, is a capital choosing body. If it is fit to make laws for a country, its majority ought to represent the general average intelligence of that country; its various members ought to represent the various special interests, special opinions, special prejudices, to be found in that community. There ought to be an advocate for every particular sect, and a vast neutral body of no sect—homogeneous and judicial, like the nation itself. Such a body, when possible, is the best selecter of executives that can be imagined. It is full of political activity; it is close to political life;

it feels the responsibility of affairs which are brought as it were to its threshold; it has as much intelligence as the society in question chances to contain. It is, what Washington and Hamilton strove to create, an electoral college of the picked men of the nation.

The best mode of appreciating its advantages is to look at the alternative. The competing constituency is the nation itself, and this is, according to theory and experience, in all but the rarest cases, a bad constituency. Mr. Lincoln, at his second election, being elected when all the Federal states had set their united hearts on one single object, was voluntarily re-elected by an actually choosing nation. He embodied the object in which every one was absorbed. But this is almost the only presidential election of which so much can be said. In almost all cases the President is chosen by a machinery of caucuses and combinations too complicated to be perfectly known, and too familiar to require description. He is not the choice of the nation, he is the choice of the wire-pullers. A very large constituency in quiet times is the necessary, almost the legitimate, subject of electioneering management: a man cannot know that he does not throw his vote away except he votes as part of some great organization; and if he votes as a part, he abdicates his electoral function in favour of the managers of that association. The nation, even if it chose for itself, would, in some degree, be an unskilled body; but when it does not choose for itself, but only as latent agitators wish, it is like a large, lazy man, with a small, vicious mind,—it moves slowly and heavily, but it moves at the bidding of a bad intention; it 'means *little*, but it means that little *ill*'.

And, as the nation is less able to choose than a parliament, so it has worse people to choose out of. The American legislators of the last century have been much blamed for not permitting the ministers of the President to be members of the Assembly; but, with reference to the specific end which they had in view, they saw clearly and decided wisely. They wished to keep 'the legislative branch absolutely distinct from the executive branch'; they believed such a separation to be essential to a good constitution; they believed such a separation to exist in the English, which the wisest of them thought the best constitution. And, to the effectual maintenance of such a separation, the exclusion of the President's ministers from the legislature is essential. If they are not excluded they become the executive, they eclipse the President himself. A legislative chamber is greedy and covetous; it acquires as much, it concedes as little as possible. The passions of its members are its rulers; the law-making faculty, the most comprehensive of the imperial faculties, is its instrument; it will *take* the administration if it can take it. Tried by their own aims, the founders of the United States were wise in excluding the ministers from Congress.

But though this exclusion is essential to the presidential system of government, it is not for that reason a small evil. It causes the degradation of public life. Unless a member of the legislature be sure of something more than speech, unless he is incited by the hope of action, and chastened by the chance of responsibility, a first-rate man will not care to take the place, and will not do much if he does take it. To belong to a debating society adhering to an executive (and this is no inapt description of a congress under a presidential constitution) is not an object to stir a noble ambition, and is a position to encourage idleness. The members of a parliament excluded from office can never be comparable, much less equal, to those of a parliament not excluded from office. The presidential government, by its nature, divides political life into two halves, an executive half and a legislative half; and, by so dividing it, makes neither half worth a man's having—worth his making it a continuous career—worthy to absorb, as cabinet government absorbs, his whole soul. The statesmen from whom a nation chooses under a presidential system are much inferior to those from whom it chooses under a cabinet system, while the selecting apparatus is also far less discerning.

All these differences are more important at critical periods, because government itself is more important. A formed public opinion, a respectable, able, and disciplined legislature, a well-chosen executive, a parliament and an administration not thwarting each other, but co-operating with each other, are of greater consequence when great affairs are in progress than when small affairs are in progress—when there is much to do than when there is little to do. But in addition to this, a parliamentary or cabinet constitution possesses an additional and special advantage in very dangerous times. It has what we may call a reserve of power fit for and needed by extreme exigencies.

The principle of popular government is that the supreme power, the determining efficacy in matters political, resides in the people—not necessarily or commonly in the whole people, in the numerical majority, but in a *chosen* people, a picked and selected people. It is so in England; it is so in all free countries. Under a cabinet constitution at a sudden emergency this people can choose a ruler for the occasion. It is quite possible and even likely that he would not be ruler *before* the occasion. The great qualities, the imperious will, the rapid energy, the eager nature fit for a great crisis are not required

—are impediments—in common times. A Lord Liverpool is better in everyday politics than a Chatham—a Louis Philippe far better than a Napoleon. By the structure of the world we often want, at the sudden occurrence of a grave tempest, to change the helmsman—to replace the pilot of the calm by the pilot of the storm. In England we have had so few catastrophes since our constitution attained maturity, that we hardly appreciate this latent excellence. We have not needed a Cavour to rule a revolution—a representative man above all men fit for a great occasion, and by a natural, legal mode brought in to rule. But even in England, at what was the nearest to a great sudden crisis which we have had of late years—at the Crimean difficulty— we used this inherent power. We abolished the Aberdeen cabinet, the ablest we have had, perhaps, since the Reform Act—a cabinet not only adapted, but eminently adapted, for every sort of difficulty save the one it had to meet—which abounded in pacific discretion, and was wanting only in the 'demonic element'; we chose a statesman who had the sort of merit then wanted, who, when he feels the steady power of England behind him, will advance without reluctance, and will strike without restraint. As was said at the time, 'We turned out the Quaker, and put in the pugilist'.

But under a presidential government you can do nothing of the kind. The American government calls itself a government of the supreme people; but at a quick crisis, the time when a sovereign power is most needed, you cannot *find* the supreme people. You have got a Congress elected for one fixed period, going out perhaps by fixed instalments, which cannot be accelerated or retarded—you have a President chosen for a fixed period, and immovable during that period: all the arrangements are for

stated times. There is no *elastic* element, everything
is rigid, specified, dated. Come what may, you can
quicken nothing and can retard nothing. You have
bespoken your government in advance, and whether
it suits you or not, whether it works well or works ill,
whether it is what you want or not, by law you must
keep it. In a country of complex foreign relations
it would mostly happen that the first and most
critical year of every war would be managed by
a peace premier, and the first and most critical years
of peace by a war premier. In each case the period of
transition would be irrevocably governed by a man
selected not for what he was to introduce, but what
he was to change—for the policy he was to abandon,
not for the policy he was to administer.

The whole history of the American civil war—
a history which has thrown an intense light on the
working of a presidential government at the time
when government is most important—is but a vast
continuous commentary on these reflections. It
would, indeed, be absurd to press against presidential
government *as such* the singular defect by which
Vice-President Johnson has become President—by
which a man elected to a sinecure is fixed in what is
for the moment the most important administrative
part in the political world. This defect, though most
characteristic of the expectations [1] of the framers of
the constitution and of its working, is but an accident
of this particular case of presidential government,
and no necessary ingredient in that government

[1] The framers of the constitution expected that the
vice-president would be elected by the Electoral College
as the second wisest man in the country. The vice-
presidentship being a sinecure, a second-rate man agreeable to the wire-pullers is always smuggled in. The
chance of succession to the presidentship is too distant
to be thought of.

itself. But the first election of Mr. Lincoln is liable to no such objection. It was a characteristic instance of the natural working of such a government upon a great occasion. And what was that working? It may be summed up—it was government by an *unknown quantity*. Hardly any one in America had any living idea what Mr. Lincoln was like, or any definite notion what he would do. The leading statesmen under the system of cabinet government are not only household words, but household *ideas*. A conception, not, perhaps, in all respects a true but a most vivid conception, what Mr. Gladstone is like, or what Lord Palmerston is like, runs through society. We have simply no notion what it would be to be left with the visible sovereignty in the hands of an unknown man. The notion of employing a man of unknown smallness at a crisis of unknown greatness is to our minds simply ludicrous. Mr. Lincoln, it is true, happened to be a man, if not of eminent ability, yet of eminent justness. There was an inner depth of Puritan nature which came out under suffering, and was very attractive. But success in a lottery is no argument for lotteries. What were the chances against a person of Lincoln's antecedents, elected as he was, proving to be what he was?

Such an incident is, however, natural to a presidential government. The President is elected by processes which forbid the election of known men, except at peculiar conjunctures, and in moments when public opinion is excited and despotic; and consequently, if a crisis comes upon us soon after he is elected, inevitably we have government by an unknown quantity—the superintendence of that crisis by what our great satirist would have called 'Statesman X'. Even in quiet times, government by a president is, for the various reasons which have been stated, inferior to government by a cabinet;

but the difficulty of quiet times is nothing as compared with the difficulty of unquiet times. The comparative deficiencies of the regular, common operation of a presidential government are far less than the comparative deficiencies in time of sudden trouble—the want of elasticity, the impossibility of a dictatorship, the total absence of a *revolutionary reserve*.

This contrast explains why the characteristic quality of cabinet governments—the fusion of the executive power with the legislative power—is of such cardinal importance. I shall proceed to show under what form and with what adjuncts it exists in England.

NO. II. THE MONARCHY

THE use of the Queen, in a dignified capacity, is incalculable. Without her in England, the present English Government would fail and pass away. Most people when they read that the Queen walked on the slopes at Windsor—that the Prince of Wales went to the Derby—have imagined that too much thought and prominence were given to little things. But they have been in error; and it is nice to trace how the actions of a retired widow and an unemployed youth become of such importance.

The best reason why Monarchy is a strong government is, that it is an intelligible government. The mass of mankind understand it, and they hardly anywhere in the world understand any other. It is often said that men are ruled by their imaginations; but it would be truer to say they are governed by the weakness of their imaginations. The nature of a constitution, the action of an assembly, the play of parties, the unseen formation of a guiding opinion, are complex facts, difficult to know, and easy to mistake. But the action of a single will, the fiat of a single mind, are easy ideas: anybody can make them out, and no one can ever forget them. When you put before the mass of mankind the question, 'Will you be governed by a king, or will you be governed by a constitution?' the inquiry comes out thus—'Will you be governed in a way you understand, or will you be governed in a way you do not understand?' The issue was put to the French people; they were asked, 'Will you be governed by Louis Napoleon, or will you be governed by an assembly?' The French people said, 'We will be governed by the one man we can imagine, and not by the many people we cannot imagine'.

The best mode of comprehending the nature of the two governments, is to look at a country in which the two have within a comparatively short space of years succeeded each other.

'The political condition,' says Mr. Grote, 'which Grecian legend everywhere presents to us, is in its principal features strikingly different from that which had become universally prevalent among the Greeks in the time of the Peloponnesian war. Historical oligarchy, as well as democracy, agreed in requiring a certain established system of government, comprising the three elements of specialized functions, temporary functionaries, and ultimate responsibility (under some forms or other) to the mass of qualified citizens—either a Senate or an Ecclesia, or both. There were, of course, many and capital distinctions between one government and another, in respect to the qualification of the citizen, the attributes and efficiency of the general assembly, the admissibility to power, &c.; and men might often be dissatisfied with the way in which these questions were determined in their own city. But in the mind of every man, some determining rule or system— something like what in modern times is called a *constitution*—was indispensable to any government entitled to be called legitimate, or capable of creating in the mind of a Greek a feeling of moral obligation to obey it. The functionaries who exercise authority under it might be more or less competent or popular; but his personal feelings towards them were commonly lost in his attachment or aversion to the general system. If any energetic man could by audacity or craft break down the constitution, and render himself permanent ruler according to his own will and pleasure, even though he might govern

well, he could never inspire the people with any
sentiment of duty towards him: his sceptre was
illegitimate from the beginning, and even the taking
of his life, far from being interdicted by that moral
feeling which condemned the shedding of blood in
other cases, was considered meritorious: he could
not even be mentioned in the language except by
a name (τύραννος, despot) which branded him as an
object of mingled fear and dislike.

'If we carry our eyes back from historical to
legendary Greece, we find a picture the reverse of
what has been here sketched. We discern a government in which there is little or no scheme or system,
still less any idea of responsibility to the governed,
but in which the mainspring of obedience on the
part of the people consists in their personal feeling
and reverence towards the chief. We remark, first
and foremost, the King; next, a limited number of
subordinate kings or chiefs; afterwards, the mass
of armed freemen, husbandmen, artisans, free-
booters, &c.; lowest of all, the free labourers for hire
and the bought slaves. The King is not distinguished by any broad, or impassable boundary from
the other chiefs, to each of whom the title Basileus
is applicable as well as to himself: his supremacy
has been inherited from his ancestors, and passes
by inheritance, as a general rule, to his eldest son,
having been conferred upon the family as a privilege
by the favour of Zeus. In war, he is the leader,
foremost in personal prowess, and directing all
military movements; in peace, he is the general
protector of the injured and oppressed; he offers up
moreover those public prayers and sacrifices which
are intended to obtain for the whole people the
favour of the gods. An ample domain is assigned
to him as an appurtenance of his lofty position, and
the produce of his fields and his cattle is consecrated

in part to an abundant, though rude hospitality. Moreover he receives frequent presents, to avert his enmity, to conciliate his favour, or to buy off his exactions; and when plunder is taken from the enemy, a large previous share, comprising probably the most alluring female captive, is reserved for him apart from the general distribution.

'Such is the position of the King in the heroic times of Greece—the only person (if we except the heralds and priests, each both special and subordinate) who is then presented to us as clothed with any individual authority—the person by whom all the executive functions, then few in number, which the society requires, are either performed or directed. His personal ascendancy—derived from divine countenance bestowed both upon himself individually and upon his race, and probably from accredited divine descent—is the salient feature in the picture: the people hearken to his voice, embrace his propositions, and obey his orders: not merely resistance, but even criticism upon his acts, is generally exhibited in an odious point of view, and is indeed never heard of except from some one or more of the subordinate princes.'

The characteristic of the English Monarchy is that it retains the feelings by which the heroic kings governed their rude age, and has added the feelings by which the constitutions of later Greece ruled in more refined ages. We are a more mixed people than the Athenians, or probably than any political Greeks. We have progressed more unequally. The slaves in ancient times were a separate order; not ruled by the same laws, or thoughts, as other men. It was not necessary to think of them in making a constitution: it was not necessary to improve them in order to make a constitution possible. The Greek legislator had not to combine in his polity men like

the labourers of Somersetshire, and men like Mr.
Grote. He had not to deal with a community in
which primitive barbarism lay as a recognized basis
to acquired civilization. *We have*. We have no
slaves to keep down by special terrors and independent legislation. But we have whole classes
unable to comprehend the idea of a constitution—
unable to feel the least attachment to impersonal
laws. Most do indeed vaguely know that there are
some other institutions besides the Queen, and some
rules by which she governs. But a vast number like
their minds to dwell more upon her than upon
anything else, and therefore she is inestimable. A
Republic has only difficult ideas in government;
a Constitutional Monarchy has an easy idea too;
it has a comprehensible element for the vacant many,
as well as complex laws and notions for the inquiring
few.

A *family* on the throne is an interesting idea also.
It brings down the pride of sovereignty to the level
of petty life. No feeling could seem more childish
than the enthusiasm of the English at the marriage
of the Prince of Wales. They treated as a great
political event, what, looked at as a matter of pure
business, was very small indeed. But no feeling
could be more like common human nature as it is,
and as it is likely to be. The women—one half the
human race at least—care fifty times more for a
marriage than a ministry. All but a few cynics like
to see a pretty novel touching for a moment the dry
scenes of the grave world. A princely marriage is
the brilliant edition of a universal fact, and as such,
it rivets mankind. We smile at the *Court Circular*;
but remember how many people read the *Court
Circular*! Its use is not in what it says, but in those
to whom it speaks. They say that the Americans
were more pleased at the Queen's letter to Mrs.

Lincoln, than at any act of the English Government.
It was a spontaneous act of intelligible feeling in the
midst of confused and tiresome business. Just so
a royal family sweetens politics by the seasonable
addition of nice and pretty events. It introduces
irrelevant facts into the business of government,
but they are facts which speak to 'men's bosoms'
and employ their thoughts.

To state the matter shortly, Royalty is a government in which the attention of the nation is concentrated on one person doing interesting actions.
A Republic is a government in which that attention
is divided between many, who are all doing uninteresting actions. Accordingly, so long as the
human heart is strong and the human reason weak,
Royalty will be strong because it appeals to diffused
feeling, and Republics weak because they appeal to
the understanding.

Secondly. The English Monarchy strengthens
our government with the strength of religion. It
is not easy to say why it should be so. Every
instructed theologian would say that it was the duty
of a person born under a Republic as much to obey
that Republic as it is the duty of one born under
a Monarchy to obey the monarch. But the mass of
the English people do not think so; they agree with
the oath of allegiance; they say it is their duty to
obey the 'Queen'; and they have but hazy notions
as to obeying laws without a queen. In former times,
when our constitution was incomplete, this notion
of local holiness in one part was mischievous. All
parts were struggling, and it was necessary each
should have its full growth. But superstition said
one should grow where it would, and no other part
should grow without its leave. The whole cavalier
party said it was their duty to obey the king,
whatever the king did. There was to be 'passive

obedience' to him, and there was no religious obedience due to any one else. He was the 'Lord's anointed', and no one else had been anointed at all. The parliament, the laws, the press were human institutions; but the Monarchy was a Divine institution. An undue advantage was given to a part of the constitution, and therefore the progress of the whole was stayed.

After the Revolution this mischievous sentiment was much weaker. The change of the line of sovereigns was at first conclusive. If there was a mystic right in any one, that right was plainly in James II ; if it was an English duty to obey any one whatever he did, he was the person to be so obeyed; if there was an inherent inherited claim in any king, it was in the Stuart king to whom the crown had come by descent, and not in the Revolution king to whom it had come by vote of Parliament. All through the reign of William III there was (in common speech) one king whom man had made, and another king whom God had made. The king who ruled had no consecrated loyalty to build upon; although he ruled in fact, according to sacred theory there was a king in France who ought to rule. But it was very hard for the English people, with their plain sense and slow imagination, to keep up a strong sentiment of veneration for a foreign adventurer. He lived under the protection of a French king; what he did was commonly stupid, and what he left undone was very often wise. As soon as Queen Anne began to reign there was a change of feeling; the old sacred sentiment began to cohere about her. There were indeed difficulties which would have baffled most people; but an Englishman whose heart is in a matter is not easily baffled. Queen Anne had a brother living and a father living, and by every rule of descent, their right was better than hers. But many people evaded both claims. They said James II had 'run away', and so abdicated, though he only ran away because he was in duress and was frightened, and though he claimed the allegiance of his subjects day by day. The Pretender, it was said, was not legitimate, though the birth was proved by evidence which any Court of Justice would have accepted. The English people were 'out of' a sacred monarch, and so they tried very hard to make a new one. Events, however, were too strong for them. They were ready and eager to take Queen Anne as the stock of a new dynasty; they were ready to ignore the claims of her father and the claims of her brother, but they could not ignore the fact that at the critical period she had no children. She had once had thirteen, but they all died in her lifetime, and it was necessary either to revert to the Stuarts or to make a new king by Act of Parliament.

According to the Act of Settlement passed by the Whigs, the crown was settled on the descendants of the 'Princess Sophia' of Hanover, a younger daughter of a daughter of James I. There were before her James II, his son, the descendants of a daughter of Charles I, and elder children of her own mother. But the Whigs passed these over because they were Catholics, and selected the Princess Sophia, who, if she was anything, was a Protestant. Certainly this selection was states-manlike, but it could not be very popular. It was quite impossible to say that it was the duty of the English people to obey the House of Hanover upon any principles which do not concede the right of the people to choose their rulers, and which do not degrade monarchy from its solitary pinnacle of majestic reverence, and make it one only among many expedient institutions. If a king is a useful public functionary who may be changed, and in whose place you may make another, you cannot regard him with mystic awe and wonder: and if you are bound to worship him, of course you cannot change him. Accordingly, during the whole reigns of George I and George II the sentiment of religious loyalty altogether ceased to support the Crown. The prerogative of the king had no strong party to support it; the Tories, who naturally would support it, disliked the actual king; and the Whigs, according to their creed, disliked the king's office. Until the accession of George III the most vigorous opponents of the Crown were the country gentlemen, its natural friends, and the representatives of quiet rural districts, where loyalty is mostly to be found, if anywhere. But after the accession of George III the common feeling came back to the same point as in Queen Anne's time. The English were ready to take the new young prince as the beginning of a sacred line of sovereigns, just as they had been willing to take an old lady who was the second cousin of his great-great-grandmother. So it is now. If you ask the immense majority of the Queen's subjects by what right she rules, they would never tell you that she rules by Parliamentary right, by virtue of 6 Anne, c. 7. They will say she rules by 'God's grace'; they believe that they have a mystic obligation to obey her. When her family came to the Crown it was a sort of treason to maintain the in-alienable right of lineal sovereignty, for it was equivalent to saying that the claim of another family was better than hers; but now, in the strange course of human events, that very sentiment has become her surest and best support.

But it would be a great mistake to believe that at the accession of George III the instinctive senti-ment of hereditary loyalty at once became as useful as now. It began to be powerful, but it hardly began to be useful. There was so much harm done by it as well as so much good, that it is quite capable of being argued whether on the whole it was beneficial or hurtful. Throughout the greater part of his life George III was a kind of 'consecrated obstruction'. Whatever he did had a sanctity different from what any one else did, and it perversely happened that he was commonly wrong. He had as good intentions as any one need have, and he attended to the business of his country, as a clerk with his bread to get attends to the business of his office. But his mind was small, his education limited, and he lived in a changing time. Accordingly he was always resisting what ought to be, and prolonging what ought not to be. He was the sinister but sacred assailant of half his ministries; and when the French revolution excited the horror of the world, and proved democracy to be 'impious', the piety of England concentrated upon him, and gave him tenfold strength. The monarchy by its religious sanction now confirms all our political order; in George III's time it confirmed little except itself. It gives now a vast strength to the entire constitution, by enlisting on its behalf the credulous obedience of enormous masses; then it lived aloof, absorbed all the holiness into itself, and turned over all the rest of the polity to the coarse justification of bare expediency.

A principal reason why the monarchy so well consecrates our whole state is to be sought in the peculiarity many Americans and many utilitarians smile at. They laugh at this 'extra', as the Yankee called it, at the solitary transcendent element. They quote Napoleon's saying, 'that he did not wish to be fatted in idleness,' when he refused to be grand elector in Sièyes' constitution, which was an office copied, and M. Thiers says, well copied, from constitutional monarchy. But such objections are wholly wrong. No doubt it was absurd enough in the Abbé Sièyes to propose that a new institution, inheriting no reverence, and made holy by no religion, should be created to fill the sort of post occupied by a constitutional king in nations of monarchical history. Such an institution, far from being so august as to spread reverence around it, is too novel and artificial to get reverence for itself; if, too, the absurdity could anyhow be augmented, it was so by offering an office of inactive uselessness and pretended sanctity to Napoleon, the most active man in France, with the greatest genius for business, only not sacred, and exclusively fit for action. But the blunder of Sièyes brings the excellence of real monarchy to the best light. When a monarch can bless, it is best that he should not be touched. It should be evident that he does no wrong. He should not be brought too closely to real measurement. He should be aloof and solitary. As the functions of English royalty are for the most part latent, it fulfils this condition. It seems to order, but it never seems to struggle. It is commonly hidden like a mystery, and sometimes paraded like a pageant, but in neither case is it contentious. The nation is divided into parties, but the Crown is of no party. Its apparent separation from business is that which removes it both from enmities and from desecration, which preserves its mystery, which enables it to combine the affection of conflicting parties—to be a visible symbol of unity to those still so imperfectly educated as to need a symbol.

Thirdly. The Queen is the head of our society. If she did not exist the Prime Minister would be the first person in the country. He and his wife would have to receive foreign ministers, and occasionally foreign princes, to give the first parties in the country; he and she would be at the head of the pageant of life; they would represent England in the eyes of foreign nations; they would represent the Government of England in the eyes of the English.

It is very easy to imagine a world in which this change would not be a great evil. In a country where people did not care for the outward show of life, where the genius of the people was untheatrical, and they exclusively regarded the substance of things, this matter would be trifling. Whether Lord and Lady Derby received the foreign ministers, or Lord and Lady Palmerston, would be a matter of indifference; whether they gave the nicest parties would be important only to the persons at those parties. A nation of unimpressible philosophers would not care at all how the externals of life were managed. Who is the showman is not material unless you care about the show.

But of all nations in the world the English are perhaps the least a nation of pure philosophers. It would be a very serious matter to us to change every four or five years the visible head of our world. We are not now remarkable for the highest sort of ambition; but we are remarkable for having a great deal of the lower sort of ambition and envy. The House of Commons is thronged with people who get there merely for 'social purposes', as the phrase goes; that is, that they and their families may go to parties else impossible. Members of Parliament are envied by thousands merely for this frivolous glory, as a thinker calls it. If the highest post in conspicuous life were thrown open to public competition, this low sort of ambition and envy would be fearfully increased. Politics would offer a prize too dazzling for mankind; clever base people would strive for it, and stupid base people would envy it. Even now a dangerous distinction is given by what is exclusively called public life. The newspapers describe daily and incessantly a certain conspicuous existence; they comment on its characters, recount its details, investigate its motives, anticipate its course. They give a precedent and a dignity to that world which they do not give to any other. The literary world, the scientific world, the philosophic world, not only are not comparable in dignity to the political world, but in comparison are hardly worlds at all. The newspaper makes no mention of them, and could not mention them. As are the papers, so are the readers; they, by irresistible sequence and association, believe that those people who constantly figure in the papers are cleverer, abler, or at any rate, somehow higher, than other people. 'I wrote books', we heard of a man saying, 'for twenty years, and I was nobody; I got into Parliament, and before I had taken my seat I had become somebody.' English politicians are the men who fill the thoughts of the English public; they are the actors on the scene, and it is hard for the admiring spectators not to believe that the admired actor is greater than themselves. In this present age and country it would be very dangerous to give the slightest addition to a force already perilously great. If the highest social rank was to be scrambled for in the House of Commons, the number of social adventurers there would be incalculably more numerous, and indefinitely more eager.

A very peculiar combination of causes has made this characteristic one of the most prominent in English society. The Middle Ages left all Europe with a social system headed by Courts. The government was made the head of all society, all intercourse, and all life; everything paid allegiance to the sovereign, and everything ranged itself round the sovereign—what was next to be greatest, and what was farthest least. The idea that the head of the government is the head of society is so fixed in the ideas of mankind that only a few philosophers regard it as historical and accidental, though when the matter is examined, that conclusion is certain and even obvious.

In the first place, society as society does not naturally need a head at all. Its constitution, if left to itself, is not monarchical, but aristocratical. Society, in the sense we are now talking of, is the union of people for amusement and conversation. The making of marriages goes on in it, as it were, incidentally, but its common and main concern is talking and pleasure. There is nothing in this which needs a single supreme head; it is a pursuit in which a single person does not of necessity dominate. By nature it creates an 'upper ten thousand'; a certain number of persons and families possessed of equal culture, and equal faculties, and equal spirit, get to be on a level—and that level a high level. By boldness, by cultivation, by 'social science' they raise themselves above others; they become the 'first families', and all the rest come to be below them. But they tend to be much about a level among one another; no one is recognized by all or by many others as superior to them all. This is society as it grew up in Greece or Italy, as it grows up now in any American or colonial town. So far from the notion of a 'head of society' being a necessary notion, in many ages it would scarcely have been an intelligible notion. You could not have made Socrates understand it. He would have said, 'If you tell me that one of my fellows is chief magistrate, and that I am bound to obey him, I understand you, and you speak well; or that another is a priest, and that he ought to offer sacrifices to the gods which I or any one not a priest ought not to offer, again I understand and agree with you. But if you tell me that there is in some citizen a hidden charm by which his words become better than my words, and his house better than my house, I do not follow you, and should be pleased if you will explain yourself.'

And even if a head of society were a natural idea, it certainly would not follow that the head of the civil government should be that head. Society as such has no more to do with civil polity than with ecclesiastical. The organization of men and women for the purpose of amusement is not necessarily identical with their organization for political purposes, any more than with their organization for religious purposes; it has of itself no more to do with the State than it has with the Church. The faculties which fit a man to be a great ruler are not those of society; some great rulers have been unintelligible like Cromwell, or brusque like Napoleon, or coarse and barbarous like Sir Robert Walpole. The light nothings of the drawing-room and the grave things of office are as different from one another as two human occupations can be. There is no naturalness in uniting the two; the end of it always is, that you put a man at the head of society who very likely is remarkable for social defects, and is not eminent for social merits.

The best possible commentary on these remarks is the 'History of English Royalty'. It has not been sufficiently remarked that a change has taken place in the structure of our society exactly analogous to the change in our polity. A Republic has insinuated itself beneath the folds of a Monarchy. Charles II was really the head of society; Whitehall, in his time, was the centre of the best talk, the best fashion, and the most curious love affairs of the age. He did not contribute good morality to society, but he set an example of infinite agreeableness. He concentrated around him all the light part of the high world of London, and London concentrated around it all the light part of the high world of England. The Court was the focus where everything fascinating gathered, and where everything exciting centred. Whitehall was an unequalled club, with female society of a very clever and sharp sort superadded. All this, as we know, is now altered. Buckingham Palace is as unlike a club as any place is likely to be. The Court is a separate part, which stands aloof from the rest of the London world, and which has but slender relations with the more amusing part of it. The two first Georges were men ignorant of English, and wholly unfit to guide and lead English society. They both preferred one or two German ladies of bad character to all else in London. George III had no social vices, but he had no social pleasures. He was a family man, and a man of business, and sincerely preferred a leg of mutton and turnips after a good day's work, to the best fashion and the most exciting talk. In consequence, society in London, though still in form under the domination of a Court, assumed in fact its natural and oligarchical structure. It, too, has become an 'upper ten thousand'; it is no more monarchical in fact than the society of New York. Great ladies give the tone to it with little reference to the particular Court world. The peculiarly masculine world of the clubs and their neighbourhood has no more to do in daily life with Buckingham Palace than with the Tuileries. Formal ceremonies of presentation and attendance are retained. The names of levee and drawing-room still sustain the memory of the time when the king's bed-chamber and the queen's 'withdrawing room' were the centres of London life, but they no longer make a part of social enjoyment: they are a sort of ritual in which nowadays almost every decent person can if he likes take part. Even Court balls, where pleasure is at least supposed to be possible, are lost in a London July. Careful observers have long perceived this, but it was made palpable to every one by the death of the Prince Consort. Since then the Court has been always in a state of suspended animation, and for a time it was quite annihilated. But everything went on as usual. A few people who had no daughters and little money made it an excuse to give fewer parties, and if very poor, stayed in the country, but upon the whole the difference was not perceptible. The queen bee was taken away, but the hive went on.

Refined and original observers have of late objected to English royalty that it is not splendid enough. They have compared it with the French Court, which is better in show, which comes to the surface everywhere so that you cannot help seeing it, which is infinitely and beyond question the most splendid thing in France. They have said, 'that in old times the English Court took too much of the nation's money, and spent it ill; but now, when it could be trusted to spend well, it does not take enough of the nation's money. There are arguments for not having a Court, and there are arguments for having a splendid Court; but there are no arguments for having a mean Court. It is better to spend a million in dazzling when you wish to dazzle, than three-quarters of a million in trying to dazzle and yet not dazzling.' There may be something in this theory; it may be that the Court of England is not quite as gorgeous as we might wish to see it. But no comparison must ever be made between it and the French Court. The Emperor represents a different idea from the Queen. He is not the head of the State; he *is* the State. The theory of his government is that every one in France is equal, and that the Emperor embodies the principle of equality. The greater you make him, the less, and therefore the more equal, you make all others. He is magnified that others may be dwarfed. The very contrary is the principle of English royalty. As in politics it would lose its principal use if it came forward into the public arena, so in society if it advertised itself it would be pernicious. We have voluntary show enough already in London; we do not wish to have it encouraged and intensified, but quieted and mitigated. Our Court is but the head of an unequal, competing, aristocratic society: its splendour would not keep others down, but incite others to come on. It is of use so long as it keeps others out of the first place, and is guarded and retired in that place. But it would do evil if it added a new example to our many examples of showy wealth—if it gave the sanction of its dignity to the race of expenditure.

Fourthly. We have come to regard the Crown as the head of our *morality*. The virtues of Queen Victoria and the virtues of George III have sunk deep into the popular heart. We have come to believe that it is natural to have a virtuous sovereign, and that the domestic virtues are as likely to be found on thrones as they are eminent when there. But a little experience and less thought show that royalty cannot take credit for domestic excellence. Neither George I, nor George II, nor William IV were patterns of family merit; George IV was a model of family demerit. The plain fact is, that to the disposition of all others most likely to go wrong, to an excitable disposition, the place of a constitutional king has greater temptations than almost any other, and fewer suitable occupations than almost any other. All the world and all the glory of it, whatever is most attractive, whatever is most seductive, has always been offered to the Prince of Wales of the day, and always will be. It is not rational to expect the best virtue where temptation is applied in the most trying form at the frailest time of human life. The occupations of a constitutional monarch are grave, formal, important, but never exciting; they have nothing to stir eager blood, awaken high imagination, work off wild thoughts. On men like George III, with a predominant taste for business occupations, the routine duties of constitutional royalty have doubtless a calm and chastening effect. The insanity with which he struggled, and in many cases struggled very successfully, during many years, would probably have burst out much oftener but for the sedative effect of sedulous employment. But how few princes have ever felt the anomalous impulse for real work; how uncommon is that impulse anywhere; how little are the circumstances of princes calculated to foster it; how little can it be relied on as an ordinary breakwater to their habitual temptations! Grave and careful men may have domestic virtues on a constitutional throne, but even these fail sometimes, and to imagine that men of more eager temperaments will commonly produce them, is to expect grapes from thorns and figs from thistles.

Lastly. Constitutional royalty has the function which I insisted on at length in my last essay, and which, though it is by far the greatest, I need not now enlarge upon again. It acts as a *disguise*. It enables our real rulers to change without heedless people knowing it. The masses of Englishmen are not fit for an elective government; if they knew how near they were to it, they would be surprised, and almost tremble.

Of a like nature is the value of constitutional royalty in times of transition. The greatest of all helps to the substitution of a cabinet government for a preceding absolute monarchy, is the accession of a king favourable to such a government, and pledged to it. Cabinet government, when new, is weak in time of trouble. The prime minister— the chief on whom everything depends, who must take responsibility if any one is to take it, who must use force if any one is to use it—is not fixed in power. He holds his place, by the essence of the government, with some uncertainty. Among a people well-accustomed to such a government such a functionary may be bold; he may rely, if not on the parliament, on the nation which understands and values him. But when that government has only recently been introduced, it is difficult for such a minister to be as bold as he ought to be. His power rests too much on human reason, and too little on human instinct. The traditional strength of the hereditary monarch is at these times of incalculable use. It would have been impossible for England to get through the first years after 1688 but for the singular ability of William III. It would have been impossible for Italy to have attained and kept her freedom without the help of Victor Emmanuel; neither the work of Cavour nor the work of Garibaldi were more necessary than his. But the failure of Louis Philippe to use his reserve power as constitutional monarch is the most instructive proof how great that reserve power is. In February, 1848, Guizot was weak because his tenure of office was insecure. Louis Philippe should have made that tenure certain. Parliamentary reform might afterwards have been conceded to instructed opinion, but nothing ought to have been conceded to the mob. The Parisian populace ought to have been put down, as Guizot wished. If Louis Philippe had been a fit king to introduce free government, he would have strengthened his ministers when they were the instruments of order, even if he afterwards discarded them when order was safe, and policy could be discussed. But he was one of the cautious men who are 'noted' to fail in old age: though of the largest experience, and of great ability, he failed and lost his crown for want of petty and momentary energy, which at such a crisis a plain man would have at once put forth.

Such are the principal modes in which the institution of royalty by its august aspect influences mankind, and in the English state of civilization they are invaluable. Of the actual business of the sovereign—the real work the Queen does—I shall speak in my next paper.

THE House of Commons has inquired into most things, but has never had a committee on 'the Queen'. There is no authentic blue-book to say what she does. Such an investigation cannot take place; but if it could, it would probably save her much vexatious routine, and many toilsome and unnecessary hours.

The popular theory of the English constitution involves two errors as to the sovereign. First, in its oldest form at least, it considers him as an 'Estate of the Realm', a separate co-ordinate authority with the House of Lords and the House of Commons. This and much else the sovereign once was, but this he is no longer. That authority could only be exercised by a monarch with a legislative veto. He should be able to reject bills, if not as the House of Commons rejects them, at least as the House of Peers rejects them. But the Queen has no such veto. She must sign her own death-warrant if the two Houses unanimously send it up to her. It is a fiction of the past to ascribe to her legislative power. She has long ceased to have any. Secondly, the ancient theory holds that the Queen is the executive. The American Constitution was made upon a most careful argument, and most of that argument assumes the king to be the administrator of the English Constitution, and an unhereditary substitute for him—viz., a president—to be peremptorily necessary. Living across the Atlantic, and misled by accepted doctrines, the acute framers of the Federal Constitution, even after the keenest attention, did not perceive the prime minister to be the principal executive of the British Constitution, and the sovereign a cog in the mechanism. There is, indeed, much excuse for the American legislators in the history of that time. They took their idea of our constitution from the time when they encountered it. But in the so-called government of Lord North, George III was the government. Lord North was not only his appointee, but his agent. The minister carried on a war which he disapproved and hated, because it was a war which his sovereign approved and liked. Inevitably, therefore, the American Convention believed the king, from whom they had suffered, to be the real executive, and not the minister, from whom they had not suffered.

If we leave literary theory, and look to our actual old law, it is wonderful how much the sovereign can do. A few years ago the Queen very wisely attempted to make life-Peers, and the House of Lords very unwisely, and contrary to its own best interests, refused to admit her claim. They said her power had decayed into non-existence; she once had it, they allowed, but it had ceased by long disuse. If any one will run over the pages of Comyn's 'Digest', or any other such book, title 'Prerogative', he will find the Queen has a hundred such powers which waver between reality and desuetude, and which would cause a protracted and very interesting legal argument if she tried to exercise them. Some good lawyer ought to write a careful book to say which of these powers are really usable, and which are obsolete. There is no authentic explicit information as to what the Queen can do, any more than of what she does.

In the bare superficial theory of free institutions this is undoubtedly a defect. Every power in a popular government ought to be known. The whole notion of such a government is that the political people—the governing people—rules as it thinks fit.

All the acts of every administration are to be canvassed by it; it is to watch if such acts seem good, and in some manner or other to interpose if they seem not good. But it cannot judge if it is to be kept in ignorance; it cannot interpose if it does not know. A secret prerogative is an anomaly—perhaps the greatest of anomalies. That secrecy is, however, essential to the utility of English royalty as it now is. Above all things our royalty is to be reverenced, and if you begin to poke about it you cannot reverence it. When there is a select committee on the Queen, the charm of royalty will be gone. Its mystery is its life. We must not let in daylight upon magic. We must not bring the Queen into the combat of politics, or she will cease to be reverenced by all combatants; she will become one combatant among many. The existence of this secret power is, according to abstract theory, a defect in our constitutional polity, but it is a defect incident to a civilization such as ours, where august and therefore unknown powers are needed, as well as known and serviceable powers.

If we attempt to estimate the working of this inner power by the evidence of those, whether dead or living, who have been brought in contact with it, we shall find a singular difference. Both the courtiers of George III and the courtiers of Queen Victoria are agreed as to the magnitude of the royal influence. It is with both an accepted secret doctrine that the Crown does more than it seems. But there is a wide discrepancy in opinion as to the quality of that action. Mr. Fox did not scruple to describe the hidden influence of George III as the undetected agency of 'an infernal spirit'. The action of the Crown at that period was the dread and terror of Liberal politicians. But now the best Liberal politicians say, '*We* shall never know, but when history is written our children may know, what we owe to the Queen and Prince Albert'. The mystery of the constitution, which used to be hated by our calmest, most thoughtful, and instructed statesmen, is now loved and reverenced by them.

Before we try to account for this change, there is one part of the duties of the Queen which should be struck out of the discussion. I mean the formal part. The Queen has to assent to and sign countless formal documents, which contain no matter of policy, of which the purport is insignificant, which any clerk could sign as well. One great class of documents George III used to read before he signed them, till Lord Thurlow told him, 'It was nonsense his looking at them, for he could not understand them'. But the worst case is that of commissions in the army. Till an Act passed only three years since, the Queen used to sign *all* military commissions, and she still signs all fresh commissions. The inevitable and natural consequence is that such commissions were, and to some extent still are, in arrears by thousands. Men have often been known to receive their commissions for the first time years after they have left the service. If the Queen had been an ordinary officer she would long since have complained, and long since have been relieved of this slavish labour. A cynical statesman is said to have defended it on the ground 'that you *may* have a fool for a sovereign, and then it would be desirable he should have plenty of occupation in which he can do no harm'. But it is in truth·childish to heap formal duties of business upon a person who has of necessity so many formal duties of society. It is a remnant of the old days when George III would know everything, however trivial, and assent to everything, however insignificant. These labours of routine may be dismissed from the discussion. It is not by them that the sovereign acquires his authority either for evil or for good.

The best mode of testing what we owe to the Queen is to make a vigorous effort of the imagination, and see how we should get on without her. Let us strip cabinet government of all its accessories, let us reduce it to its two necessary constituents—a representative assembly (a House of Commons) and a cabinet appointed by that assembly—and examine how we should manage with them only. We are so little accustomed to analyse the constitution; we are so used to ascribe the whole effect of the constitution to the whole constitution, that a great many people will imagine it to be impossible that a nation should thrive or even live with only these two simple elements. But it is upon that possibility that the general imitability of the English Government depends. A monarch that can be truly reverenced, a House of Peers that can be really respected, are historical accidents nearly peculiar to this one island, and entirely peculiar to Europe. A new country, if it is to be capable of a cabinet government, if it is not to degrade itself to presidential government, must create that cabinet out of its native resources— must not rely on these old world debris.

Many modes might be suggested by which a parliament might do in appearance what our parliament does in reality, viz., appoint a premier. But I prefer to select the simplest of all modes. We shall then see the bare skeleton of this polity, perceive in what it differs from the royal form, and be quite free from the imputation of having selected an unduly charming and attractive substitute.

Let us suppose the House of Commons—existing alone and by itself—to appoint the premier quite simply, just as the shareholders of a railway choose a director. At each vacancy, whether caused by death or resignation, let any member or members have the right of nominating a successor; after a proper interval, such as the time now commonly occupied by a ministerial crisis, ten days or a fortnight, let the members present vote for the candidate they prefer; then let the Speaker count the votes, and the candidate with the greatest number be premier. This mode of election would throw the whole choice into the hands of party organization, just as our present mode does, except in so far as the Crown interferes with it; no outsider would ever be appointed, because the immense number of votes which every great party brings into the field would far outnumber every casual and petty minority. The premier should not be appointed for a fixed time, but during good behaviour or the pleasure of parliament. *Mutatis mutandis*, subject to the differences now to be investigated, what goes on now would go on then. The premier then, as now, must resign upon a vote of want of confidence, but the volition of parliament would then be the overt and single force in the selection of a successor, whereas it is now the predominant though latent force.

It will help the discussion very much if we divide it into three parts. The whole course of a representative government has three stages—first, when a ministry is appointed; next, during its continuance; last, when it ends. Let us consider what is the exact use of the Queen at each of these stages, and how our present form of government differs in each, whether for good or for evil, from that simpler form of cabinet government which might exist without her.

At the beginning of an administration there would not be much difference between the royal and unroyal species of cabinet governments when there were only two great parties in the State, and when the greater of those parties was thoroughly agreed within itself who should be its parliamentary leader, and who therefore should be its premier. The sovereign must now accept that recognized leader; and if the choice were directly made by the House of Commons, the House must also choose him; its supreme section, acting compactly and harmoniously, would sway its decisions without substantial resistance, and perhaps without even apparent competition. A predominant party, rent by no intestine demarcation, would be despotic. In such a case cabinet government would go on without friction whether there was a queen or whether there was no queen. The best sovereign could then achieve no good, and the worst effect no harm.

But the difficulties are far greater when the predominant party is not agreed who should be its leader. In the royal form of cabinet government the sovereign then has sometimes a substantial selection; in the unroyal, who would choose? There must be a meeting at 'Willis's Rooms'; there must be that sort of interior despotism of the majority over the minority within the party, by which Lord John Russell in 1859 was made to resign his pretensions to the supreme government, and to be content to serve as a subordinate to Lord Palmerston. The tacit compression which a party anxious for office would exercise over leaders who divided its strength, would be used and must be used. Whether such a party would always choose precisely the best man may well be doubted. In a party once divided it is very difficult to secure unanimity in favour of the very person whom a disinterested bystander would recommend. All manner of jealousies and enmities are immediately awakened, and it is always difficult, often impossible, to get them to sleep again. But though such a party might not select the very best leader, they have the strongest motives to select a very good leader. The maintenance of their rule depends on it. Under a presidential constitution the preliminary caucuses which choose the president need not care as to the ultimate fitness of the man they choose. They are solely concerned with his attractiveness as a candidate; they need not regard his efficiency as a ruler. If they elect a man of weak judgement, he will reign his stated term; even though he show the best judgement, at the end of that term there will be by constitutional destiny another election. But under a ministerial government there is no such fixed destiny. The government is a removable government; its tenure depends upon its conduct. If a party in power were so foolish as to choose a weak man for its head, it would cease to be in power. Its judgement is its life. Suppose in 1859 that the Whig Party had determined to set aside both Earl Russell and Lord Palmerston, and to choose for its head an incapable nonentity, the Whig Party would probably have been exiled from office at the Schleswig-Holstein difficulty. The nation would have deserted them, and Parliament would have deserted them, too; neither would have endured to see a secret negotiation, on which depended the portentous alternative of war or peace, in the hands of a person who was thought to be weak—who had been promoted because of his mediocrity—whom his own friends did not respect. A ministerial government, too, is carried on in the face of day. Its life is in debate. A president may be a weak man; yet if he keep good ministers to the end of his administration, he may not be found out—it may still be a dubious controversy whether he is wise or foolish. But a prime minister must show what he is. He must meet the House of Commons in debate; he must be able to guide that assembly in the management of its business, to gain its ear in every emergency, to rule it in its hours of excitement. He is conspicuously submitted to a searching test, and if he fails he must resign.

Nor would any party like to trust to a weak man the great power which a cabinet government commits to its premier. The premier, though elected by parliament, can dissolve parliament. Members would be naturally anxious that the power which might destroy their coveted dignity should be lodged in fit hands. They dare not place in unfit hands a power which, besides hurting the nation, might altogether ruin them. We may be sure, therefore, that whenever the predominant party is divided, the *un*-royal form of cabinet government would secure for us a fair and able parliamentary leader—that it would give us a good premier, if not the very best. Can it be said that the royal form does more?

In one case I think it may. If the constitutional monarch be a man of singular discernment, of unprejudiced disposition, and great political knowledge, he may pick out from the ranks of the divided party its very best leader, even at a time when the party, if left to itself, would not nominate him. If the sovereign be able to play the part of that thoroughly intelligent but perfectly disinterested spectator who is so prominent in the works of certain moralists, he may be able to choose better for his subjects than they would choose for themselves. But if the monarch be not so exempt from prejudice, and have not this nearly miraculous discernment, it is not likely that he will be able to make a wiser choice than the choice of the party itself. He certainly is not under the same motive to choose wisely. His place is fixed whatever happens, but the failure of an appointing party depends on the capacity of their appointee.

There is great danger, too, that the judgement of the sovereign may be prejudiced. For more than forty years the personal antipathies of George III materially impaired successive administrations. Almost at the beginning of his career he discarded Lord Chatham: almost at the end he would not permit Mr. Pitt to coalesce with Mr. Fox. He always preferred mediocrity; he generally disliked high ability; he always disliked great ideas. If constitutional monarchs be ordinary men of restricted experience and common capacity (and we have no right to suppose that *by miracle* they will be more), the judgement of the sovereign will often be worse than the judgement of the party, and he will be very subject to the chronic danger of preferring a respectful commonplace man, such as Addington, to an independent first-rate man, such as Pitt.

We shall arrive at the same sort of mixed conclusion if we examine the choice of a premier under both systems in the critical case of cabinet government—the case of three parties. This is the case in which that species of government is most sure to exhibit its defects, and least likely to exhibit its merits. The defining characteristic of that government is the choice of the executive ruler by the legislative assembly; but when there are three parties a satisfactory choice is impossible. A really good selection is a selection by a large majority which trusts those it chooses, but when there are three parties there is no such trust. The numerically weakest has the casting vote—it can determine which candidate shall be chosen. But it does so under a penalty. It forfeits the right of voting for its own candidate. It settles which of other people's favourites shall be chosen, on condition of abandoning its own favourite. A choice based on such self-denial can never be a firm choice—it is a choice at any moment liable to be revoked. The events of 1858, though not a perfect illustration of what I mean, are a sufficient illustration. The Radical Party, acting apart from the moderate Liberal Party, kept Lord Derby in power. The ultra-movement party thought it expedient to combine with the non-movement party. As one of them coarsely but clearly put it, 'We get more of our way under these men than under the other men'; he meant that, in his judgement, the Tories would be more obedient to the Radicals than the Whigs. But it is obvious that a union of opposites so marked could not be durable. The Radicals bought it by choosing the men whose principles were most adverse to them; the Conservatives bought it by agreeing to measures whose scope was most adverse to them. After a short interval the Radicals returned to their natural alliance and their natural discontent with the moderate Whigs. They used their determining vote first for a government of one opinion and then for a government of the contrary opinion.

I am not blaming this policy. I am using it merely as an illustration. I say that if we imagine this sort of action greatly exaggerated and greatly prolonged parliamentary government becomes impossible. If there are three parties, no two of which will steadily combine for mutual action, but of which the weakest gives a rapidly oscillating preference to the two others, the primary condition of a cabinet polity is not satisfied. We have not a parliament fit to choose; we cannot rely on the selection of a sufficiently permanent executive, because there is no fixity in the thoughts and feelings of the choosers.

Under every species of cabinet government, whether the royal or the unroyal, this defect can be cured in one way only. The moderate people of

every party must combine to support the government which, on the whole, suits every party best.
This is the mode in which Lord Palmerston's administration has been lately maintained: a ministry
in many ways defective, but more beneficially
vigorous abroad, and more beneficially active at
home, than the vast majority of English ministries.
The moderate Conservatives and the moderate
Radicals have maintained a steady government by
a sufficiently coherent union with the moderate
Whigs. Whether there is a king or no king, this
preservative self-denial is the main force on which
we must rely for the satisfactory continuance of a
parliamentary government at this its period of
greatest trial. Will that moderation be aided or
impaired by the addition of a sovereign? Will it be
more effectual under the royal sort of ministerial
government, or will it be less effectual?

If the sovereign has a genius for discernment, the
aid which he can give at such a crisis will be great.
He will select for his minister, and if possible
maintain as his minister, the statesman upon whom
the moderate party will ultimately fix their choice,
but for whom at the outset it is blindly searching;
being a man of sense, experience, and tact, he will
discern which is the combination of equilibrium,
which is the section with whom the milder members
of the other sections will at last ally themselves.
Amid the shifting transitions of confused parties, it
is probable that he will have many opportunities of
exercising a selection. It will rest with him to call
either on A B to form an administration or upon
X Y, and either may have a chance of trial. A disturbed state of parties is inconsistent with fixity, but
it abounds in momentary tolerance. Wanting something, but not knowing with precision what, parties
will accept for a brief period anything, to see

whether it may be that unknown something—to see what it will do. During the long succession of weak governments which begins with the resignation of the Duke of Newcastle in 1762 and ends with the accession of Mr. Pitt in 1784, the vigorous will of George III was an agency of the first magnitude. If at a period of complex and protracted division of parties, such as are sure to occur often and last long in every enduring parliamentary government, the extrinsic force of royal selection were always exercised discreetly, it would be a political benefit of incalculable value.

But will it be so exercised? A constitutional sovereign must in the common course of government be a man of but common ability. I am afraid, looking to the early acquired feebleness of hereditary dynasties, that we must expect him to be a man of inferior ability. Theory and experience both teach that the education of a prince can be but a poor education, and that a royal family will generally have less ability than other families. What right have we then to expect the perpetual entail on any family of an exquisite discretion, which if it be not a sort of genius, is at least as rare as genius?

Probably in most cases the greatest wisdom of a constitutional king would show itself in well considered inaction. In the confused interval between 1857 and 1859 the Queen and Prince Albert were far too wise to obtrude any selection of their own. If they had chosen, perhaps they would not have chosen Lord Palmerston. But they saw, or may be believed to have seen, that the world was settling down without them, and that by interposing an extrinsic agency, they would but delay the beneficial crystallization of intrinsic forces. There is, indeed, a permanent reason which would make the wisest king, and the king who feels most sure of his wisdom.

very slow to use that wisdom. The responsibility of parliament should be felt by parliament. So long as parliament thinks it is the sovereign's business to find a government it will be sure not to find a government itself. The royal form of ministerial government is the worst of all forms if it erect the subsidiary apparatus into the principal force, if it induce the assembly which ought to perform paramount duties to expect some one else to perform them.

It should be observed, too, in fairness to the unroyal species of cabinet government, that it is exempt from one of the greatest and most characteristic defects of the royal species. Where there is no court there can be no evil influence from a court. What these influences are every one knows; though no one, hardly the best and closest observer, can say with confidence and precision how great their effect is. Sir Robert Walpole, in language too coarse for our modern manners, declared after the death of Queen Caroline, that he would pay no attention to the king's daughters ('those girls', as he called them), but would rely exclusively on Madame de Walmoden, the king's mistress.' 'The king', says a writer in George IV's time, 'is in our favour, and what is more to the purpose, the Marchioness of Conyngham is so too.' Everybody knows to what sort of influences several Italian changes of government since the unity of Italy have been attributed. These sinister agencies are likely to be most effective just when everything else is troubled, and when, therefore, they are particularly dangerous. The wildest and wickedest king's mistress would not plot against an invulnerable administration. But very many will intrigue when parliament is perplexed, when parties are divided, when alternatives are many, when many evil things are possible, when cabinet government must be difficult.

It is very important to see that a good administration can be started without a sovereign, because some colonial statesmen have doubted it. 'I can conceive', it has been said, 'that a ministry would go on well enough without a governor when it was launched, but I do not see how to launch it.' It has even been suggested that a colony which broke away from England, and had to form its own government, might not unwisely choose a governor for life, and solely trusted with selecting ministers, something like the Abbé Sièyes's grand elector. But the introduction of such an officer into such a colony would in fact be the voluntary erection of an artificial encumbrance to it. He would inevitably be a party man. The most dignified post in the State must be an object of contest to the great sections into which every active political community is divided. These parties mix in everything and meddle in everything; and they neither would nor could permit the most honoured and conspicuous of all stations to be filled, except at their pleasure. They know, too, that the grand elector, the great chooser of ministries, might be, at a sharp crisis, either a good friend or a bad enemy. The strongest party would select some one who would be on their side when he had to take a side, who would incline to them when he did incline, who should be a constant auxiliary to them and a constant impediment to their adversaries. It is absurd to choose by contested party election an impartial chooser of ministers.

But it is during the continuance of a ministry, rather than at its creation, that the functions of the sovereign will mainly interest most persons, and that most people will think them to be of the gravest importance. I own I am myself of that opinion. I think it may be shown that the post of sovereign over an intelligent and political people under a constitutional monarchy is the post which a wise man would choose above any other—where he would find the intellectual impulses best stimulated and the worst intellectual impulses best controlled.

On the duties of the Queen during an administration we have an invaluable fragment from her own hand. In 1851 Louis Napoleon had his *coup d'état*; in 1852 Lord John Russell had his—he expelled Lord Palmerston. By a most instructive breach of etiquette he read in the House a royal memorandum on the duties of his rival. It is as follows: 'The Queen requires, first that Lord Palmerston will distinctly state what he proposes in a given case, in order that the Queen may know as distinctly to what she is giving her royal sanction. Secondly, having once given her sanction to such a measure that it be not arbitrarily altered or modified by the minister. Such an act she must consider as failing in sincerity towards the Crown, and justly to be visited by the exercise of her constitutional right of dismissing that minister. She expects to be kept informed of what passes between him and foreign ministers before important decisions are taken based upon that intercourse; to receive the foreign dispatches in good time; and to have the drafts for her approval sent to her in sufficient time to make herself acquainted with their contents before they must be sent off.'

In addition to the control over particular ministers, and especially over the foreign minister, the Queen has a certain control over the Cabinet. The first minister, it is understood, transmits to her authentic information of all the most important decisions, together with what the newspapers would do equally well, the more important votes in Parliament. He is bound to take care that she knows everything which there is to know as to the passing politics of the nation. She has by rigid usage a right to complain if she does not know of every great act of her ministry, not only before it is done, but while there is yet time to consider it—while it is still possible that it may not be done.

To state the matter shortly, the sovereign has, under a constitutional monarchy such as ours, three rights—the right to be consulted, the right to encourage, the right to warn. And a king of great sense and sagacity would want no others. He would find that his having no others would enable him to use these with singular effect. He would say to his minister: 'The responsibility of these measures is upon you. Whatever you think best must be done. Whatever you think best shall have my full and effectual support. *But* you will observe that for this reason and that reason what you propose to do is bad; for this reason and that reason what you do not propose is better. I do not oppose, it is my duty not to oppose; but observe that I *warn*.' Supposing the king to be right, and to have what kings often have, the gift of effectual expression, he could not help moving his minister. He might not always turn his course, but he would always trouble his mind.

In the course of a long reign a sagacious king would acquire an experience with which few ministers could contend. The king could say: 'Have you referred to the transactions which happened during such and such an administration, I think about fourteen years ago? They afford an instructive example of the bad results which are sure to attend the policy which you propose. You did not at that time take so prominent a part in public life as you now do, and it is possible you do not fully remember all the events. I should recommend you to recur to them, and to discuss them with your older colleagues who took part in them. It is unwise to recommence

a policy which so lately worked so ill.' The king
would indeed have the advantage which a permanent
under-secretary has over his superior the parliamentary secretary—that of having shared in the
proceedings of the previous parliamentary secretaries. These proceedings were part of his own life;
occupied the best of his thoughts, gave him perhaps
anxiety, perhaps pleasure, were commenced in spite
of his dissuasion, or were sanctioned by his approval.
The parliamentary secretary vaguely remembers
that something was done in the time of some of his
predecessors, when he very likely did not know the
least or care the least about that sort of public
business. He has to begin by learning painfully and
imperfectly what the permanent secretary knows by
clear and instant memory. No doubt a parliamentary secretary always can, and sometimes does,
silence his subordinate by the tacit might of his
superior dignity. He says: 'I do not think there is
much in all that. Many errors were committed at
the time you refer to which we need not now discuss.'
A pompous man easily sweeps away the suggestions
of those beneath him. But though a minister may so
deal with his subordinate, he cannot so deal with
his king. The social force of admitted superiority
by which he overturned his under-secretary is now
not with him but against him. He has no longer to
regard the deferential hints of an acknowledged
inferior, but to answer the arguments of a superior
to whom he has himself to be respectful. George
III in fact knew the forms of public business as well
or better than any statesman of his time. If, in
addition to his capacity as a man of business and to
his industry, he had possessed the higher faculties
of a discerning statesman, his influence would have
been despotic. The old Constitution of England
undoubtedly gave a sort of power to the Crown

which our present Constitution does not give. While a majority in parliament was principally purchased by royal patronage, the king was a party to the bargain either with his minister or without his minister. But even under our present Constitution a monarch like George III, with high abilities, would possess the greatest influence. It is known to all Europe that in Belgium King Leopold has exercised immense power by the use of such means as I have described.

It is known, too, to every one conversant with the real course of the recent history of England, that Prince Albert really did gain great power in precisely the same way. He had the rare gifts of a constitutional monarch. If his life had been prolonged twenty years, his name would have been known to Europe as that of King Leopold is known. While he lived he was at a disadvantage. The statesmen who had most power in England were men of far greater experience than himself. He might, and no doubt did, exercise a great, if not a commanding influence over Lord Malmesbury, but he could not rule Lord Palmerston. The old statesman who governed England, at an age when most men are unfit to govern their own families, remembered a whole generation of statesmen who were dead before Prince Albert was born. The two were of different ages and different natures. The elaborateness of the German prince—an elaborateness which has been justly and happily compared with that of Goethe—was wholly alien to the half-Irish, half-English, statesman. The somewhat boisterous courage in minor dangers, and the obtrusive use of an always effectual, but not always refined, commonplace, which are Lord Palmerston's defects, doubtless grated on Prince Albert, who had a scholar's caution and a scholar's courage. The facts will be known to our children's children, though not to us. Prince Albert did much, but he died ere he could have made his influence felt on a generation of statesmen less experienced than he was, and anxious to learn from him.

It would be childish to suppose that a conference between a minister and his sovereign can ever be a conference of pure argument. 'The divinity which doth hedge a king' may have less sanctity than it had, but it still has much sanctity. No one, or scarcely any one, can argue with a cabinet minister in his own room as well as he would argue with another man in another room. He cannot make his own points as well; he cannot unmake as well the points presented to him. A monarch's room is worse. The best instance is Lord Chatham, the most dictatorial and imperious of English statesmen, and almost the first English statesman who was borne into power against the wishes of the king and against the wishes of the nobility—the first popular minister. We might have expected a proud tribune of the people to be dictatorial to his sovereign—to be to the king what he was to all others. On the contrary, he was the slave of his own imagination; there was a kind of mystic enchantment in vicinity to the monarch which divested him of his ordinary nature. 'The last peep into the king's closet', said Mr. Burke, 'intoxicates him, and will to the end of his life.' A wit said that, even at the levee, he bowed so low that you could see the tip of his hooked nose between his legs. He was in the habit of kneeling at the bedside of George III while transacting business. Now no man can *argue* on his knees. The same superstitious feeling which keeps him in that physical attitude will keep him in a corresponding mental attitude. He will not refute the bad arguments of the king as he will refute another man's bad arguments. He will not state his own best arguments effectively and incisively when he knows that the king would not like to hear them. In a nearly balanced argument the king must always have the better, and in politics many most important arguments are nearly balanced. Whenever there was much to be said for the king's opinion it would have its full weight; whatever was said for the minister's opinions would only have a lessened and enfeebled weight.

The king, too, possesses a power, according to theory, for extreme use on a critical occasion, but which he can in law use on any occasion. He can dissolve; he can say to his minister in fact, if not in words, 'This parliament sent you here, but I will see if I cannot get another parliament to send some one else here'. George III well understood that it was best to take his stand at times and on points when it was perhaps likely, or at any rate not unlikely, the nation would support him. He always made a minister that he did not like tremble at the shadow of a possible successor. He had a cunning in such matters like the cunning of insanity. He had conflicts with the ablest men of his time, and he was hardly ever baffled. He understood how to help a feeble argument by a tacit threat, and how best to address it to an habitual deference.

Perhaps such powers as these are what a wise man would most seek to exercise and least fear to possess. To wish to be a despot, 'to hunger after tyranny', as the Greek phrase had it, marks in our day an uncultivated mind. A person who so wishes cannot have weighed what Butler calls the 'doubtfulness things are involved in'. To be sure you are right to impose your will, or to wish to impose it, with violence upon others; to see your own ideas vividly and fixedly, and to be tormented till you can apply them in life and practice, not to like to hear the opinions of others, to be unable to sit down and weigh the truth they have, are but crude states of intellect in our present civilization. We know, at least, that facts are many; that progress is complicated; that burning ideas (such as young men have) are mostly false and always incomplete. The notion of a far-seeing and despotic statesman, who can lay down plans for ages yet unborn, is a fancy generated by the pride of the human intellect to which facts give no support. The plans of Charlemagne died with him; those of Richelieu were mistaken; those of Napoleon gigantesque and frantic. But a wise and great constitutional monarch attempts no such vanities. His career is not in the air; he labours in the world of sober fact; he deals with schemes which can be effected—schemes which are desirable— schemes which are worth the cost. He says to the ministry his people send to him, to ministry after ministry, 'I think so and so; do you see if there is anything in it. I have put down my reasons in a certain memorandum, which I will give you. Probably it does not exhaust the subject, but it will suggest materials for your consideration.' By years of discussion with ministry after ministry, the best plans of the wisest king would certainly be adopted, and the inferior plans, the impracticable plans, rooted out and rejected. He could not be uselessly beyond his time, for he would have been obliged to convince the representatives, the characteristic men of his time. He would have the best means of proving that he was right on all new and strange matters, for he would have won to his side probably, after years of discussion, the chosen agents of the commonplace world—men who were where they were, because they had pleased the men of the existing age, who will never be much disposed to new conceptions or profound thoughts. A sagacious and original constitutional monarch might go to his grave in peace if any man could. He would know that his best laws were in harmony with his age; that they suited the people who were to work them, the people who were to be benefited by them. And he would have passed a happy life. He would have passed a life in which he could always get his arguments heard, in which he could always make those who had the responsibility of action think of them before they acted—in which he could know that the schemes which he had set at work in the world were not the casual accidents of an individual idiosyncrasy, which are mostly much wrong, but the likeliest of all things to be right—the ideas of one very intelligent man at last accepted and acted on by the ordinary intelligent many.

But can we expect such a king, or, for that is the material point, can we expect a lineal series of such kings? Every one has heard the reply of the Emperor Alexander to Madame de Stael, who favoured him with a declamation in praise of beneficent despotism. 'Yes, Madame, but it is only a happy accident.' He well knew that the great abilities and the good intentions necessary to make an efficient and good despot never were continuously combined in any line of rulers. He knew that they were far out of reach of hereditary human nature. Can it be said that the characteristic qualities of a constitutional monarch are more within its reach? I am afraid it cannot. We found just now that the characteristic use of an hereditary constitutional monarch, at the outset of an administration, greatly surpassed the ordinary competence of hereditary faculties. I fear that an impartial investigation will establish the same conclusion as to his uses during the continuance of an administration.

If we look at history, we shall find that it is only during the period of the present reign that in England the duties of a constitutional sovereign have ever been well performed. The first two Georges were ignorant of English affairs, and wholly unable to guide them, whether well or ill; for many years in their time the Prime Minister had, over and above the labour of managing parliament, to manage the woman—sometimes the queen, sometimes the mistress—who managed the sovereign; George III interfered unceasingly, but he did harm unceasingly; George IV and William IV gave no steady continuing guidance, and were unfit to give it. On the Continent, in first-class countries, constitutional royalty has never lasted out of one generation. Louis Philippe, Victor Emmanuel, and Leopold are the founders of their dynasties; we must not reckon in constitutional monarchy any more than in despotic monarchy on the permanence in the descendants of the peculiar genius which founded the race. As far as experience goes, there is no reason to expect an hereditary series of useful limited monarchs.

If we look to theory, there is even less reason to expect it. A monarch is useful when he gives an effectual and beneficial guidance to his ministers. But these ministers are sure to be among the ablest men of their time. They will have had to conduct the business of parliament so as to satisfy it: they will have to speak so as to satisfy it. The two together cannot be done save by a man of very great and varied ability. The exercise of the two gifts is sure to teach a man much of the world; and if it did not, a parliamentary leader has to pass through a magnificent training before he becomes a leader. He has to gain a seat in parliament; to gain the ear of parliament; to gain the confidence of parliament;

to gain the confidence of his colleagues. No one can achieve these—no one, still more, can both achieve them and retain them—without a singular ability, nicely trained in the varied detail of life. What chance has an hereditary monarch such as nature forces him to be, such as history shows he is, against men so educated and so born? He can but be an average man to begin with; sometimes he will be clever, but sometimes he will be stupid; in the long run he will be neither clever nor stupid: he will be the simple, common man who plods the plain routine of life from the cradle to the grave. His education will be that of one who has never had to struggle; who has always felt that he has nothing to gain; who has had the first dignity given him; who has never seen common life as in truth it is. It is idle to expect an ordinary man born in the purple to have greater genius than an extraordinary man born out of the purple; to expect a man whose place has always been fixed to have a better judgement than one who has lived by his judgement; to expect a man whose career will be the same whether he is discreet or whether he is indiscreet to have the nice discretion of one who has risen by his wisdom, who will fall if he ceases to be wise.

The characteristic advantage of a constitutional king is the permanence of his place. This gives him the opportunity of acquiring a consecutive knowledge of complex transactions, but it gives only an opportunity. The king must use it. There is no royal road to political affairs: their detail is vast, disagreeable, complicated, and miscellaneous. A king, to be the equal of his ministers in discussion, must work as they work; he must be a man of business as they are men of business. Yet a constitutional prince is the man who is most tempted to pleasure, and the least forced to business. A despot must feel that he is the pivot of the State. The stress of his kingdom is upon him. As he is, so are his affairs. He may be seduced into pleasure; he may neglect all else; but the risk is evident. He will hurt himself; he may cause a revolution. If he becomes unfit to govern, some one else who is fit may conspire against him. But a constitutional king need fear nothing. He may neglect his duties, but he will not be injured. His place will be as fixed, his income as permanent, his opportunities of selfish enjoyment as full as ever. Why should he work? It is true he will lose the quiet and secret influence which in the course of years industry would gain for him; but an eager young man, on whom the world is squandering its luxuries and its temptations, will not be much attracted by the distant prospect of a moderate influence over dull matters. He may form good intentions; he may say, 'Next year I *will* read these papers; I will try and ask more questions; I will not let these women talk to me so'. But they will talk to him. The most hopeless idleness is that most smoothed with excellent plans. 'The Lord Treasurer', says Swift, 'promised he will settle it to-night, and so he will say a hundred nights.' We may depend upon it, the ministry whose power will be lessened by the prince's attention will not be too eager to get him to attend.

So it is if the prince come young to the throne; but the case is worse when he comes to it old or middle-aged. He is then unfit to work. He will then have spent the whole of youth and the first part of manhood in idleness, and it is unnatural to expect him to labour. A pleasure-loving lounger in middle life will not begin to work as George III worked, or as Prince Albert worked. The only fit material for a constitutional king is a prince who begins early to reign—who in his youth is superior to pleasure—who in his youth is willing to labour—who has by nature a genius for discretion. Such kings are among God's greatest gifts, but they are also among His rarest.

An ordinary idle king on a constitutional throne will leave no mark on his time; he will do little good and as little harm; the royal form of cabinet government will work in his time pretty much as the unroyal. The addition of a cipher will not matter though it take precedence of the significant figures. But *corruptio optima pessima*. The most evil case of the royal form is far worse than the most evil case of the unroyal. It is easy to imagine, upon a constitutional throne, an active and meddling fool who always acts when he should not, who never acts when he should, who warns his ministers against their judicious measures, who encourages them in their injudicious measures. It is easy to imagine that such a king should be the tool of others; that favourites should guide him; that mistresses should corrupt him; that the atmosphere of a bad court should be used to degrade free government.

We have had an awful instance of the dangers of constitutional royalty. We have had the case of a meddling maniac. During great part of his life George III's reason was half upset by every crisis. Throughout his life he had an obstinacy akin to that of insanity. He was an obstinate and an evil influence; he could not be turned from what was inexpedient; by the aid of his station he turned truer but weaker men from what was expedient. He gave an excellent moral example to his contemporaries, but he is an instance of those whose good dies with them, while their evil lives after them. He prolonged the American war, perhaps he caused the American war, so we inherit the vestiges of an American hatred; he forbad Mr. Pitt's wise plans, so we inherit an Irish difficulty. He would not let us do right in time, so now our attempts at right are out of time and fruitless. Constitutional royalty under an active and half-insane king is one of the worst of governments. There is in it a secret power which is always eager, which is generally obstinate, which is often wrong, which rules ministers more than they know themselves, which overpowers them much more than the public believe, which is irresponsible because it is inscrutable, which cannot be prevented because it cannot be seen. The benefits of a good monarch are almost invaluable, but the evils of a bad monarch are almost irreparable.

We shall find these conclusions confirmed if we examine the powers and duties of an English monarch at the break-up of an administration. But the power of dissolution and the prerogative of creating peers, the cardinal powers of that moment, are too important and involve too many complex matters to be sufficiently treated at the very end of a paper as long as this.

NO. IV. THE HOUSE OF LORDS

In my last essay I showed that it was possible for a constitutional monarch to be, when occasion served, of first-rate use both at the outset and during the continuance of an administration; but that in matter of fact it was not likely that he would be useful. The requisite ideas, habits, and faculties far surpass the usual competence of an average man, educated in the common manner of sovereigns. The same arguments are entirely applicable at the close of an administration. But at that conjuncture the two most singular prerogatives of an English king—the power of creating new peers and the power of dissolving the Commons—come into play; and we cannot duly criticize the use or misuse of these powers till we know what the peers are and what the House of Commons is.

The use of the House of Lords—or, rather, of the Lords, in its dignified capacity—is very great. It does not attract so much reverence as the Queen, but it attracts very much. The office of an order of nobility is to impose on the common people—not necessarily to impose on them what is untrue, yet less what is hurtful; but still to impose on their quiescent imaginations what would not otherwise be there. The fancy of the mass of men is incredibly weak; it can see nothing without a visible symbol, and there is much that it can scarcely make out with a symbol. Nobility is the symbol of mind. It has the marks from which the mass of men always used to infer mind, and often still infer it. A common clever man who goes into a country place will get no reverence; but the 'old squire' will get reverence. Even after he is insolvent, when every one knows that his ruin is but a question of time, he will get five times as much respect from the common peasantry as the newly-made rich man who sits beside him. The common peasantry will listen to his nonsense more submissively than to the new man's sense. An old lord will get infinite respect. His very existence is so far useful that it awakens the sensation of obedience to a *sort* of mind in the coarse, dull, contracted multitude, who could neither appreciate or perceive any other.

The order of nobility is of great use, too, not only in what it creates, but in what it prevents. It prevents the rule of wealth—the religion of gold. This is the obvious and natural idol of the Anglo-Saxon. He is always trying to make money; he reckons everything in coin; he bows down before a great heap, and sneers as he passes a little heap. He has a 'natural instinctive admiration of wealth for its own sake'. And within good limits the feeling is quite right. So long as we play the game of industry vigorously and eagerly (and I hope we shall long play it, for we must be very different from what we are if we do anything better), we shall of necessity respect and admire those who play successfully, and a little despise those who play unsuccessfully. Whether this feeling be right or wrong, it is useless to discuss; to a certain degree, it is involuntary: it is not for mortals to settle whether we will have it or not; nature settles for us that, within moderate limits, we must have it. But the admiration of wealth in many countries goes far beyond this; it ceases to regard in any degree the skill of acquisition; it respects wealth in the hands of the inheritor just as much as in the hands of the maker; it is a simple envy and love of a heap of gold as a heap of gold. From this our aristocracy preserves us. There is no country where a 'poor devil of a millionaire is so ill off as in England'. The experiment is tried every day, and every day it is proved that money alone —money *pur et simple*—will not buy 'London Society'. Money is kept down, and, so to say, cowed by the predominant authority of a different power.

But it may be said that this is no gain; that worship for worship, the worship of money is as good as the worship of rank. Even granting that it were so, it is a great gain to society to have two idols; in the competition of idolatries, the true worship gets a chance. But it is not true that the reverence for rank—at least, for hereditary rank—is as base as the reverence for money. As the world has gone, manner has been half-hereditary in certain castes, and manner is one of the fine arts. It is the *style* of society; it is in the daily-spoken intercourse of human beings what the art of literary expression is in their occasional written intercourse. In reverencing wealth we reverence not a man, but an appendix to a man; in reverencing inherited nobility, we reverence the probable possession of a great faculty —the faculty of bringing out what is in one. The unconscious grace of life *may* be in the middle classes: finely-mannered persons are born everywhere; but it *ought* to be in the aristocracy; and a man must be born with a hitch in his nerves if he has not some of it. It is a physiological possession of the race, though it is sometimes wanting in the individual.

There is a third idolatry from which that of rank preserves us, and perhaps it is the worst of any— that of office. The basest deity is a subordinate *employé*, and yet just now in civilized governments it is the commonest. In France and all the best of the Continent it rules like a superstition. It is to no purpose that you prove that the pay of petty

officials is smaller than mercantile pay; that their
work is more monotonous than mercantile work;
that their mind is less useful and their life more
tame. They are still thought to be greater and better.
They are *decorés*; they have a little red on the left
breast of their coat, and no argument will answer
that. In England, by the odd course of our society,
what a theorist would desire has in fact turned up.
The great offices, whether permanent or parliamentary, which require mind now give social prestige, and almost only those. An Under-Secretary
of State with £2,000 a-year is a much greater man
than the director of a finance company with £5,000,
and the country saves the difference. But except
in a few offices like the Treasury, which were once
filled with aristocratic people, and have an odour of
nobility at second-hand, minor place is of no social
use. A big grocer despises the exciseman; and what
in many countries would be thought impossible,
the exciseman envies the grocer. Solid wealth tells
where there is no artificial dignity given to petty
public functions. A clerk in the public service is
'nobody'; and you could not make a common
Englishman see why he should be anybody.

But it must be owned that this turning of society
into a political expedient has half spoiled it. A great
part of the 'best' English people keep their mind in
a state of decorous dullness. They maintain their
dignity; they get obeyed; they are good and charit-
able to their dependants. But they have no notion
of *play* of mind; no conception that the charm of
society depends upon it. They think cleverness an
antic, and have a constant though needless horror
of being thought to have any of it. So much does
this stiff dignity give the tone, that the few Englishmen capable of social brilliancy mostly secrete it.
They reserve it for persons whom they can trust,

and whom they know to be capable of appreciating its *nuances*. But a good government is well worth a great deal of social dullness. The dignified torpor of English society is inevitable if we give precedence, not to the cleverest classes, but to the oldest classes, and we have seen how useful that is.

The social prestige of the aristocracy is, as every one knows, immensely less than it was a hundred years or even fifty years since. Two great movements—the two greatest of modern society—have been unfavourable to it. The rise of industrial wealth in countless forms has brought in a competitor which has generally more mind, and which would be supreme were it not for awkwardness and intellectual *gêne*. Every day our companies, our railways, our debentures, and our shares, tend more and more to multiply these *surroundings* of the aristocracy, and in time they will hide it. And while this undergrowth has come up, the aristocracy have come down. They have less means of standing out than they used to have. Their power is in their theatrical exhibition, in their state. But society is every day becoming less stately. As our great satirist has observed, 'The last Duke of St. David's used to cover the north road with his carriages; landladies and waiters bowed before him. The present Duke sneaks away from a railway station, smoking a cigar, in a brougham.' The aristocracy cannot lead the old life if they would; they are ruled by a stronger power. They suffer from the tendency of all modern society to raise the average, and to lower—comparatively, and perhaps absolutely, to lower—the summit. As the picturesqueness, the featureliness, of society diminishes, aristocracy loses the single instrument of its peculiar power.

If we remember the great reverence which used to be paid to nobility as such, we shall be surprised that the House of Lords, as an assembly, has always been inferior; that it was always just as now, not the first, but the second of our assemblies. I am not, of course, now speaking of the Middle Ages; I am not dealing with the embryo or the infant form of our Constitution; I am only speaking of its adult form. Take the times of Sir R. Walpole. He was Prime Minister because he managed the House of Commons; he was turned out because he was beaten on an election petition in that House; he ruled England because he ruled that House. Yet the nobility were then the governing power in England. In many districts the word of some lord was law. The 'wicked Lord Lowther', as he was called, left a name of terror in Westmoreland during the memory of men now living. A great part of the borough members and a great part of the county members were their nominees; an obedient, un-questioning deference was paid them. As indivi-duals the peers were the greatest people; as a House the collected peers were but the second House.

Several causes contributed to create this anomaly, but the main cause was a natural one. The House of Peers has never been a House where the most important peers were most important. It could not be so. The qualities which fit a man for marked eminence, in a deliberative assembly, are not here-ditary, and are not coupled with great estates. In the nation, in the provinces, in his own province, a Duke of Devonshire, or a Duke of Bedford, was a much greater man than Lord Thurlow. They had great estates, many boroughs, innumerable re-tainers, followings like a court. Lord Thurlow had no boroughs, no retainers; he lived on his salary. Till the House of Lords met, the dukes were not only the greatest, but immeasurably the greatest. But as soon as the House met, Lord Thurlow became the greatest. He could speak, and the others could not speak. He could transact business in half an hour which they could not have transacted in a day, or could not have transacted at all. When some foolish peer, who disliked his domination, sneered at his birth, he had words to meet the case: he said it was better for any one to owe his place to his own exertions than to owe it to descent, to being the 'accident of an accident'. But such a House as this could not be pleasant to great noblemen. They could not like to be second in their own assembly (and yet that was their position from age to age) to a lawyer who was of yesterday,—whom everybody could remember without briefs,—who had talked for 'hire',—who had 'hungered after six-and-eightpence'. Great peers did not gain glory from the House; on the contrary, they lost glory when they were in the House. They devised two expedients to get out of this difficulty; they invented proxies which enabled them to vote without being present,—without being offended by vigour and invective,—without being vexed by ridicule,—without leaving the rural mansion or the town palace where they were demigods. And what was more effectual still, they used their influence in the House of Commons instead of the House of Lords. In that indirect manner a rural potentate, who half returned two county members, and wholly returned two borough members,—who perhaps gave seats to members of the Government, who possibly seated the leader of the Opposition,—became a much greater man than by sitting on his own bench, in his own House, hearing a chancellor talk. The House of Lords was a second-rate force, even when the peers were a first-rate force, because the greatest peers, those who had the greatest social importance, did not care for their own House, or like it, but gained great part of their political power by a hidden but potent influence in the competing House.

When we cease to look at the House of Lords under its dignified aspect, and come to regard it under its strictly useful aspect, we find the literary theory of the English Constitution wholly wrong, as usual. This theory says that the House of Lords is a co-ordinate estate of the realm, of equal rank with the House of Commons; that it is the aristocratic branch, just as the Commons is the popular branch; and that by the principle of our Constitution the aristocratic branch has equal authority with the popular branch. So utterly false is this doctrine that it is a remarkable peculiarity, a capital excellence of the British Constitution, that it contains a sort of Upper House, which is not of equal authority to the Lower House, yet still has some authority.

The evil of two co-equal Houses of distinct natures is obvious. Each House can stop all legislation, and yet some legislation may be necessary At this moment we have the best instance of this which could be conceived. The Upper House of our Victorian Constitution, representing the rich woolgrowers, has disagreed with the Lower Assembly, and most business is suspended. But for a most curious stratagem the machine of government would stand still. Most constitutions have committed this blunder. The two most remarkable Republican institutions in the world commit it. In both the American and the Swiss Constitutions the Upper House has as much authority as the second; it could produce the maximum of impediment—the deadlock, if it liked; if it does not do so, it is owing not to the goodness of the legal constitution, but to the discreetness of the members of the Chamber. In both these constitutions this dangerous division is defended by a peculiar doctrine with which I have nothing to do now. It is said that there must be in a Federal Government some institution, some authority, some body possessing a veto in which the separate States composing the Confederation are all equal. I confess this doctrine has to me no self-evidence, and it is assumed, but not proved. The State of Delaware is *not* equal in power or influence to the State of New York, and you cannot make it so by giving it an equal veto in an Upper Chamber. The history of such an institution is indeed most natural. A little State will like, and must like, to see some token, some memorial mark of its old independence preserved in the Constitution by which that independence is extinguished. But it is one thing for an institution to be natural, and another for it to be expedient. If indeed it be that a Federal Government compels the erection of an Upper Chamber of conclusive and co-ordinate authority, it is one more in addition to the many other inherent defects of that kind of government. It may be necessary to have the blemish, but it is a blemish just as much.

There ought to be in every Constitution an available authority somewhere. The sovereign power must be *come-at-able*. And the English have made it so. The House of Lords, at the passing of the Reform Act of 1832, was as unwilling to concur with the House of Commons as the Upper Chamber at Victoria to concur with the Lower Chamber. But it did concur. The Crown has the authority to create new peers; and the king of the day had promised the ministry of the day to create them. The House of Lords did not like the precedent, and they passed the Bill. The power was not used, but its existence was as useful as its energy. Just as the knowledge that his men *can* strike makes a master yield in order that they may not strike, so the knowledge that their House could be swamped at the will of the king—at the will of the people—made the Lords yield to the people.

From the Reform Act the function of the House of Lords has been altered in English history. Before that Act it was, if not a directing Chamber, at least a Chamber of Directors. The leading nobles, who had most influence in the Commons, and swayed the Commons, sat there. Aristocratic influence was so powerful in the House of Commons, that there never was any serious breach of unity. When the Houses quarrelled, it was, as in the great Aylesbury case, about their respective privileges, and not about the national policy. The influence of the nobility was then so potent, that it was not necessary to exert it. The English Constitution, though then on this point very different from what it now is, did not even then contain the blunder of the Victorian or of the Swiss Constitution. It had not two Houses of distinct origin; it had two Houses of common origin—two Houses in which the predominant element was the same. The danger of discordance was obviated by a latent unity.

Since the Reform Act the House of Lords has become a revising and suspending House. It can alter Bills; it can reject Bills on which the House of Commons is not yet thoroughly in earnest—upon which the nation is not yet determined. Their veto is a sort of hypothetical veto. They say, We reject your Bill for this once, or these twice, or even these thrice; but if you keep on sending it up, at last we won't reject it. The House has ceased to be one of latent directors, and has become one of temporary rejectors and palpable alterers.

It is the sole claim of the Duke of Wellington to the name of a statesman that he presided over this change. He wished to guide the Lords to their true position, and he did guide them. In 1846, in the crisis of the Corn-Law struggle, and when it was a question whether the House of Lords should resist or yield, he wrote a very curious letter to the late Lord Derby:—

'For many years, indeed from the year 1830, when I retired from office, I have endeavoured to manage the House of Lords upon the principle on which I conceive that the institution exists in the Constitution of the country, that of Conservatism. I have invariably objected to all violent and extreme measures, which is not exactly the mode of acquiring influence in a political party in England, particularly one in opposition to Government. I have invariably supported Government in Parliament upon important occasions, and have always exercised my personal influence to prevent the mischief of anything like a difference or division between the two Houses,—of which there are some remarkable instances, to which I will advert here, as they will tend to show you the nature of my management, and possibly, in some degree, account for the extraordinary power which I have for so many years exercised, without any apparent claim to it.

'Upon finding the difficulties in which the late King William was involved by a promise made to create peers, the number, I believe, indefinite, I determined myself, and I prevailed upon others, the number very large, to be absent from the House in the discussion of the last stages of the Reform Bill, after the negotiations had failed for the formation of a new Administration. This course gave at the time great dissatisfaction to the party; notwithstanding that I believe it saved the existence of the House of Lords at the time and the Constitution of the country.

'Subsequently, throughout the period from 1835 to 1841, I prevailed upon the House of Lords to depart from many principles and systems which they as well as I had adopted and voted on Irish tithes, Irish corporations, and other measures, much to the vexation and annoyance of many. But I recollect one particular measure, the union of the provinces of Upper and Lower Canada, in the early stages of which I had spoken in opposition to the measure, and had protested against it; and in the last stages of it I prevailed upon the House to agree to, and pass it, in order to avoid the injury to the public interests of a dispute between the Houses upon a question of such importance. Then I supported the measures of the Government, and protected the servant of the Government, Captain Elliot, in China. All of which tended to weaken my influence with some of the party; others, possibly a majority, might have approved of the course which I took. It was at the same time well known that, from the commencement at least of Lord Melbourne's Government, I was in constant communication with it, upon all military matters, whether occurring at home or abroad, at all events. But likewise upon many others.

'All this tended, of course, to diminish my influence in the Conservative party, while it tended essentially to the ease and satisfaction of the Sovereign, and to the maintenance of good order. At length came the resignation of the Government by Sir Robert Peel, in the month of December last, and the Queen desiring Lord John Russell to form an Administration. On the 12th of December the Queen wrote to me the letter of which I enclose the copy, and the copy of my answer of the same date; of which it appears that you have never seen copies, although I communicated them immediately to

Sir Robert Peel. It was impossible for me to act otherwise than is indicated in my letter to the Queen. I am the servant of the Crown and people. I have been paid and rewarded, and I consider myself retained; and that I can't do otherwise than serve as required, when I can do so without dishonour, that is to say, as long as I have health and strength to enable me to serve. But it is obvious that there is, and there must be, an end of all connection and counsel between party and me. I might with consistency, and some may think that I ought to, have declined to belong to Sir Robert Peel's Cabinet on the night of the 20th of December. But my opinion is, that if I had, Sir Robert Peel's Government would not have been framed; that we should have had —— and —— in office next morning.

'But, at all events, it is quite obvious that when that arrangement comes, which sooner or later must come, there will be an end to all influence on my part over the Conservative party, if I should be so indiscreet as to attempt to exercise any. You will see, therefore, that the stage is quite clear for you, and that you need not apprehend the consequences of differing in opinion from me when you will enter upon it; as in truth I have, by my letter to the Queen of the 12th of December, put an end to the connection between the party and me, when the party will be in opposition to her Majesty's Government.

'My opinion is, that the great object of all is that you should assume the station, and exercise the influence, which I have so long exercised in the House of Lords. The question is, how is that object to be attained? By guiding their opinion and decision, or by following it? You will see that I have endeavoured to guide their opinion, and have succeeded upon some most remarkable occasions. But it has been by a good deal of management.

'Upon the important occasion and question now before the House, I propose to endeavour to induce them to avoid to involve the country in the additional difficulties of a difference of opinion, possibly a dispute between the Houses, on a question in the decision of which it has been frequently asserted that their lordships had a personal interest; which assertion, however false as affecting each of them personally, could not be denied as affecting the proprietors of land in general. I am aware of the difficulty, but I don't despair of carrying the Bill through. You must be the best judge of the course which you ought to take, and of the course most likely to conciliate the confidence of the House of Lords. My opinion is, that you should advise the House to vote that which would tend most to public order, and would be most beneficial to the immediate interests of the country.'

This is the mode in which the House of Lords came to be what it now is, a chamber with (in most cases) a veto of delay, with (in most cases) a power of revision, but with no other rights or powers. The question we have to answer is, 'The House of Lords being such, what is the use of the Lords?'

The common notion evidently fails, that it is a bulwark against imminent revolution. As the Duke's letter in every line evinces, the wisest members, the guiding members of the House, know that the House must yield to the people if the people is determined. The two cases—that of the Reform Act and the Corn Laws—were decisive cases. The great majority of the Lords thought Reform revolution, Free-trade confiscation, and the two together ruin. If they could ever have been trusted to resist the people, they would then have resisted it. But

in truth it is idle to expect a second chamber—
a chamber of notables—ever to resist a popular
chamber, a nation's chamber, when that chamber
is vehement and the nation vehement too. There
is no strength in it for that purpose. Every class
chamber, every minority chamber, so to speak, feels
weak and helpless when the nation is excited. In
a time of revolution there are but two powers, the
sword and the people. The executive commands
the sword; the great lesson which the fiirst Napoleon
taught the Parisian populace—the contribution he
made to the theory of revolutions at the 18th
Brumaire—is now well known. Any strong soldier
at the head of the army can use the army. But
a second chamber cannot use it. It is a pacific
assembly, composed of timid peers, aged lawyers,
or, as abroad, clever *littérateurs*. Such a body has
no force to put down the nation, and if the nation
will have it do something it must do it.

The very nature, too, as has been seen, of the
Lords in the English Constitution, shows that it
cannot stop revolution. The constitution contains
an exceptional provision to prevent its stopping it.
The executive, the appointee of the popular chamber
and the nation, can make new peers, and so create
a majority in the peers; it can say to the Lords, 'Use
the powers of your House as we like, or you shall
not use them at all. We will find others to use
them; your virtue shall go out of you if it is not
used as we like, and stopped when we please.' An
assembly under such a threat cannot arrest, and
could not be intended to arrest, a determined and
insisting executive.

In fact the House of Lords, as a House, is not
a bulwark that will keep out revolution, but an index
that revolution is unlikely. Resting as it does upon
old deference and inveterate homage, it shows that

the spasm of new forces, the outbreak of new agencies, which we call revolution, is for the time simply impossible. So long as many old leaves linger on the November trees, you know that there has been little frost and no wind: just so while the House of Lords retains much power, you may know that there is no desperate discontent in the country, no wild agency likely to cause a great demolition.

There used to be a singular idea that two chambers—a revising chamber and a suggesting chamber—were essential to a free government. The first person who threw a hard stone—an effectually hitting stone—against the theory was one very little likely to be favourable to democratic influence, or to be blind to the use of aristocracy; it was the present Lord Grey. He had to look at the matter practically. He was the first great colonial minister of England who ever set himself to introduce representative institutions into *all* her capable colonies, and the difficulty stared him in the face that in those colonies there were hardly enough good people for one assembly, and not near enough good people for two assemblies. It happened—and most naturally happened—that a second assembly was mischievous. The second assembly was either the nominee of the Crown, which in such places naturally allied itself with better instructed minds, or was elected by people with a higher property qualification—some peculiarly well-judging people. Both these choosers choose the best men in the colony, and put them into the second assembly. But thus the popular assembly was left without those best men. The popular assembly was denuded of those guides and those leaders who would have led and guided it best. Those superior men were put aside to talk to one another, and perhaps dispute with one another; they were a concentrated instance of high but neutralized forces. They wished to do good, but they could do nothing. The Lower House, with all the best people in the colony extracted, did what it liked. The democracy was strengthened rather than weakened by the isolation of its best opponents in a weak position. As soon as experience had shown this, or seemed to show it, the theory that two chambers were essential to a good and free government vanished away.

With a perfect Lower House it is certain that an Upper House would be scarcely of any value. If we had an ideal House of Commons perfectly representing the nation, always moderate, never passionate, abounding in men of leisure, never omitting the slow and steady forms necessary for good consideration, it is certain that we should not need a higher chamber. The work would be done so well that we should not want any one to look over or revise it. And whatever is unnecessary in government is pernicious. Human life makes so much complexity necessary that an artificial addition is sure to do harm: you cannot tell where the needless bit of machinery will catch and clog the hundred needful wheels; but the chances are conclusive that it will impede them somewhere, so nice are they and so delicate. But though beside an ideal House of Commons the Lords would be unnecessary, and therefore pernicious, beside the actual House a revising and leisured legislature is extremely useful, if not quite necessary.

At present the chance majorities on minor questions in the House of Commons are subject to no effectual control. The nation never attends to any but the principal matters of policy and state. Upon these it forms that rude, rough, ruling judgement which we call public opinion; but upon other things it does not think at all, and it would be useless for it to think. It has not the materials for forming a judgement: the detail of Bills, the instrumental part of policy, the latent part of legislation, are wholly out of its way. It knows nothing about them, and could not find time or labour for the careful investigation by which alone they can be apprehended. A casual majority of the House of Commons has therefore dominant power: it can legislate as it wishes. And though the whole House of Commons upon great subjects very fairly represents public opinion, and though its judgement upon minor questions is, from some secret excellences in its composition, remarkably sound and good; yet, like all similar assemblies, it is subject to the sudden action of selfish combinations. There are said to be two hundred 'members for the railways' in the present Parliament. If these two hundred choose to combine on a point which the public does not care for, and which they care for because it affects their purse, they are absolute. A formidable sinister interest may always obtain the complete command of a dominant assembly by some chance and for a moment, and it is therefore of great use to have a second chamber of an opposite sort, differently composed, in which that interest in all likelihood will not rule.

The most dangerous of all sinister interests is that of the executive Government, because it is the most powerful. It is perfectly possible—it has happened, and will happen again—that the Cabinet, being very powerful in the Commons, may inflict minor measures on the nation which the nation did not like, but which it did not understand enough to forbid. If, therefore, a tribunal of revision can be found in which the executive, though powerful, is less powerful, the government will be the better; the retarding chamber will impede minor instances of parliamentary tyranny, though it will not prevent or much impede revolution.

Every large assembly is, moreover, a fluctuating body; it is not one house, so to say, but a set of houses; it is one set of men to-night and another to-morrow night. A certain unity is doubtless preserved by the duty which the executive is supposed to undertake, and does undertake, of keeping a house; a constant element is so provided about which all sorts of variables accumulate and pass away. But even after due allowance for the full weight of this protective machinery, our House of Commons is, as all such chambers must be, subject to sudden turns and bursts of feeling, because the members who compose it change from time to time. The pernicious result is perpetual in our legislation; many acts of Parliament are medleys of different motives, because the majority which passed one set of its clauses is different from that which passed another set.

But the greatest defect of the House of Commons is that it has no leisure. The life of the House is the worst of all lives—a life of distracting routine. It has an amount of business brought before it such as no similar assembly ever has had. The British empire is a miscellaneous aggregate, and each bit of the aggregate brings its bit of business to the House of Commons. It is India one day and Jamaica the next: then again China, and then Schleswig-Holstein. Our legislation touches on all subjects, because our country contains all ingredients. The mere questions which are asked of the ministers run over half human affairs; the Private Bill Acts, the mere *privilegia* of our Government—subordinate as they ought to be—probably give the House of Commons more absolute work than the whole business, both national and private, of any other assembly which has ever sat. The whole scene is so encumbered with changing business, that it is hard to keep your head in it.

Whatever, too, may be the case hereafter, when a better system has been struck out, at present the House does all the work of legislation, all the detail, and all the clauses itself. One of the most helpless exhibitions of helpless ingenuity and wasted mind is a committee of the whole House on a Bill of many clauses which eager enemies are trying to spoil, and various friends are trying to mend. An Act of Parliament is at least as complex as a marriage settlement; and it is made much as a settlement would be if it were left to the vote and settled by the major part of persons concerned, including the unborn children. There is an advocate for every interest, and every interest clamours for every advantage. The executive Government by means of its disciplined forces, and the few invaluable members who sit and think, preserves some sort of unity. But the result is very imperfect. The best test of a machine is the work it turns out. Let any one who knows what legal documents ought to be, read first a will he has just been making and then an Act of Parliament; he will certainly say, 'I would have dismissed my attorney if he had done my business as the legislature has done the nation's business'. While the House of Commons is what it is, a good revising, regulating, and retarding House would be a benefit of great magnitude.

But is the House of Lords such a chamber? Does it do this work? This is almost an undiscussed question. The House of Lords, for thirty years at least, has been in popular discussion an accepted matter. Popular passion has not crossed the path, and no vivid imagination has been excited to clear the matter up.

The House of Lords has the greatest merit which such a chamber can have; it is *possible*. It is incredibly difficult to get a revising assembly, because it is difficult to find a class of respected revisers. A federal Senate, a second House, which represents State Unity, has this advantage; it embodies a feeling at the root of society—a feeling which is older than complicated politics, which is stronger a thousand times over than common political feelings—the *local* feeling. 'My shirt', said the Swiss state-right patriot, 'is dearer to me than my coat.' Every State in the American Union would feel that disrespect to the Senate was disrespect to itself. Accordingly, the Senate is respected: whatever may be the merits or demerits of its action, it can act; it is real, independent, and efficient. But in common governments it is fatally difficult to make an *un*popular entity powerful in a popular government.

It is almost the same thing to say that the House of Lords is independent. It would not be powerful, it would not be possible, unless it were known to be independent. The Lords are in several respects more independent than the Commons; their judgement may not be so good a judgement, but it is emphatically their own judgement. The House of Lords, as a body, is accessible to no social bribe. And this, in our day, is no light matter. Many members of the House of Commons, who are to be influenced by no other manner of corruption, are much influenced by this its most insidious sort. The conductors of the press and the writers for it are worse—at least the more influential who come near the temptation; for 'position', as they call it, for a certain intimacy with the aristocracy, some of them would do almost anything and say almost anything. But the Lords are those who give social bribes, and not those who take them. They are above corruption because they are the corruptors. They have no constituency to fear or wheedle; they have the best means of forming a disinterested and cool judgement of any class in the country. They have, too, leisure to form it. They have no occupations to distract them which are worth the name. Field sports are but playthings, though some Lords put an Englishman's seriousness into them. Few Englishmen can bury themselves in science or literature; and the aristocracy have less, perhaps, of that impetus than the middle classes. Society is too correct and dull to be an occupation, as in other times and ages it has been. The aristocracy live in the fear of the middle classes—of the grocer and the merchant. They dare not frame a society of enjoyment as the French aristocracy once formed it. Politics are the only occupation a peer has worth the name. He may pursue them undistractedly. The House of Lords, besides independence to revise judicially and position to revise effectually, has leisure to revise intellectually.

These are great merits; and, considering how difficult it is to get a good second chamber, and how much with our present first chamber we need a second, we may well be thankful for them. But we must not permit them to blind our eyes. Those merits of the Lords have faults close beside them which go far to make them useless. With its wealth, its place, and its leisure, the House of Lords would, on the very surface of the matter, rule us far more than it does if it had not secret defects which hamper and weaken it.

The first of these defects is hardly to be called secret, though, on the other hand, it is not well known. A severe though not unfriendly critic of our institutions said that 'the *cure* for admiring the House of Lords was to go and look at it'—to look at it not on a great party field-day, or at a time of parade, but in the ordinary transaction of business. There are perhaps ten peers in the House, possibly only six; three is the quorum for transacting business. A few more may dawdle in or not dawdle in; those are the principal speakers, the lawyers (a few years ago when Lyndhurst, Brougham, and Campbell were in vigour, they were by far the predominant talkers) and a few statesmen whom every one knows. But the mass of the House is nothing. This is why orators trained in the Commons detest to speak in the Lords. Lord Chatham used to call it the 'Tapestry'. The House of Commons is a scene of life if ever there was a scene of life. Every member in the throng, every atom in the medley, has his own objects (good or bad), his own purposes (great or petty); his own notions, such as they are, of what is; his own notions, such as they are, of what ought to be. There is a motley confluence of vigorous elements, but the result is one and good. There is a 'feeling of the House', a 'sense' of the House, and no one who knows anything of it can despise it. A very shrewd man of the world went so far as to say that 'the House of Commons has more sense than any one in it'. But there is no such 'sense' in the House of Lords, because there is no life. The Lower Chamber is a chamber of eager politicians; the Upper (to say the least) of *not* eager ones,

This apathy is not, indeed, as great as the outside show would indicate. The committees of the Lords (as is well known) do a great deal of work, and do it very well. And such as it is, the apathy is very natural. A House composed of rich men who can vote by proxy without coming will not come very much.[1] But after every abatement the real indiffer-

[1] In accordance with a recent resolution of the House of Lords, proxies are now disused.—*Note* to second edition.

E

ence to their duties of most peers is a great defect, and the apparent indifference is a dangerous defect. As far as politics go there is profound truth in Lord Chesterfield's axiom, that 'the world must judge of you by what you seem, not by what you are'. The world knows what you seem; it does not know what you are. An assembly—a revising assembly especially—which does not assemble, which looks as if it does not care how it revises, is defective in a main political ingredient. It may be of use, but it will hardly convince mankind that it is so.

The next defect is even more serious; it affects not simply the apparent work of the House of Lords but the real work. For a revising legislature, it is too uniformly made up. Errors are of various kinds; but the constitution of the House of Lords only guards against a single error—that of too quick change. The Lords—leaving out a few lawyers and a few outcasts—are all landowners of more or less wealth. They all have more or less the opinions, the merits, the faults of that one class. They revise legislation, as far as they do revise it, exclusively according to the supposed interests, the predominant feelings, the inherited opinions, of that class. Since the Reform Act, this uniformity of tendency has been very evident. The Lords have felt—it would be harsh to say hostile, but still dubious, as to the new legislation. There was a spirit in it alien to their spirit, and which when they could they have tried to cast out. That spirit is what has been termed the 'modern spirit'. It is not easy to concentrate its essence in a phrase: it lives in our life, animates our actions, suggests our thoughts. We all know what it means, though it would take an essay to limit it and define it. To this the Lords object; wherever it is concerned, they are not impartial revisers, but biased revisers.

This singleness of composition would be no fault, it would be, or might be, even a merit, if the criticism of the House of Lords, though a suspicious criticism, were yet a criticism of great understanding. The characteristic legislation of every age must have characteristic defects; it is the outcome of a character, of necessity faulty and limited. It must mistake some kind of things; it must overlook some other. If we could get hold of a complemental critic, a critic who saw what the age did not see, and who saw rightly what the age mistook, we should have a critic of inestimable value. But is the House of Lords that critic? Can it be said that its unfriendliness to the legislation of the age is founded on a perception of what the age does not see, and a rectified perception of what the age does see? The most extreme partisan, the most warm admirer of the Lords, if of fair and tempered mind, cannot say so. The evidence is too strong. On free trade, for example, no one can doubt that the Lords—in opinion, in what they wished to do, and would have done, if they had acted on their own minds—were utterly wrong. This is the clearest test of the 'modern spirit'. It is easier here to be sure it is right than elsewhere. Commerce is like war; its result is patent. Do you make money or do you not make it? There is as little appeal from figures as from battle. Now no one can doubt that England is a great deal better off because of free trade; that it has more money, and that its money is diffused more as we should wish it diffused. In the one case in which we can unanswerably test the modern spirit, it was right, and the dubious Upper House— the House which would have rejected it, if possible —was wrong.

There is another reason. The House of Lords, being an hereditary chamber, cannot be of more than common ability. It may contain—it almost always has contained, it almost always will contain —extraordinary men. But its average born law-makers cannot be extraordinary. Being a set of eldest sons picked out by chance and history, it cannot be very wise. It would be a standing miracle if such a chamber possessed a knowledge of its age superior to the other men of the age; if it possessed a superior and supplemental knowledge; if it descried what they did not discern, and saw truly that which they saw, indeed, but saw untruly.

The difficulty goes deeper. The task of revising, of adequately revising the legislation of this age, is not only that which an aristocracy has no facility in doing, but one which it has a difficulty in doing. Look at the statute book for 1865—the statutes at large for the year. You will find, not pieces of literature, not nice and subtle matters, but coarse matters, crude heaps of heavy business. They deal with trade, with finance, with statute law reform, with common law reform; they deal with various sorts of business, but with business always. And there is no educated human being less likely to know business, worse placed for knowing business, than a young lord. Business is really more agreeable than pleasure; it interests the whole mind, the aggregate nature of man more continuously, and more deeply. But it does not *look* as if it did. It is difficult to convince a young man, who can have the best of pleasure, that it will. A young lord just come into £30,000 a year will not, as a rule, care much for the law of patents, for the law of 'passing tolls', or the law of prisons. Like Hercules, he may choose virtue, but hardly Hercules could choose business. He has everything to allure him from it, and nothing to allure him to it. And even if he wish to give himself to business, he has indifferent means.

Pleasure is near him, but business is far from him. Few things are more amusing than the ideas of a well-intentioned young man, who is born out of the business world, but who wishes to take to business, about business. He has hardly a notion in what it consists. It really is the adjustment of certain particular means to equally certain particular ends. But hardly any young man destitute of experience is able to separate end and means. It seems to him a kind of mystery; and it is lucky if he do not think that the forms are the main part, and that the end is but secondary. There are plenty of business men, falsely so called, who will advise him so. The subject seems a kind of maze. 'What would you recommend me to *read*?' the nice youth asks; and it is impossible to explain to him that reading has nothing to do with it, that he has not yet the original ideas in his mind to read about; that administration is an art as painting is an art; and that no book can teach the practice of either.

Formerly this defect in the aristocracy was hidden by their other advantages. Being the only class at ease for money and cultivated in mind they were without competition; and though they might not be, as a rule, and extraordinary ability excepted, excellent in State business, they were the best that could be had. Even in old times, however, they sheltered themselves from the greater pressure of coarse work. They appointed a manager—a Peel or a Walpole, anything but an aristocrat in manner or in nature— to act for them and manage for them. But now a class is coming up trained to thought, full of money, and yet trained to business. As I write, two members of this class have been appointed to stations considerable in themselves, and sure to lead (if anything is sure in politics) to the Cabinet and power. This is the class of highly-cultivated men of business who, after a few years, are able to leave business and begin ambition. As yet these men are few in public life, because they do not know their own strength. It is like Columbus and the egg once again; a few original men will show it can be done, and then a crowd of common men will follow. These men know business partly from tradition, and this is much. There are University families—families who talk of fellowships, and who invest their children's ability in Latin verses as soon as they discover it; there used to be Indian families of the same sort, and probably will be again when the competitive system has had time to foster a new breed. Just so there are business families to whom all that concerns money, all that concerns administration, is as familiar as the air they breathe. All Americans, it has been said, know business; it is in the air of their country. Just so certain classes know business here; and a lord can hardly know it. It is as great a difficulty to learn business in a palace as it is to learn agriculture in a park.

To one kind of business, indeed, this doctrine does not apply. There is one kind of business in which our aristocracy have still, and are likely to retain long, a certain advantage. This is the business of diplomacy. Napoleon, who knew men well, would never, if he could help it, employ men of the Revolution in missions to the old courts; he said, 'They spoke to no one, and no one spoke to them'; and so they sent home no information. The reason is obvious. The old-world diplomacy of Europe was largely carried on in drawing-rooms, and, to a great extent, of necessity still is so. Nations touch at their summits. It is always the highest class which travels most, knows most of foreign nations, has the least of the territorial sectarianism which calls itself patriotism, and is often thought to be so. Even here, indeed, in England the new trade-class is in real merit equal to the aristocracy. Their knowledge of foreign things is as great, and their contact with them often more. But, notwith-standing, the new race is not as serviceable for diplomacy as the old race. An ambassador is not simply an agent; he is also a spectacle. He is sent abroad for show as well as for substance; he is to represent the Queen among foreign courts and foreign sovereigns. An aristocracy is in its nature better suited to such work: it is trained to the theatrical part of life; it is fit for that if it is fit for anything.

But, with this exception, an aristocracy is necessar-ily inferior in business to the classes nearer business; and it is not, therefore, a suitable class, if we had our choice of classes, out of which to frame a cham-ber for revising matters of business. It is indeed a singular example how natural business is to the English race, that the House of Lords works as well as it does. The common appearance of the 'whole House' is a jest—a dangerous anomaly, which Mr. Bright will sometimes use; but a great deal of sub-stantial work is done in 'Committees', and often very well done. The great majority of the Peers do none of their appointed work, and could do none of it; but a minority—a minority never so large and never so earnest as in this age—do it, and do it well. Still no one, who examines the matter without prejudice, can say that the work is done perfectly. In a country so rich in mind as England, far more intellectual power can be, and ought to be, applied to the revision of our laws.

And not only does the House of Lords do its work imperfectly, but often, at least, it does it timidly. Being only a section of the nation, it is afraid of the nation. Having been used for years and years, on the greatest matters to act contrary to its own judgement, it hardly knows when to act on that judgement. The depressing languor with which it damps an earnest young Peer is at times ridiculous. 'When the Corn Laws are gone, and the rotten boroughs, why tease about Clause IX in the Bill to regulate Cotton Factories?' is the latent thought of many Peers. A word from the leaders, from 'the Duke', or Lord Derby, or Lord Lyndhurst, will rouse on any matters the sleeping energies; but most Lords are feeble and forlorn.

These grave defects would have been at once lessened, and in the course of years nearly effaced, if the House of Lords had not resisted the proposal of Lord Palmerston's first government to create peers for life. The expedient was almost perfect. The difficulty of reforming an old institution like the House of Lords is necessarily great; its possibility rests on continuous caste and ancient deference. And if you begin to agitate about it, to bawl at meetings about it, that deference is gone, its peculiar charm lost, its reserved sanctity gone. But, by an odd fatality, there was in the recesses of the Constitution an old prerogative which would have rendered agitation needless—which would have effected, without agitation, all that agitation could have effected. Lord Palmerston was—now that he is dead, and his memory can be calmly viewed— as firm a friend to an aristocracy, as thorough an aristocrat, as any in England; yet he proposed to use that power. If the House of Lords had still been under the rule of the Duke of Wellington, perhaps they would have acquiesced. The Duke would not indeed have reflected on all the considerations which a philosophic statesman would have set out before him; but he would have been brought right by one of his peculiarities. He disliked, above all things, to oppose the Crown. At a great crisis, at the crisis of the Corn Laws, what he considered was not what other people were thinking of, the economical issue under discussion, the welfare of the country hanging in the balance, but the Queen's ease. He thought the Crown so superior a part in the Constitution, that, even on vital occasions, he looked solely—or said he looked solely—to the momentary comfort of the present sovereign. He never was comfortable in opposing a conspicuous act of the Crown. It is very likely that, if the Duke had still been the President of the House of Lords, they would have permitted the Crown to prevail in its well-chosen scheme. But the Duke was dead, and his authority —or some of it—had fallen to a very different person. Lord Lyndhurst had many great qualities; he had a splendid intellect—as great a faculty of finding truth as any one in his generation; but he had no love of truth. With this great faculty of finding truth, he was a believer in error—in what his own party now admit to be error—all his life through. He could have found the truth as a statesman just as he found it when a judge; but he never did find it. He never looked for it. He was a great partisan, and he applied a capacity of argument, and a faculty of intellectual argument rarely equalled, to support the tenets of his party. The proposal to create life-peers was proposed by the antagonistic party—was at the moment likely to injure his own party. To him this was a great opportunity. The speech he delivered on that occasion lives in the memory of those who heard it. His eyes did not at that time let him read, so he repeated by memory, and quite accurately, all the black-letter authorities bearing on the question. So great an intellectual effort has rarely been seen in an English assembly. But the result was deplorable. Not by means of his black-letter authorities, but by means of his recognized authority and his vivid impression, he induced the House of Lords to reject the proposition of the Government. Lord Lyndhurst said the Crown could not now create life-peers, and so there are no life-peers. The House of Lords rejected the inestimable, the unprecedented opportunity of being tacitly reformed. Such a chance does not come twice. The life-peers who would have been then introduced would have been among the first men in the country. Lord Macaulay was to have been among the first; Lord Wensleydale—the most learned and not the least logical of our lawyers—to be the very first. Thirty or forty such men, added judiciously and sparingly as years went on, would have given to the House of Lords the very element which, as a criticizing Chamber, it needs so much. It would have given it critics. The most accomplished men in each department might then, without irrelevant considerations of family and of fortune, have been added to the Chamber of Review. The very element which was wanted to the House of Lords was, as it were, by a constitutional providence, offered to the House of Lords, and they refused it. By what species of effort that error can be repaired, I cannot tell; but, unless it is repaired, the intellectual capacity can never be what it would have been, will never be what it ought to be, will never be sufficient for its work.

Another reform ought to have accompanied the creation of life-peers. Proxies ought to have been abolished. Some time or other the slack attendance of the House of Lords will destroy the House of Lords. There are occasions in which appearances are realities, and this is one of them. The House of Lords on most days looks so unlike what it ought to be, that most people will not believe it is what it ought to be. The attendance of considerate peers will, for obvious reasons, be larger when it can no longer be overpowered by the *non*-attendance, by the commissioned votes, of inconsiderate peers. The abolition of proxies would have made the House of Lords a real House; the addition of life-peers would have made it a good House.

The greater of these changes would have most materially aided the House of Lords in the performance of its subsidiary functions. It always perhaps happens in a great nation, that certain bodies of sensible men, posted prominently in its constitution, acquire functions, and usefully exercise functions, which, at the outset, no one expected from them, and which do not identify themselves with their original design. This has happened to the House of Lords especially. The most obvious instance is the judicial function. This is a function which no theorist would assign to a second chamber in a new constitution, and which is matter of accident in ours. Gradually, indeed, the unfitness of the second chamber for judicial functions has made itself felt. Under our present arrangements this function is not entrusted to the House of Lords, but to a Committee of the House of Lords. On one occasion only, the trial of O'Connell, the whole House, or some few in the whole House, wished to vote, and they were told they could not, or they would destroy the judicial prerogative. No one, indeed, would venture *really* to place the judicial function in the chance majorities of a fluctuating assembly; it is so by a sleepy theory; it is not so in living fact. As a legal question, too, it is a matter of grave doubt whether there ought to be two supreme courts in this country—the Judicial Committee of the Privy Council, and (what is in fact though not in name) the Judicial Committee of the

House of Lords. Up to a very recent time one committee might decide that a man was sane as to money, and the other committee might decide that he was insane as to land. This absurdity has been cured; but the error from which it arose has not been cured—the error of having two supreme courts, to both of which, as time goes on, the same question is sure often enough to be submitted, and each of which is sure every now and then to decide it differently. I do not reckon the judicial function of the House of Lords as one of its true subsidiary functions, first because it does not in fact exercise it, next because I wish to see it in appearance deprived of it. The supreme court of the English people ought to be a great conspicuous tribunal, ought to rule all other courts, ought to have no competitor, ought to bring our law into unity, ought not to be hidden beneath the robes of a legislative assembly.

The real subsidiary functions of the House of Lords are, unlike its judicial functions, very analogous to its substantial nature. The first is the faculty of criticizing the executive. An assembly in which the mass of the members have nothing to lose, where most have nothing to gain, where every one has a social position firmly fixed, where no one has a constituency, where hardly any one cares for the minister of the day, is the very assembly in which to look for, from which to expect, independent criticism. And in matter of fact, we find it. The criticism of the acts of late administrations by Lord Grey has been admirable. But such criticism, to have its full value, should be many-sided. Every man of great ability puts his own mark on his own criticism; it will be full of thought and feeling, but then it is of idiosyncratic thought and feeling. We want many critics of ability and knowledge in the

Upper House—not equal to Lord Grey, for they would be hard to find—but like Lord Grey. They should resemble him in impartiality; they should resemble him in clearness; they should most of all resemble him in taking the supplemental view of a subject. There is an actor's view of a subject which (I speak of mature and discussed action—of Cabinet action) is nearly sure to include everything old and new—everything ascertained and determinate. But there is also a bystander's view, which is likely to omit some one or more of these old and certain elements, but also to contain some new or distant matter which the absorbed and occupied actor could not see. There ought to be many life-peers in our secondary chamber capable of giving us this higher criticism. I am afraid we shall not soon see them, but as a first step we should learn to wish for them.

The second subsidiary action of the House of Lords is even more important. Taking the House of Commons, not after possible but most unlikely improvements, but in matter of fact and as it stands, it is overwhelmed with work. The task of managing it falls upon the Cabinet, and that task is very hard. Every member of the Cabinet in the Commons has to 'attend the House'; to contribute by his votes, if not by his voice, to the management of the House. Even in so small a matter as the education department, Mr. Lowe, a consummate observer, spoke of the desirability of finding a chief 'not exposed to the prodigious labour of attending the House of Commons'. It is all but necessary that certain members of the Cabinet should be exempt from its toil, and untouched by its excitement. But it is also necessary that they should have the power of explaining their views to the nation; of being heard as other people are heard. There are various plans for so doing, which I may discuss a little in speaking of the House of Commons. But so much is evident: the House of Lords, for its own members, attains this object; it gives them a voice; it gives them what no competing plan does give them—*position*. The leisured members of the Cabinet speak in the Lords with authority and power. They are not administrators with a right to speech—clerks (as is sometimes suggested) brought down to lecture a House, but not to vote in it; but they are the equals of those they speak to; they speak as they like, and reply as they choose; they address the House, not with the 'bated breath' of subordinates, but with the force and dignity of sure rank. Life-peers would enable us to use this faculty of our Constitution more freely and more variously. It would give us a larger command of able leisure; it would improve the Lords as a political pulpit, for it would enlarge the list of its select preachers.

The danger of the House of Commons is, perhaps, that it will be reformed too rashly; the danger of the House of Lords certainly is, that it may never be reformed. Nobody asks that it should be so; it is quite safe against rough destruction, but it is not safe against inward decay. It may lose its veto as the Crown has lost its veto. If most of its members neglect their duties, if all its members continue to be of one class, and that not quite the best; if its doors are shut against genius that cannot found a family, and ability which has not five thousand a year, its power will be less year by year, and at last be gone, as so much kingly power is gone—no one knows how. Its danger is not in assassination, but atrophy; not abolition, but decline.

THE dignified aspect of the House of Commons is altogether secondary to its efficient use. It *is* dignified: in a government in which the most prominent parts are good because they are very stately, any prominent part, to be good at all, must be somewhat stately. The human imagination exacts keeping in government as much as in art; it will not be at all influenced by institutions which do not match with those by which it is principally influenced. The House of Commons needs to be impressive, and impressive it is: but its use resides not in its appearance, but in its reality. Its office is not to win power by aweing mankind, but to use power in governing mankind.

The main function of the House of Commons is one which we know quite well, though our common constitutional speech does not recognize it. The House of Commons is an electoral chamber; it is the assembly which chooses our president. Washington and his fellow-politicians contrived an electoral college, to be composed (as was hoped) of the wisest people in the nation, which, after due deliberation, was to choose for President the wisest man in the nation. But that college is a sham; it has no independence and no life. No one knows, or cares to know, who its members are. They never discuss, and never deliberate. They were chosen to vote that Mr. Lincoln be President, or that Mr. Breckenridge

---

[1] I reprint this chapter substantially as it was first written. It is too soon, as I have explained in the introduction, to say what changes the late Reform Act will make in the House of Commons.

be President; they do so vote, and they go home. But our House of Commons is a real choosing body; it elects the people it likes. And it dismisses whom it likes too. No matter that a few months since it was chosen to support Lord Aberdeen or Lord Palmerston; upon a sudden occasion it ousts the statesman to whom it at first adhered, and selects an opposite statesman whom it at first rejected. Doubtless in such cases there is a tacit reference to probable public opinion; but certainly also there is much free will in the judgement of the Commons. The House only goes where it thinks in the end the nation will follow; but it takes its chance of the nation following or not following; it assumes the initiative, and acts upon its discretion or its caprice.

When the American nation has chosen its President, its virtue goes out of it, and out of the Transmissive College through which it chooses. But because the House of Commons has the power of dismissal in addition to the power of election, its relations to the Premier are incessant. They guide him, and he leads them. He is to them what they are to the nation. He only goes where he believes they will go after him. But he has to take the lead; he must choose his direction, and begin the journey. Nor must he flinch. A good horse likes to feel the rider's bit; and a great deliberative assembly likes to feel that it is under worthy guidance. A minister who succumbs to the House,—who ostentatiously seeks its pleasure,—who does not try to regulate it,—who will not boldly point out plain errors to it, seldom thrives. The great leaders of Parliament have varied much, but they have all had a certain firmness. A great assembly is as soon spoiled by over-indulgence as a little child. The whole life of English politics is the action and reaction between the Ministry and the Parliament. The appointees strive to guide, and the appointors surge under the guidance.

The elective is now the most important function of the House of Commons. It is most desirable to insist, and be tedious, on this, because our tradition ignores it. At the end of half the sessions of Parliament, you will read in the newspapers, and you will hear even from those who have looked close at the matter and should know better, 'Parliament has done nothing this session. Some things were promised in the Queen's speech, but they were only little things; and most of them have not passed.' Lord Lyndhurst used for years to recount the small outcomings of legislative achievement; and yet those were the days of the first Whig Governments, who had more to do in legislation, and did more, than any Government. The true answer to such harangues as Lord Lyndhurst's by a Minister should have been in the first person. He should have said firmly, 'Parliament has maintained ME, and that was its greatest duty; Parliament has carried on what, in the language of traditional respect, we call the Queen's Government; it has maintained what wisely or unwisely it deemed the best Executive of the English nation'.

The second function of the House of Commons is what I may call an expressive function. It is its office to express the mind of the English people on all matters which come before it. Whether it does so well or ill I shall discuss presently.

The third function of Parliament is what I may call—preserving a sort of technicality even in familiar matters for the sake of distinctness—the teaching function. A great and open council of considerable men cannot be placed in the middle of a society without altering that society. It ought to alter it for the better. It ought to teach the nation what it does not know. How far the House of Commons can so teach, and how far it does so teach, are matters for subsequent discussion.

Fourthly, the House of Commons has what may be called an informing function—a function which though in its present form quite modern is singularly analogous to a medieval function. In old times one office of the House of Commons was to inform the Sovereign what was wrong. It laid before the Crown the grievances and complaints of particular interests. Since the publication of the Parliamentary debates a corresponding office of Parliament is to lay these same grievances, these same complaints, before the nation, which is the present sovereign. The nation needs it quite as much as the king ever needed it. A free people is indeed mostly fair, liberty practises men in a give-and-take, which is the rough essence of justice. The English people, possibly even above other free nations, is fair. But a free nation rarely can be—and the English nation is not—quick of apprehension. It only comprehends what is familiar to it—what comes into its own experience, what squares with its own thoughts. 'I never heard of such a thing in my life', the middle-class Englishman says, and he thinks he so refutes an argument. The common disputant cannot say in reply that his experience is but limited, and that the assertion may be true, though he had never met with anything at all like it. But a great debate in Parliament *does* bring home something of this feeling. Any notion, any creed, any feeling, any grievance which can get a decent number of English members to stand up for it, is felt by almost all Englishmen to be perhaps a false and pernicious opinion, but at any rate possible—an opinion within the intellectual sphere, an opinion to be reckoned with. And it is an immense achievement. Practical diplomatists say that a free government is harder to deal with than a despotic government: you may be able to get the despot to hear the other side; his ministers, men of trained intelligence, will be sure to know what makes against them; and they *may* tell him. But a free nation never hears any side save its own. The newspapers only repeat the side their purchasers like: the favourable arguments are set out, elaborated, illustrated; the adverse arguments maimed, misstated, confused. The worst judge, they say, is a deaf judge; the most dull government is a free government on matters its ruling classes will not hear. I am disposed to reckon it as the second function of Parliament in point of importance, that to some extent it makes us hear what otherwise we should not.

Lastly, there is the function of legislation, of which of course it would be preposterous to deny the great importance, and which I only deny to be *as* important as the executive management of the whole state, or the political education given by Parliament to the whole nation. There are, I allow, seasons when legislation is more important than either of these. The nation may be misfitted with its laws, and need to change them: some particular corn law may hurt all industry, and it may be worth a thousand administrative blunders to get rid of it. But generally the laws of a nation suit its life; special adaptations of them are but subordinate; the administration and conduct of that life is the matter which presses most. Nevertheless, the statute book of every great nation yearly contains many important new laws, and the English statute book does so above any. An immense mass, indeed, of the legislation is not, in the proper language of jurisprudence, legislation at all. A law is a general command applicable to many cases. The 'special acts' which crowd the statute-book and weary parliamentary committees are applicable to one case only. They do not lay down rules according to which railways shall be made, they enact that such a railway shall be made from this place to that place, and they have no bearing upon any other transaction. But after every deduction and abatement, the annual legislation of Parliament is a result of singular importance; were it not so, it could not be, as it often is considered, the sole result of its annual assembling.

Some persons will perhaps think that I ought to enumerate a sixth function of the House of Commons—a financial function. But I do not consider that, upon broad principle, and omitting legal technicalities, the House of Commons has any special function with regard to financial different from its functions with respect to other legislation. It is to rule in both, and to rule in both through the Cabinet. Financial legislation is of necessity a yearly recurring legislation; but frequency of occurrence does not indicate a diversity of nature or compel an antagonism of treatment.

In truth, the principal peculiarity of the House of Commons in financial affairs is nowadays not a special privilege, but an exceptional disability. On common subjects any member can propose anything, but not on money—the minister only can propose to tax the people. This principle is commonly involved in medieval metaphysics as to the prerogative of the Crown, but it is as useful in the nineteenth century as in the fourteenth, and rests on as sure a principle. The House of Commons—now that it is the true sovereign, and appoints the real executive—has long ceased to be the checking, sparing, economical body it once was. It now is more apt to spend money than the minister of the day. I have heard a very experienced financier say, 'If you want to raise a certain cheer in the House of Commons, make a general panegyric on economy; if you want to invite a sure defeat, propose a particular saving'. The process is simple. Every expenditure of public money has some apparent public object; those who wish to spend the money expatiate on that object; they say, 'What is £50,000 to this great country? Is this a time for cheeseparing objection? Our industry was never so productive; our resources never so immense. What is £50,000 in comparison with this great national interest?' The members who are for the expenditure always come down; perhaps a constituent or a friend who will profit by the outlay, or is keen on the object, has asked them to attend; at any rate, there is a popular vote to be given, on which the newspapers—always philanthropic, and sometimes talked over—will be sure to make encomiums. The members against the expenditure rarely come down of themselves; why should they become unpopular without reason? The object seems decent; many of its advocates are certainly sincere: a hostile vote will make enemies, and be censured by the journals. If there were not some check, the 'people's house' would soon outrun the people's money.

That check is the responsibility of the Cabinet for the national finance. If any one could propose a tax, they might let the House spend it as it would, and wash their hands of the matter; but now, for whatever expenditure is sanctioned—even when it is sanctioned against the ministry's wish—the ministry must find the money. Accordingly, they have the strongest motive to oppose extra outlay. They will have to pay the bill for it; they will have to impose taxation, which is always disagreeable, or suggest loans which, under ordinary circumstances, are shameful. The ministry is (so to speak) the bread-winner of the political family, and has to meet the cost of philanthropy and glory, just as the head of a family has to pay for the charities of his wife and the toilette of his daughters.

In truth, when a Cabinet is made the sole executive, it follows it must have the sole financial charge, for all action costs money, all policy depends on money, and it is in adjusting the relative goodness of action and policies that the executive is employed.

From a consideration of these functions, it follows that we are ruled by the House of Commons; we are, indeed, so used to be so ruled, that it does not seem to be at all strange. But of all odd forms of government, the oddest really is government by a *public meeting*. Here are 658 persons, collected from all parts of England, different in nature, different in interests, different in look and language. If we think what an empire the English is, how various are its components, how incessant its concerns, how immersed in history its policy: if we think what a vast information, what a nice discretion, what a consistent will ought to mark the rulers of that empire,—we shall be surprised when we see them. We see a changing body of miscellaneous persons, sometimes few, sometimes many, never the same for an hour; sometimes excited, but mostly dull and half weary,—impatient of eloquence, catching at any joke as an alleviation. These are the persons who rule the British empire,—who rule England,—who rule Scotland,—who rule Ireland,—who rule a great deal of Asia,—who rule a great deal of Polynesia,—who rule a great deal of America, and scattered fragments everywhere.

Paley said many shrewd things, but he never said a better thing than that it was much harder to make

men see a difficulty than comprehend the explanation of it.   The key to the difficulties of most
discussed and unsettled questions is commonly in
their undiscussed parts; they are like the background
of a picture which looks obvious, easy, just what any
one might have painted, but which, in fact, sets the
figures in their right position, chastens them, and
makes them what they are.   Nobody will understand
parliament government who fancies it an easy thing,
a natural thing, a thing not needing explanation.
You have not a perception of the first elements in
this matter till you know that government by a *club*
is a standing wonder.

There has been a capital illustration lately how
helpless many English gentlemen are when called
together on a sudden.   The Government, rightly or
wrongly, thought fit to entrust the quarter-sessions
of each county with the duty of combating its cattle
plague; but the scene in most 'shire halls' was un-
satisfactory.   There was the greatest difficulty in
getting, not only a right decision, but *any* decision.
I saw one myself which went thus.   The chairman
proposed a very complex resolution, in which there
was much which every one liked, and much which
every one disliked, though, of course, the favourite
parts of some were the objectionable parts to others.
This resolution got, so to say, wedged in the meeting; everybody suggested amendments; one amendment was carried which none were satisfied with,
and so the matter stood over.   It is a saying in
England, 'a big meeting never does anything'; and
yet we are governed by the House of Commons—
by 'a big meeting'.

It may be said that the House of Commons does
not rule, it only elects the rulers.   But there must be
something special about it to enable it to do that.
Suppose the Cabinet were elected by a London club,

what confusion there would be, what writing and answering! 'Will you speak to So-and-So, and ask him to vote for my man?' would be heard on every side. How the wife of A and the wife of B would plot to confound the wife of C! Whether the club elected under the dignified shadow of a queen, or without the shadow, would hardly matter at all; if the substantial choice was in them, the confusion and intrigue would be there too. I propose to begin this paper by asking, not why the House of Commons governs well? but the fundamental—almost unasked question—how the House of Commons comes to be able to govern at all?

The House of Commons can do work which the quarter-sessions or clubs cannot do, because it is an organized body, while quarter-sessions and clubs are unorganized. Two of the greatest orators in England—Lord Brougham and Lord Bolingbroke—spent much eloquence in attacking party government. Bolingbroke probably knew what he was doing; he was a consistent opponent of the power of the Commons; he wished to attack them in a vital part. But Lord Brougham does not know; he proposes to amend parliamentary government by striking out the very elements which make parliamentary government possible. At present the majority of Parliament obey certain leaders; what those leaders propose they support, what those leaders reject they reject. An old Secretary of the Treasury used to say, 'This is a bad case, an indefensible case. We must apply our *majority* to this question.' That secretary lived fifty years ago, before the Reform Bill, when majorities were very blind, and very 'applicable'. Nowadays, the power of leaders over their followers is strictly and wisely limited: they can take their followers but a little way, and that only in certain directions. Yet still there are leaders and followers. On the Conservative side of the House there are vestiges of the despotic leadership even now. A cynical politician is said to have watched the long row of county members, so fresh and respectable-looking, and muttered, 'By Jove, they are the finest brute votes in Europe!' But all satire apart, the principle of Parliament is obedience to leaders. Change your leader if you will, take another if you will, but obey No. 1 while you serve No. 1, and obey No. 2 when you have gone over to No. 2. The penalty of not doing so, is the penalty of impotence. It is not that you will not be able to do any good, but you will not be able to do anything at all. If everybody does what he thinks right, there will be 657 amendments to every motion, and none of them will be carried or the motion either.

The moment, indeed, that we distinctly conceive that the House of Commons is mainly and above all things an elective assembly, we at once perceive that party is of its essence. There never was an election without a party. You cannot get a child into an asylum without a combination. At such places you may see 'Vote for orphan A' upon a placard, and 'Vote for orphan B (also an idiot!!!)' upon a banner, and the party of each is busy about its placard and banner. What is true at such minor and momentary elections must be much more true in a great and constant election of rulers. The House of Commons lives in a state of perpetual potential choice: at any moment it can choose a ruler and dismiss a ruler. And therefore party is inherent in it, is bone of its bone, and breath of its breath.

Secondly, though the leaders of party no longer have the vast patronage of the last century with which to bribe, they can coerce by a threat far more potent than any allurement—they can dissolve.

This is the secret which keeps parties together. Mr. Cobden most justly said, 'He had never been able to discover what was the proper moment, according to members of Parliament, for a dissolution. He had heard them say they were ready to vote for everything else, but he had never heard them say they were ready to vote for that.' Efficiency in an assembly requires a solid mass of steady votes; and these are *collected* by a deferential attachment to particular men, or by a belief in the principles those men represent, and they are *maintained* by fear of those men—by the fear that if you vote against them, you may yourself soon not have a vote at all.

Thirdly, it may seem odd to say so, just after inculcating that party organization is the vital principle of representative government, but that organization is permanently efficient, because it is not composed of warm partisans. The body is eager, but the atoms are cool. If it were otherwise, parliamentary government would become the worst of governments—a sectarian government. The party in power would go all the lengths their orators proposed—all that their formulae enjoined, as far as they had ever said they would go. But the partisans of the English Parliament are not of such a temper. They are Whigs, or Radicals, or Tories, but they are much else too. They are common Englishmen, and, as Father Newman complains, 'hard to be worked up to the dogmatic level'. They are not eager to press the tenets of their party to impossible conclusions. On the contrary, the way to lead them—the best and acknowledged way—is to affect a studied and illogical moderation. You may hear men say, 'Without committing myself to the tenet that $3 + 2$ make 5, though I am free to admit that the honourable member for Bradford has advanced very grave arguments in behalf of it, I think I may, with the permission of the Committee, assume that $2+3$ do not make 4, which will be a sufficient basis for the important propositions which I shall venture to submit on the present occasion'. This language is very suitable to the greater part of the House of Commons. Most men of business love a sort of twilight. They have lived all their lives in an atmosphere of probabilities and of doubt, where nothing is very clear, where there are some chances for many events, where there is much to be said for several courses, where nevertheless one course must be determinedly chosen and fixedly adhered to. They like to hear arguments suited to this intellectual haze. So far from caution or hesitation in the statement of the argument striking them as an indication of imbecility, it seems to them a sign of practicality. They got rich themselves by transactions of which they could not have stated the argumentative ground—and all they ask for is a distinct, though moderate conclusion, that they can repeat when asked; something which they feel *not* to be abstract argument, but abstract argument diluted and dissolved in real life. 'There seem to me', an impatient young man once said, 'to be no stays in Peel's arguments.' And that was why Sir Robert Peel was the best leader of the Commons in our time; we like to have the rigidity taken out of an argument, and the substance left.

Nor indeed, under our system of government, are the leaders themselves of the House of Commons, for the most part, eager to carry party conclusions too far. They are in contact with reality. An Opposition, on coming into power, is often like a speculative merchant whose bills become due. Ministers have to make good their promises, and they find a difficulty in so doing. They have said the state of things is so-and-so, and if you give us the power we will do thus and thus. But when they come to handle the official documents, to converse with the permanent under-secretary—familiar with disagreeable facts, and though in manner most respectful, yet most imperturbable in opinion—very soon doubts intervene. Of course, something must be done: the speculative merchant cannot forget his bills; the late Opposition cannot, in office, forget those sentences which terrible admirers in the country still quote. But just as the merchant asks his debtor, 'Could you not take a bill at four months?' so the new minister says to the permanent under-secretary, 'Could you not suggest a middle course? I am of course not bound by mere sentences used in debate; I have never been accused of letting a false ambition of consistency warp my conduct; but', &c., &c. And the end always is, that a middle course is devised which *looks* as much as possible like what was suggested in opposition, but which *is* as much as possible what patent facts—facts which seem to live in the office, so teasing and unceasing are they—prove ought to be done.

Of all modes of enforcing moderation on a party, the best is to contrive that the members of that party shall be intrinsically moderate, careful, and almost shrinking men; and the next best to contrive, that the leaders of the party, who have protested most in its behalf, shall be placed in the closest contact with the actual world. Our English system contains both contrivances: it makes party government permanent and possible in the sole way in which it can be so, by making it mild.

But these expedients, though they sufficiently remove the defects which make a common club or quarter-sessions impotent, would not enable the House of Commons to govern England. A representative public meeting is subject to a defect over and above those of other public meetings. It may not be independent. The constituencies may not let it alone. But if they do not, all the checks which have been enumerated upon the evils of a party organization would be futile. The feeling of a constituency is the feeling of a dominant party, and that feeling is elicited, stimulated, sometimes even manufactured by the local political agent. Such an opinion could not be moderate; could not be subject to effectual discussion; could not be in close contact with pressing facts; could not be framed under a chastening sense of near responsibility; could not be formed as those form their opinions who have to act upon them. Constituency government is the precise opposite of parliamentary government. It is the government of immoderate persons far from the scene of action, instead of the government of moderate persons close to the scene of action; it is the judgement of persons judging in the last resort and without a penalty, in lieu of persons judging in fear of a dissolution, and ever conscious that they are subject to an appeal.

Most persons would admit these conditions of parliamentary government when they read them, but two at least of the most prominent ideas in the public mind are inconsistent with them. The scheme to which the arguments of our demagogues distinctly tend, and the scheme to which the predilections of some most eminent philosophers cleave, are both so. They would not only make parliamentary government work ill, but they would prevent its working at all; they would not render it bad, for they would make it impossible.

The first of these is the ultra-democratic theory. This theory demands that every man of twenty-one years of age (if not every woman, too) should have an equal vote in electing Parliament. Suppose that last year there were twelve millions adult males in England. Upon this theory each man is to have one twelve-millionth share in electing a Parliament; the rich and wise are not to have, by explicit law, more votes than the poor and stupid; nor are any latent contrivances to give them an influence equivalent to more votes. The machinery for carrying out such a plan is very easy. At each census the country ought to be divided into 658 electoral districts, in each of which the number of adult males should be the same; and these districts ought to be the only constituencies, and elect the whole Parliament. But if the above prerequisites are needful for parliamentary government, that Parliament would not work.

Such a Parliament could not be composed of moderate men. The electoral districts would be, some of them, in purely agricultural places, and in these the parson and the squire would have almost unlimited power. They would be able to drive or send to the poll an entire labouring population. These districts would return an unmixed squirearchy. The scattered small towns, which now send so many members to Parliament, would be lost in the clownish mass; their votes would send to Parliament no distinct members. The agricultural part of England would choose its representatives from quarter sessions exclusively. On the other hand, a large part of the constituencies would be town districts; and these would send up persons representing the beliefs or the unbeliefs of the lowest classes in their towns. They would, perhaps, be divided between the genuine representatives of the artisans—not possibly of the best of the artisans, who are a select and intellectual class, but of the common order of workpeople—and the merely pretended members for that class, whom I may call the members for the public-houses. In all big towns in which there is electioneering these houses are the centres of illicit corruption and illicit management. There are pretty good records of what that corruption and management are, but there is no need to describe them here. Everybody will understand what sort of things I mean, and the kind of unprincipled members that are returned by them. Our new Parliament, therefore, would be made up of two sorts of representatives from the town lowest class, and one sort of representatives from the agricultural lowest class. The genuine representatives of the country would be men of one marked sort, and the genuine representatives for the county men of another marked sort, but very opposite: one would have the prejudices of town artisans, and the other the prejudices of county magistrates. Each class would speak a language of its own; each would be unintelligible to the other; and the only thriving class would be the immoral representatives, who were chosen by corrupt machination, and who would probably get a good profit on the capital they laid out in that corruption. If it be true that a parliamentary government is possible only when the overwhelming majority of the representatives are men essentially moderate, of no marked varieties, free from class prejudices, this ultra-democratic Parliament could not maintain that government, for its members would be remarkable for two sorts of moral violence and one sort of immoral.

I do not for a moment rank the scheme of Mr. Hare with the scheme of the ultra-democrats. One can hardly help having a feeling of romance about it. The world seems growing young when grave old lawyers and mature philosophers propose a scheme promising so much. It is from these classes that young men suffer commonly the chilling demonstration that their fine plans are opposed to rooted obstacles, that they are repetitions of other plans which failed long ago, and that we must be content with the very moderate results of tried machinery. But Mr. Hare and Mr. Mill offer as the effect of their new scheme results as large and improvements as interesting as a young enthusiast ever promised to himself in his happiest mood.

I do not give any weight to the supposed impracticability of Mr. Hare's scheme because it is new. Of course it cannot be put in practice till it is old. A great change of this sort happily cannot be sudden; a free people cannot be confused by new institutions which they do not understand, for they will not adopt them till they understand them. But if Mr. Hare's plan would accomplish what its friends say, or half what they say, it would be worth working for, if it were not adopted till the year 1966. We ought incessantly to popularize the principle by writing; and, what is better than writing, small preliminary bits of experiment. There is so much that is wearisome and detestable in all other election machineries, that I well understand, and wish I could share, the sense of relief with which the believers in this scheme throw aside all their trammels, and look to an almost ideal future, when this captivating plan is carried.

Mr. Hare's scheme cannot be satisfactorily discussed in the elaborate form in which he presents it. No common person readily apprehends all the details in which, with loving care, he has embodied it. He was so anxious to prove what could be done, that he has confused most people as to what it is. I have heard a man say, 'He never could remember it two days running'. But the difficulty which I feel is fundamental, and wholly independent of detail.

There are two modes in which constituencies may be made. First, the law may make them, as in England and almost everywhere: the law may say such and such qualifications shall give a vote for constituency X; those who have that qualification shall *be* constituency X. These are what we may call compulsory constituencies, and we know all about them. Or, secondly, the law may leave the electors themselves to make them. The law may say all the adult males of a country shall vote, or those males who can read and write, or those who have £50 a year, or any persons any way defined, and then leave those voters to group themselves as they like. Suppose there were 658,000 voters to elect the House of Commons; it is possible for the legislature to say, 'We do not care how you combine. On a given day let each set of persons give notice in what group they mean to vote; if every voter gives notice, and every one looks to make the most of his vote, each group will have just 1,000. But the law shall not make this necessary—it shall take the 658 most numerous groups, no matter whether they have 2,000, or 1,000, or 900, or 800 votes—the most numerous groups, whatever their number may be; and these shall be the constituencies of the nation.' These are voluntary constituencies, if I may so call them; the simplest kind of voluntary constituencies. Mr. Hare proposes a far more complex kind; but to show the merits and demerits of the voluntary principle the simplest form is much the best.

The temptation to that principle is very plain. Under the compulsory form of constituency the votes of the minorities are thrown away. In the city of London, now, there are many Tories, but all the members are Whigs; every London Tory, therefore, is by law and principle misrepresented: his city sends to Parliament not the member whom he wished to have, but the member he wished *not* to have. But upon the voluntary system the London Tories, who are far more than 1,000 in number, may combine; they may make a constituency, and return a member. In many existing constituencies the disfranchisement of minorities is hopeless and chronic. I have myself had a vote for an agricultural county for twenty years, and I am a Liberal; but two Tories have always been returned, and all my life will be returned. As matters now stand, my vote is of no use. But if I could combine with 1 000 other Liberals in that and other Conservative counties, we might choose a Liberal member.

Again, this plan gets rid of all our difficulties as to the size of constituencies. It is said to be unreasonable that Liverpool should return only the same number of members as King's Lynn or Lyme Regis; but upon the voluntary plan, Liverpool could come down to King's Lynn. The Liberal minority in King's Lynn could communicate with the Liberal minority in Liverpool, and make up 1,000; and so everywhere. The numbers of popular places would gain what is called their legitimate advantage; they would, when constituencies are voluntarily made, be able to make, and be willing to make, the greatest number of constituencies.

Again, the admirers of a great man could make a worthy constituency for him. As it is, Mr. Mill was returned by the electors of Westminster; and they have never, since they had members, done themselves so great an honour. But what did the electors of Westminster know of Mr. Mill? What fraction of his mind could be imagined by any percentage of their minds? A great deal of his genius most of them would not like. They meant to do homage to mental ability, but it was the worship of an unknown god—if ever there was such a thing in this world. But upon the voluntary plan, one thousand out of the many thousand students of Mr. Mill's book could have made an appreciating constituency for him.

I could reckon other advantages, but I have to object to the scheme, not to recommend it. What are the counterweights which overpower these merits? I reply that the voluntary composition of constituencies appears to me inconsistent with the necessary prerequisites of parliamentary government as they have been just laid down.

Under the voluntary system, the crisis of politics is not the election of the member, but the making the constituency. President-making is already a trade in America; and constituency-making would, under the voluntary plan, be a trade here. Every party would have a numerical problem to solve. The leaders would say, 'We have 350,000 votes, we must take care to have 350 members'; and the only way to obtain them is to organize. A man who wanted to compose part of a Liberal constituency must not himself hunt for 1,000 other Liberals; if he did, after writing 10,000 letters, he would probably find he was making part of a constituency of 100, all whose votes would be thrown away, the constituency being too small to be reckoned. Such a Liberal must write to the great Registration Association in Parliament Street; he must communicate with its able managers, and they would soon use his vote for him. They would say, 'Sir, you are late; Mr. Gladstone, sir, is full. He got his 1,000 last year. Most of the gentlemen you read of in the papers are full. As soon as a gentleman makes a nice speech, we get a heap of letters to say, "Make us into that gentleman's constituency". But we cannot do that. Here is our list. If you do not want to throw your vote away, you must be guided by us: here are three very satisfactory gentlemen (and one is an Honourable): you may vote for either of these, and we will write your name down; but if you go voting wildly, you'll be thrown out altogether.'

The evident result of this organization would be the return of party men mainly. The member-makers would look, not for independence, but for subservience—and they could hardly be blamed for so doing. They are agents for the Liberal Party; and, as such, they should be guided by what they take to be the wishes of their principal. The mass of the Liberal Party wishes measure A, measure B, measure C. The managers of the registration—the skilled manipulators—are busy men. They would say, 'Sir, here is our card; if you want to get into parliament on our side, you must go for that card; it was drawn up by Mr. Lloyd; he used to be engaged on railways, but since they passed this new voting plan, we get him to attend to us; it is a sound card; stick to that and you will be right'. Upon this (in theory) voluntary plan, you would get together a set of members bound hard and fast with party bands and fetters, infinitely tighter than any members now.

Whoever hopes anything from desultory popular action if matched against systematized popular action, should consider the way in which the American President is chosen. The plan was that the citizens at large should vote for the statesman they liked best. But no one does· anything of the sort. They vote for the ticket made by 'the caucus', and the caucus is a sort of representative meeting which sits voting and voting till they have cut out all the known men against whom much is to be said, and agreed on some unknown man against whom there is nothing known, and therefore nothing to be alleged. Caucuses, or their equivalent, would be far worse here in constituency-making than there in President-making, because on great occasions the American nation can fix on some one great man whom it knows, but the English nation could not fix on 658 great men and choose them. It does not know so many, and if it did, would go wrong in the difficulties of the manipulation.

But though a common voter could only be ranged in an effectual constituency, and a common candidate only reach a constituency by obeying the orders of the political election-contrivers upon his side, certain voters and certain members would be quite independent of both. There are organizations in this country which would soon make a set of constituencies for themselves. Every chapel would be an office for vote transferring before the plan had been known three months. The Church would be much slower in learning it, and much less handy in using it; but would learn. At present the Dissenters are a most energetic and valuable component of the Liberal Party; but under the voluntary plan they would not be a component—they would be a separate, independent element. We now propose to group boroughs; but then they would combine chapels. There would be a member for the Baptist congregation of Tavistock cum Totnes cum, &c., &c.

The full force of this cannot be appreciated except by referring to the former proof that the mass of a Parliament ought to be men of moderate sentiments, or they will elect an immoderate ministry, and enact violent laws. But upon the plan suggested, the House would be made up of party politicians selected by a party committee, chained to that committee and pledged to party violence, and of characteristic, and therefore immoderate repre-

sentatives, for every 'ism' in all England. Instead
of a deliberate assembly of moderate and judicious
men, we should have a various compound of all
sorts of violence.

I may seem to be drawing a caricature, but I have
not reached the worst. Bad as these members
would be, if they were left to themselves—if, in
a free Parliament, they were confronted with the
perils of government, close responsibility might
improve them and make them tolerable. But they
would not be left to themselves. A voluntary constituency will nearly always be a despotic constituency. Even in the best case, where a set of earnest
men choose a member to expound their earnestness,
they will look after him to see that he does expound
it. The members will be like the minister of
a dissenting congregation. That congregation is
collected by a unity of sentiment in doctrine A, and
the preacher is to preach doctrine A; if he does not,
he is dismissed. At present the member is free
because the constituency is not in earnest: no
constituency has an acute, accurate doctrinal creed
in politics. The law made the constituencies by geographical divisions; and they are not bound
together by close unity of belief. They have vague
preferences for particular doctrines; and that is all.
But a voluntary constituency would be a church
with tenets; it would make its representative the
messenger of its mandates, and the delegate of its
determinations. As in the case of a dissenting
congregation, one great minister sometimes rules
it, while ninety-nine ministers in the hundred
are ruled by it, so here one noted man would rule
his electors, but the electors would rule all the
others.

Thus, the members for a good voluntary constituency would be hopelessly enslaved, because of its

goodness; but the members for a bad voluntary constituency would be yet more enslaved because of its badness. The makers of these constituencies would keep the despotism in their own hands. In America there is a division of politicians into wire-pullers and blowers; under the voluntary system the member of Parliament would be the only momentary mouth-piece—the impotent blower; while the constituency-maker would be the latent wire-puller—the constant autocrat. He would write to gentlemen in Parliament, and say, 'You were elected upon "the Liberal ticket"; if you deviate from that ticket you cannot be chosen again'. And there would be no appeal for a common-minded man. He is no more likely to make a constituency for himself than a mole is likely to make a planet.

It may indeed be said that against a septennial Parliament such machinations would be powerless; that a member elected for seven years might defy the remonstrances of an earnest constituency, or the imprecations of the latent manipulators. But after the voluntary composition of constituencies, there would soon be but short-lived Parliaments. Earnest constituencies would exact frequent elections; they would not like to part with their virtue for a long period; it would anger them to see it used contrary to their wishes, amid circumstances which at the election no one thought of. A seven years' Parliament is often chosen in one political period, lasts through a second, and is dissolved in a third. A constituency collected by law and on compulsion endures this change because it has no collective earnestness; it does not mind seeing the power it gave used in a manner that it could not have foreseen. But a self-formed constituency of eager opinions, a missionary constituency, so to speak, would object; it would think it its bounden duty to object; and the crafty manipulators, though they said nothing, in silence would object still more. The two together would enjoin annual elections, and would rule their members unflinchingly.

The voluntary plan, therefore, when tried in this easy form, is inconsistent with the extrinsic independence as well as with the inherent moderation of a Parliament—two of the conditions which, as we have seen, are essential to the bare possibility of parliamentary government. The same objections, as is inevitable, adhere to that principle under its more complicated forms. It is in vain to pile detail on detail when the objection is one of first principle. If the above reasoning be sound, compulsory constituencies are necessary, voluntary constituencies destructive; the optional transferability of votes is not a salutary aid, but a ruinous innovation.

I have dwelt upon the proposal of Mr. Hare and upon the ultra-democratic proposal, not only because of the high intellectual interest of the former and the possible practical interest of the latter, but because they tend to bring into relief two at least of the necessary conditions of parliamentary government. But besides these necessary qualities which are needful before a parliamentary government can work at all, there are some additional prerequisites before it can work well. That a House of Commons may work well it must perform, as we saw, five functions well: it must elect a ministry well, legislate well, teach the nation well, express the nation's will well, bring matters to the nation's attention well.

The discussion has a difficulty of its own. What is meant by 'well'? Who is to judge? Is it to be some panel of philosophers, some fancied posterity, or some other outside authority? I answer, no philosophy, no posterity, no external authority, but the English nation here and now.

Free government is self-government—a government of the people by the people. The best government of this sort is that which the people think best. An imposed government, a government like that of the English in India, may very possibly be better; it may represent the views of a higher race than the governed race; but it is not therefore a free government. A free government is that which the people subject to it voluntarily choose. In a casual collection of loose people the only possible free government is a democratic government. Where no one knows, or cares for, or respects any one else, all must rank equal; no one's opinion can be more potent than that of another. But, as has been explained, a deferential nation has a structure of its own. Certain persons are by common consent agreed to be wiser than others, and their opinion, is by consent, to rank for much more than its numerical value. We may in these happy nations weigh votes as well as count them, though in less favoured countries we can count only. But in free nations, the votes so weighed or so counted must decide. A perfect free government is one which decides perfectly according to those votes; an imperfect, one which so decides imperfectly; a bad, one which does not so decide at all. Public opinion is the test of this polity; the best opinion which, with its existing habits of deference, the nation will accept: if the free government goes by that opinion, it is a good government of its species; if it contravenes that opinion, it is a bad one.

Tried by this rule the House of Commons does its appointing business well. It chooses rulers as we wish rulers to be chosen. If it did not, in a speaking and writing age we should soon know. I have heard a great Liberal statesman say, 'The time was coming when we must advertise for a grievance'.[1] What a good grievance it would be were the ministry appointed and retained by the Parliament a ministry detested by the nation. An anti-present government league would be instantly created, and it would be more instantly powerful and more instantly success-ful than the Anti-Corn Law League.

It has, indeed, been objected that the choosing business of Parliament is done ill, because it does not choose strong governments. And it is certain that when public opinion does not definitely decide upon a marked policy, and when in consequence parties in the Parliament are nearly even, individual cupidity and changeability may make Parliament change its appointees too often; may induce them never enough to trust any of them; may make it keep all of them under a suspended sentence of coming dismissal. But the experience of Lord Palmerston's second Government proves, I think, that these fears are exaggerated. When the choice of a nation is really fixed on a statesman, Parliament will fix upon him too. The parties in the Parliament of 1859 were as nearly divided as in any probable Parliament; a great many Liberals did not much like Lord Palmerston, and they would have gladly co-operated in an attempt to dethrone him. But the same influence acted on Parliament within which acted on the nation without. The moderate men of both parties were satisfied that Lord Palmerston's was the best government, and they therefore pre-served it though it was hated by the immoderate on both sides. We have then found by a critical instance that a government supported by what I may call 'the common element',—by the like-

[1] This was said in 1858.

minded men of unlike parties,—will be retained in power, though parties are even, and though, as Treasury counting reckons, the majority is imperceptible. If happily, by its intelligence and attractiveness, a cabinet can gain a hold upon the great middle part of Parliament, it will continue to exist notwithstanding the hatching of small plots and the machinations of mean factions.

On the whole, I think it indisputable that the selecting task of Parliament is performed as well as public opinion wishes it to be performed; and if we want to improve that standard, we must first improve the English nation, which imposes that standard. Of the substantial part of its legislative task the same, too, may I think, be said. The manner of our legislation is indeed detestable, and the machinery for settling that manner odious. A committee of the whole House, dealing, or attempting to deal, with the elaborate clauses of a long Bill, is a wretched specimen of severe but misplaced labour. It is sure to wedge some clause into the Act, such as that which the judge said 'seemed to have fallen by itself, *perhaps*, from heaven, into the mind of the legislature', so little had it to do with anything on either side or around it. At such times government by a public meeting displays its inherent defects, and is little restrained by its necessary checks. But the essence of our legislature may be separated from its accidents. Subject to two considerable defects I think Parliament passes laws as the nation wishes to have them passed.

Thirty years ago this was not so. The nation had outgrown its institutions, and was cramped by them. It was a man in the clothes of a boy; every limb wanted more room, and every garment to be fresh made. 'D-mn me,' said Lord Eldon in the dialect of his age, 'if I had to begin life again I would begin as an agitator.' The shrewd old man saw that the best life was that of a miscellaneous objector to the old world, though he loved that world, believed in it, could imagine no other. But he would not say so now. There is no worse trade than agitation at this time. A man can hardly get an audience if he wishes to complain of anything. Nowadays, not only does the mind and policy of Parliament (subject to the exceptions before named) possess the common sort of moderation essential to the possibility of parliamentary government, but also that exact gradation, that precise species of moderation, most agreeable to the nation at large. Not only does the nation endure a parliamentary government, which it would not do if Parliament were immoderate, but it likes parliamentary government. A sense of satisfaction permeates the country because most of the country feels it has got the precise thing that suits it.

The exceptions are two. First. That Parliament leans too much to the opinions of the landed interest. The Cattle Plague Act is a conspicuous instance of this defect. The details of that Bill may be good or bad, and its policy wise or foolish. But the manner in which it was hurried through the House savoured of despotism. The cotton trade or the wine trade could not, in their maximum of peril, have obtained such aid in such a manner. The House of Commons would hear of no pause and would heed no arguments. The greatest number of them feared for their incomes. The land of England returns many members annually for the counties; these members the constitution gave them. But what is curious is that the landed interest gives no seats to other classes, but takes plenty of seats *from* other classes. Half the boroughs in England are represented by considerable landowners, and when rent is in question, as in the cattle case, they think more of themselves than of those who sent them. In number the landed gentry in the House far surpass any other class. They have, too, a more intimate connexion with one another; they were educated at the same schools; know one another's family name from boyhood; form a society; are the same kind of men; marry the same kind of women. The merchants and manufacturers in Parliament are a motley race—one educated here, another there, a third not educated at all; some are of the second generation of traders, who consider self-made men intruders upon an hereditary place; others are self-made, and regard the men of inherited wealth, which they did not make and do not augment, as beings of neither mind nor place, inferior to themselves because they have no brains, and inferior to lords because they have no rank. Traders have no bond of union, no habits of intercourse; their wives, if they care for society, want to see not the wives of other such men, but 'better people', as they say—the wives of men certainly with land, and, if Heaven help, with the titles. Men who study the structure of Parliament, not in abstract books, but in the concrete London world, wonder not that the landed interest is very powerful, but that it is not despotic. I believe it would be despotic if it were clever, or rather if its representatives were so, but it has a fixed device to make them stupid. The counties not only elect landowners, which is natural, and perhaps wise, but also elect only landowners *of their own county*, which is absurd. There is no free trade in the agricultural mind; each county prohibits the import of able men from other counties. This is why eloquent sceptics —Bolingbroke and Disraeli—have been so apt to lead the unsceptical Tories. They *will* have people with a great piece of land in a particular spot, and of course these people generally cannot speak, and often cannot think. And so eloquent men who laugh at the party come to lead the party. The landed interest has much more influence than it should have; but it wastes that influence so much that the excess is, except on singular occurrences (like the cattle plague), of secondary moment.

It is almost another side of the same matter to say that the structure of Parliament gives too little weight to the growing districts of the country and too much to the stationary. In old times the south of England was not only the pleasantest but the greatest part of England. Devonshire was a great maritime county when the foundations of our representation were fixed; Somersetshire and Wiltshire great manufacturing counties. The harsher climate of the northern counties was associated with a ruder, a sterner, and a sparser people. The immense preponderance which our Parliament gave before 1832, and, though pruned and mitigated, still gives to England south of the Trent, then corresponded to a real preponderance in wealth and mind. How opposite the present contrast is we all know. And the case gets worse every day. The nature of modern trade is to give to those who have much and take from those who have little. Manufacture goes where manufacture is, because there and there alone it finds attendant and auxiliary manufacture. Every railway takes trade from the little town to the big town, because it enables the customer to buy in the big town. Year by year the North (as we may roughly call the new industrial world) gets more important, and the South (as we may call the pleasant remnant of old times) gets less important. It is a grave objection to our existing parliamentary constitution that it gives much power to regions of past greatness, and refuses equal power to regions of present greatness.

I think (though it is not a popular notion) that by far the greater part of the cry for parliamentary reform is due to this inequality. The great capitalists, Mr. Bright and his friends, believe they are sincere in asking for more power for the working man, but, in fact, they very naturally and very properly want more power for themselves. They cannot endure—they ought not to endure—that a rich, able manufacturer should be a less man than a small, stupid squire. The notions of political equality which Mr. Bright puts forward are as old as political speculation, and have been refuted by the first efforts of that speculation. But for all that they are likely to last as long as political society, because they are based upon indelible principles in human nature. Edmund Burke called the first East Indians 'Jacobins to a man', because they did not feel their 'present importance equal to their real wealth'. So long as there is an uneasy class, a class which has not its just power, it will rashly clutch and blindly believe the notion that all men should have the same power.

I do not consider the exclusion of the working classes from effectual representation a defect in *this* aspect of our parliamentary representation. The working classes contribute almost nothing to our corporate public opinion, and therefore, the fact of their want of influence in Parliament does not impair the coincidence of Parliament with public opinion. They are left out in the representation, and also in the thing represented.

Nor do I think the number of persons of aristocratic descent in Parliament impairs the accordance of Parliament with public opinion. No doubt the direct descendants and collateral relatives of noble families supply members to Parliament in far greater proportion than is warranted by the number of such families in comparison with the whole nation. But I do not believe that these families have the least corporate character, or any common opinions, different from others of the landed gentry. They have the opinions of the propertied rank in which they were born. The English aristocracy have never been a caste apart, and are not a caste apart now. They would keep up nothing that other landed gentlemen would not. And if any landed gentlemen are to be sent to the House of Commons, it is desirable that many should be men of some rank. As long as we keep up a double set of institutions,—one dignified and intended to impress the many, the other efficient and intended to govern the many,—we should take care that the two match nicely, and hide where the one begins and where the other ends. This is in part effected by conceding some subordinate power to the august part of our polity, but it is equally aided by keeping an aristocratic element in the useful part of our polity. In truth, the deferential instinct secures both. Aristocracy is a power in the 'constituencies'. A man who is an honourable or a baronet, or better yet, perhaps, a real earl, though Irish, is coveted by half the electing bodies; and, *cæteris paribus*, a manufacturer's son has no chance with him. The reality of the deferential feeling in the community is tested by the actual election of the class deferred to, where there is a large free choice betwixt it and others.

Subject therefore to the two minor, but still not inconsiderable, defects I have named, Parliament conforms itself accurately enough, both as a chooser of executives and as a legislature, to the formed opinion of the country. Similarly, and subject to the same exceptions, it expresses the nation's opinion in words well, when it happens that words, not laws, are wanted. On foreign matters, where we cannot legislate, whatever the English nation thinks, or thinks it thinks, as to the critical events of the world, whether in Denmark, in Italy, or America, and no matter whether it thinks wisely or unwisely, that same something, wise or unwise, will be thoroughly well said in Parliament. The lyrical function of Parliament, if I may use such a phrase, is well done; it pours out in characteristic words the characteristic heart of the nation. And it can do little more useful. Now that free government is in Europe so rare and in America so distant, the opinion, even the incomplete, erroneous, rapid opinion of the free English people is invaluable. It may be very wrong, but it is sure to be unique; and if it is right it is sure to contain matter of great magnitude, for it is only a first-class matter in distant things which a free people ever sees or learns. The English people must miss a thousand minutiae that continental bureaucracies know even too well; but if they see a cardinal truth which those bureaucracies miss, that cardinal truth may greatly help the world.

But if in these ways, and subject to these exceptions, Parliament by its policy and its speech well embodies and expresses public opinion, I own I think it must be conceded that it is not equally successful in elevating public opinion. The teaching task of Parliament is the task it does worst. Probably at this moment it is natural to exaggerate this defect. The greatest teacher of all in Parliament, the head master of the nation, the great elevator of the country—so far as Parliament elevates it—must be the Prime Minister; he has an influence, an authority, a facility in giving a great tone to discussion, or a mean tone, which no other man has. Now Lord

Palmerston for many years steadily applied his mind to giving, not indeed a mean tone, but a light tone, to the proceedings of Parliament. One of his greatest admirers has since his death told a story of which he scarcely sees, or seems to see, the full effect. When Lord Palmerston was first made leader of the House, his jaunty manner was not at all popular, and some predicted failure. 'No,' said an old member, 'he will soon educate us *down* to his level; the House will soon prefer this Ha! Ha! style to the wit of Canning and the gravity of Peel.' I am afraid that we must own that the prophecy was accomplished. No prime minister, so popular and so influential, has ever left in the public memory so little noble teaching. Twenty years hence, when men inquire as to the then fading memory of Palmerston, we shall be able to point to no great truth which he taught, no great distinct policy which he embodied, no noble words which once fascinated his age, and which, in after years, men would not willingly let die. But we shall be able to say 'he had a genial manner, a firm, sound sense; he had a kind of cant of insincerity, but we always knew what he meant; he had the brain of a ruler in the clothes of a man of fashion'. Posterity will hardly understand the words of the aged reminiscent, but we now feel their effect. The House of Commons, since it caught its tone from such a statesman, has taught the nation worse, and elevated it less, than usual.

I think, however, that a correct observer would decide that in general, and on principle, the House of Commons does not teach the public as much as it might teach it, or as the public would wish to learn. I do not wish very abstract, very philosophical, very hard matters to be stated in Parliament. The teaching there given must be popular, and to be popular it must be concrete, embodied, short.

The problem is to know the highest truth which the people will bear, and to inculcate and preach that. Certainly Lord Palmerston did not preach it. He a little degraded us by preaching a doctrine just below our own standard;—a doctrine not enough below us to repel us much, but yet enough below to harm us by augmenting a worldliness which needed no addition, and by diminishing a love of principle and philosophy which did not want deduction.

In comparison with the debates of any other assembly, it is true the debates by the English Parliament are most instructive. The debates in the American Congress have little teaching efficacy; it is the characteristic vice of Presidential Government to deprive them of that efficacy; in that government a debate in the legislature has little effect, for it cannot turn out the executive, and the executive can veto all it decides. The French Chambers [1] are suitable appendages to an Empire which desires the power of despotism without its shame; they prevent the enemies of the Empire being quite correct when they say there is no free speech: a few permitted objectors fill the air with eloquence, which every one knows to be often true, and always vain. The debates in an English Parliament fill a space in the world which, in these auxiliary chambers, is not possible. But I think any one who compares the discussions on great questions in the higher part of the press, with the discussions in Parliament, will feel that there is (of course amid much exaggeration and vagueness) a greater vigour and a higher meaning in the writing than in the speech; a vigour which the public appreciate—a meaning that they like to hear.

[1] This of course relates to the assemblies of the Empire.

The *Saturday Review* said, some years since, that the ability of Parliament was a 'protected ability'; that there was at the door a differential duty of at least £2,000 a year. Accordingly the House of Commons, representing only mind coupled with property, is not equal in mind to a legislature chosen for mind only, and whether accompanied by wealth or not. But I do not for a moment wish to see a representation of pure mind; it would be contrary to the main thesis of this essay. I maintain that Parliament ought to embody the public opinion of the English nation; and, certainly, that opinion is much more fixed by its property than by its mind. The 'too clever by half' people, who live in 'Bohemia', ought to have no more influence in Parliament than they have in England, and they can scarcely have less. Only, after every great abatement and deduction, I think the country would bear a little more mind; and that there is a profusion of opulent dullness in Parliament which might a little— though only a little—be pruned away.

The only function of Parliament which remains to be considered is the informing function, as I just now called it: the function which belongs to it, or to members of it, to bring before the nation the ideas, grievances, and wishes of special classes. This must not be confounded with what I have called its teaching function. In life, no doubt, the two run one into another. But so do many things which it is very important in definition to separate. The fact of two things being often found together is rather a reason for, than an objection to, separating them in idea. Sometimes they are *not* found together, and then we may be puzzled if we have not trained ourselves to separate them. The teaching function brings true ideas before the nation, and is the function of its highest minds. The expressive function brings only special ideas, and is the function of but special minds. Each class has its ideas, wants, and notions; and certain brains are ingrained with them. Such sectarian conceptions are not those by which a determining nation should regulate its action, nor arc orators, mainly animated by such conceptions, safe guides in policy. But those orators should be heard; those conceptions should be kept in sight. The great maxim of modern thought is not only the toleration of everything, but the examination of everything. It is by examining very bare, very dull, very unpromising things, that modern science has come to be what it is. There is a story of a great chemist who said he owed half his fame to his habit of examining, after his experiments, what was going to be thrown away; everybody knew the result of the experiment itself, but in the refuse matter there were many little facts and unknown changes, which suggested the discoveries of a famous life to a person capable of looking for them. So with the special notions of neglected classes. They may contain elements of truth which, though small, are the very elements which we now require, because we already know all the rest.

This doctrine was well known to our ancestors. They laboured to give a *character* to the various constituencies, or to many of them. They wished that the shipping trade, the wool trade, the linen trade, should each have their spokesman: that the unsectional Parliament should know what each section in the nation thought before it gave the national decision. This is the true reason for admitting the working classes to a share in the representation, at least as far as the composition of Parliament is to be improved by that admission. A great many ideas, a great many feelings, have gathered among the town artisans—a peculiar intellectual life has sprung up among them. They believe that they have interests which are misconceived or neglected; that they know something which others do not know; that the thoughts of Parliament are not as their thoughts. They ought to be allowed to try to convince Parliament; their notions ought to be stated as those of other classes are stated; their advocates should be heard as other people's advocates are heard. Before the Reform Bill, there was a recognized machinery for that purpose. The member for Westminster, and other members, were elected by universal suffrage (or what was in substance such); those members did, in their day, state what were the grievances and ideas—or were thought to be the grievances and ideas—of the working classes. It was the single, unbending franchise introduced in 1832 that has caused this difficulty, as it has others.

Until such a change is made the House of Commons will be defective, just as the House of Lords was defective. It will not *look* right. As long as the Lords do not come to their own House, we may prove on paper that it is a good revising chamber, but it will be difficult to make the literary argument felt. Just so, as long as a great class, congregated in political localities, and known to have political thoughts and wishes, is without notorious and palpable advocates in Parliament, we may prove on paper that our representation is adequate, but the world will not believe it. There is a saying of the eighteenth century, that in politics 'gross appearances are great realities'. It is in vain to demonstrate that the working classes have no grievances; that the middle classes have done all that is possible for them, and so on with a crowd of arguments which I need not repeat, for the newspapers keep them in type, and we can say them by heart. But so long as the 'gross appearance' is that there are no evident, incessant representatives to speak the wants of artisans, the 'great reality' will be a diffused dissatisfaction. Thirty years ago it was vain to prove that Gatton and Old Sarum were valuable seats, and sent good members. Everybody said, 'Why, there are no people there'. Just so, everybody must say now, 'Our representative system must be imperfect, for an immense class has no members to speak for it'. The only answer to the cry against constituencies *without* inhabitants was to transfer their power to constituencies *with* inhabitants. Just so, the way to stop the complaint that artisans have no members is to give them members,—to create a body of representatives, chosen by artisans, be-lieving, as Mr. Carlyle would say, 'that artisanism is the one thing needful'.

NO. VI. ON CHANGES OF MINISTRY

THERE is one error as to the English Constitution which crops-up periodically. Circumstances which often, though irregularly, occur naturally suggest that error, and as surely as they happen it revives. The relation of Parliament, and especially of the House of Commons, to the Executive Government is the specific peculiarity of our constitution, and an event which frequently happens much puzzles some people as to it.

That event is a change of ministry. All our administrators go out together. The whole executive government changes—at least, all the heads of it change in a body, and at every such change some speculators are sure to exclaim that such a habit is foolish. They say, 'No doubt Mr. Gladstone and Lord Russell may have been wrong about Reform; no doubt Mr. Gladstone may have been cross in the House of Commons; but why should either or both of these events change all the heads of all our practical departments? What could be more absurd than what happened in 1858? Lord Palmerston was for once in his life over-buoyant; he gave rude answers to stupid inquiries; he brought into the Cabinet a nobleman concerned in an ugly trial about a woman; he, or his Foreign Secretary, did not answer a French dispatch by a dispatch, but told our ambassador to reply orally. And because of these trifles, or at any rate, these isolated *un*-administrative mistakes, all our administration had fresh heads. The Poor Law Board had a new chief, the Home Department a new chief, the Public Works a new chief. Surely this was absurd.' Now, is this objection good or bad? Speaking generally, is it wise so to change all our rulers?

The practice produces three great evils. First, it brings in on a sudden new persons and untried persons to preside over our policy. A little while ago Lord Cranborne [1] had no more idea that he would now be Indian Secretary than that he would be a bill broker. He had never given any attention to Indian affairs; he can get them up, because he is an able educated man who can get up anything. But they are not 'part and parcel' of his mind; not his subjects of familiar reflection, nor things of which he thinks by predilection, of which he cannot help thinking. But because Lord Russell and Mr. Gladstone did not please the House of Commons about Reform, there he is. A perfectly inexperienced man, so far as Indian affairs go, rules all our Indian empire. And if all our heads of offices change together, so very frequently it must be. If twenty offices are vacant at once, there are almost never twenty tried, competent, clever men ready to take them. The difficulty of making up a government is very much like the difficulty of putting together a Chinese puzzle: the spaces do not suit what you have to put into them. And the difficulty of matching a ministry is more than that of fitting a puzzle, because the ministers to be put in can object, though the bits of a puzzle cannot. One objector can throw out the combination. In 1847 Lord Grey would not join Lord John Russell's projected government if Lord Palmerston was to be Foreign Secretary; Lord Palmerston *would* be Foreign Secretary, and so the government was not formed. The cases in which a single refusal prevents a government are rare, and there must be many concurrent circumstances to make it effectual. But the cases in which refusals impair or spoil a government are very

[1] Now Lord Salisbury, who when this was written was Indian Secretary.—*Note* to second edition.

common. It almost never happens that the ministry-maker can put into his offices whom he would like; a number of placemen are always too proud, too eager, or too obstinate to go just where they should.

Again, this system not only makes new ministers ignorant, but keeps present ministers indifferent. A man cannot feel the same interest that he might in his work if he knows that by events over which he has no control,—by errors in which he had no share,—by metamorphoses of opinion which belong to a different sequence of phenomena, he may have to leave that work in the middle, and may very likely never return to it. The new man put into a fresh office ought to have the best motive to learn his task thoroughly, but, in fact, in England, he has not at all the best motive. The last wave of party and politics brought him there, the next may take him away. Young and eager men take, even at this disadvantage, a keen interest in office work, but most men, especially old men, hardly do so. Many a battered minister may be seen to think much more of the vicissitudes which make him and unmake him, than of any office matter.

Lastly, a sudden change of ministers may easily cause a mischievous change of policy. In many matters of business, perhaps in most, a continuity of mediocrity is better than a hotch-potch of excellences. For example, now that progress in the scientific arts is revolutionizing the instruments of war, rapid changes in our head-preparers for land and sea war are most costly and most hurtful. A single competent selector of new inventions would probably in the course of years, after some experience, arrive at something tolerable; it is in the nature of steady, regular, experimenting ability to diminish, if not vanquish, such difficulties. But a quick succession of chiefs has no similar facility.

They do not learn from each other's experience;—
you might as well expect the new head boy at
a public school to learn from the experience of the
last head boy. The most valuable result of many
years is a nicely-balanced mind instinctively heedful
of various errors; but such a mind is the incommunicable gift of individual experience, and an outgoing
minister can no more leave it to his successor than
an elder brother can pass it on to a younger. Thus
a desultory and incalculable policy may follow from
a rapid change of ministers.

These are formidable arguments, but four things
may, I think, be said in reply to, or mitigation of
them. A little examination will show that this
change of ministers is essential to a Parliamentary
government;—that something like it will happen in
all elective governments, and that worse happens
under presidential government;—that it is not
necessarily prejudicial to a good administration, but
that, on the contrary, something like it is a prerequisite of good administration;—that the evident evils
of English administration are not the results of Parliamentary government, but of grave deficiencies in
other parts of our political and social state; —that,
in a word, they result not from what we have, but
from what we have *not*.

As to the first point, those who wish to remove
the choice of ministers from Parliament have not
adequately considered what a Parliament is. A
Parliament is nothing less than a big meeting of
more or less idle people. In proportion as you give
it power it will inquire into everything, settle everything, meddle in everything. In an ordinary despotism, the powers of a despot are limited by his bodily
capacity, and by the calls of pleasure; he is but one
man;—there are but twelve hours in his day, and he
is not disposed to employ more than a small part in

dull business;—he keeps the rest for the court, or the harem, or for society. He is at the top of the world, and all the pleasures of the world are set before him. Mostly there is only a very small part of political business which he cares to understand, and much of it (with the shrewd sensual sense belonging to the race) he knows that he will never understand. But a Parliament is composed of a great number of men by no means at the top of the world. When you establish a predominant Parliament, you give over the rule of the country to a despot who has unlimited time,—who has unlimited vanity,—who has, or believes he has, unlimited comprehension, whose pleasure is in action, whose life is work. There is no limit to the curiosity of Parliament. Sir Robert Peel once suggested that a list should be taken down of the questions asked of him in a single evening; they touched more or less on fifty subjects, and there were a thousand other subjects which by parity of reason might have been added too. As soon as bore A ends, bore B begins. Some inquire from genuine love of knowledge, or from a real wish to improve what they ask about,—others to see their name in the papers,—others to show a watchful constituency that they are alert,—others to get on and to get a place in the government,—others from an accumulation of little motives they could not themselves analyse, or because it is their habit to ask things. And a proper reply must be given. It was said that 'Darby Griffith destroyed Lord Palmerston's first Government', and undoubtedly the cheerful impertinence with which in the conceit of victory that minister answered grave men much hurt his Parliamentary power. There is one thing which no one will permit to be treated lightly,—himself. And so there is one too which a sovereign assembly will never permit to be lessened or ridiculed,—its own power. The minister of the day will have to give an account in Parliament of all branches of adminis- tration, to say why they act when they do, and why they do not when they don't.

Nor is chance inquiry all a public department has most to fear. Fifty members of Parliament may be zealous for a particular policy affecting the depart- ment, and fifty others for another policy, and between them they may divide its action, spoil its favourite aims, and prevent its consistently working out either of their own aims. The process is very simple. Every department at times looks as if it was in a scrape; some apparent blunder, perhaps some real blunder, catches the public eye. At once the antagonist Parliamentary sections, which want to act on the department, seize the opportunity. They make speeches, they move for documents, they amass statistics. They declare 'that in no other country is such a policy possible as that which the department is pursuing; that it is medieval; that it costs money; that it wastes life; that America does the contrary; that Prussia does the contrary'. The newspapers follow according to their nature. These bits of administrative scandal amuse the public. Articles on them are very easy to write, easy to read, easy to talk about. They please the vanity of man- kind. We think as we read, 'Thank God, *I* am not as that man; *I* did not send green coffee to the Crimea; *I* did not send patent cartridge to the common guns, and common cartridge to the breech- loaders. *I* make money; that miserable public functionary only wastes money.' As for the defence of the department, no one cares for it or reads it. Naturally at first hearing it does not sound true. The opposition have the unrestricted selection of the point of attack, and they seldom choose a case in which the department, upon the surface of the matter, seems to be right. The case of first impression will always be that something shameful has happened; that such and such men did die; that this and that gun would not go off; that this or that ship will not sail. All the pretty reading is unfavourable, and all the praise is very dull.

Nothing is more helpless than such a department in Parliament if it has no authorized official defender. The wasps of the House fasten on it; here they perceive is something easy to sting, and safe, for it cannot sting in return. The small grain of foundation for complaint germinates, till it becomes a whole crop. At once the minister of the day is appealed to; he is at the head of the administration, and he must put the errors right, if such they are. The opposition leader says, 'I put it to the right honourable gentleman, the First Lord of the Treasury. He is a man of business. I do not agree with him in his choice of ends, but he is an almost perfect master of methods and means. What he wishes to do he does do. Now I appeal to him whether such gratuitous errors, such fatuous incapacity, are to be permitted in the public service. Perhaps the right honourable gentleman will grant me his attention while I show from the very documents of the department', &c., &c. What is the minister to do? He never heard of this matter; he does not care about the matter. Several of the supporters of the Government are interested in the opposition to the department; a grave man, supposed to be wise, mutters, 'This is *too* bad'. The Secretary of the Treasury tells him, 'The House is uneasy. A good many men are shaky. A. B. said yesterday he had been dragged through the dirt four nights following. Indeed I am disposed to think myself that the department has been somewhat lax. Perhaps an inquiry', &c., &c. And upon that the Prime Minister rises and says, 'That Her Majesty's Government having given very serious and grave consideration to this most important subject, are not prepared to say that in so complicated a matter the department has been perfectly exempt from error. He does not indeed concur in all the statements which have been made; it is obvious that several of the charges advanced are inconsistent with one another. If A. had really died from eating green coffee on the Tuesday, it is plain he could not have suffered from insufficient medical attendance on the following Thursday. However, on so complex a subject, and one so foreign to common experience, he will not give a judgement. And if the honourable member would be satisfied with having the matter inquired into by a committee of that House, he will be prepared to accede to the suggestion.'

Possibly the outlying department, distrusting the ministry, crams a friend. But it is happy indeed if it chances on a judicious friend. The persons most ready to take up that sort of business are benevolent amateurs, very well intentioned, very grave, very respectable, but also rather dull. Their words are good, but about the joints their arguments are weak. They speak very well, but while they are speaking, the decorum is so great that everybody goes away. Such a man is no match for a couple of House of Commons gladiators. They pull what he says to shreds. They show or say that he is wrong about his facts. Then he rises in a fuss and must explain: but in his hurry he mistakes, and cannot find the right paper, and becomes first hot, then confused, next inaudible, and so sits down. Probably he leaves the House with the notion that the defence of the department has broken down, and so *The Times* announces to all the world as soon as it awakes.

Some thinkers have naturally suggested that the heads of departments should as such have the right of speech in the House. But the system when it has been tried has not answered. M. Guizot tells us from his own experience that such a system is not effectual. A great popular assembly has a corporate character; it has its own privileges, prejudices, and notions. And one of these notions is that its own members—the persons it sees every day—whose qualities it knows, whose minds it can test, are those whom it can most trust. A clerk speaking from without would be an unfamiliar object. He would be an outsider. He would speak under suspicion; he would speak without dignity. Very often he would speak as a victim. All the bores of the House would be upon him. He would be put upon examination. He would have to answer interrogatories. He would be put through the figures and cross-questioned in detail. The whole effect of what he said would be lost in *quæstiunculæ* and hidden in a controversial detritus.

Again, such a person would rarely speak with great ability. He would speak as a scribe. His habits must have been formed in the quiet of an office; he is used to red tape, placidity, and the respect of subordinates. Such a person will hardly ever be able to stand the hurly-burly of a public assembly. He will lose his head—he will say what he should not. He will get hot and red; he will feel he is a sort of culprit. After being used to the flattering deference of deferential subordinates, he will be pestered by fuss and confounded by invective. He will hate the House as naturally as the House does not like him. He will be an incompetent speaker addressing a hostile audience.

And what is more, an outside administrator addressing Parliament, can move Parliament only by the goodness of his arguments. He has no votes to back them up with. He is sure to be at chronic war with some active minority of assailants or others. The natural mode in which a department is improved on great points and new points is by external suggestion; the worst foes of a department are the plausible errors which the most visible facts suggest, and which only half visible facts confute. Both the good ideas and the bad ideas are sure to find advocates first in the press and then in Parliament. Against these a permanent clerk would have to contend by argument alone. The Minister, the head of the parliamentary Government, will not care for him. The Minister will say in some undress soliloquy, 'These permanent "fellows" must look after themselves. I cannot be bothered. I have only a majority of nine, and a very shaky majority, too. I cannot afford to make enemies for those whom I did not appoint. They did nothing for me, and I can do nothing for them.' And if the permanent clerk come to ask his help he will say in decorous language, 'I am sure that if the department can evince to the satisfaction of Parliament that its past management has been such as the public interests require, no one will be more gratified than myself. I am not aware if it will be in my power to attend in my place on Monday; but if I can be so fortunate, I shall listen to your official statement with my very best attention.' And so the permanent public servant will be teased by the wits, oppressed by the bores, and massacred by the innovators of Parliament.

The incessant tyranny of Parliament over the public offices is prevented, and can only be prevented, by the appointment of a parliamentary head, connected by close ties with the present ministry and the ruling party in Parliament. The parliamentary head is a protecting machine. He and the friends he brings stand between the department and the busy-bodies and crotchet-makers of the House and the country. So long as at any moment the policy of an office could be altered by chance votes in either House of Parliament, there is no security for any consistency. Our guns and our ships are not, perhaps, very good now. But they would be much worse if any thirty or forty advocates for this gun or that gun could make a motion in Parliament, beat the department, and get their ships or their guns adopted. The 'Black Breech Ordnance Company' and the 'Adamantine Ship Company' would soon find representatives in Parliament, if forty or fifty members would get the national custom for their rubbish. But this result is now prevented by the parliamentary head of the department. As soon as the opposition begins the attack, he looks up his means of defence. He studies the subject, compiles his arguments, and builds little piles of statistics, which he hopes will have some effect. He has his reputation at stake, and he wishes to show that he is worth his present place, and fit for future pro-motion. He is well known, perhaps liked, by the House—at any rate the House attends to him; he is one of the regular speakers whom they hear and heed. He is sure to be able to get himself heard, and he is sure to make the best defence he can. And after he has settled his speech he loiters up to the Secretary of the Treasury, and says quietly, 'They have got a motion against me on Tuesday, you know. I hope you will have your men here. A lot of fellows have crotchets, and though they do not agree a bit with one another, they are all against the depart-ment; they will all vote for the inquiry.' And the Secretary answers, 'Tuesday, you say; no (looking at a paper), I do not think it will come on on Tuesday. There is Higgins on Education. He is good for a long time. But anyhow it shall be all right.' And then he glides about and speaks a word here and a word there, in consequence of which, when the anti-official motion is made, a considerable array of steady, grave faces sits behind the Treasury Bench—nay, possibly a rising man who sits in outlying independence below the gangway rises to defend the transaction; the department wins by thirty-three, and the management of that business pursues its steady way.

This contrast is no fancy picture. The experiment of conducting the administration of a public department by an independent unsheltered authority has often been tried, and always failed. Parliament always poked at it, till it made it impossible. The most remarkable is that of the Poor Law. The administration of that law is not now very good, but it is not too much to say that almost the whole of its goodness has been preserved by its having an official and party protector in the House of Commons. Without that contrivance we should have drifted back into the errors of the old Poor Law, and superadded to them the present meanness and incompetence in our large towns. All would have been given up to local management. Parliament would have interfered with the central board till it made it impotent, and the local authorities would have been despotic. The first administration of the new Poor Law was by 'Commissioners'—the three kings of Somerset House, as they were called. The system was certainly not tried in untrustworthy hands. At the crisis Mr. Chadwick, one of the most active and best administrators in England, was the secretary and the motive power: the principal Commissioner was Sir George Lewis, perhaps the best selective administrator of our time. But the House of Commons would not let the Commission alone. For a long time it was defended because the Whigs had made the Commission, and felt bound as a party to protect it. The new law started upon a certain intellectual impetus, and till that was spent its administration was supported in a rickety existence by an abnormal strength. But afterwards the Commissioners were left to their intrinsic weakness. There were members for all the localities, but there were none for them. There were members for every crotchet and corrupt interest, but there were none for them. The rural guardians would have liked to eke out wages by rates; the city guardians hated control, and hated to spend money. The Commission had to be dissolved, and a parliamentary head was added; the result is not perfect, but it is an amazing improvement on what would have happened in the old system. The new system has not worked well because the central authority has too little power; but under the previous system the central authority was getting to have, and by this time would have had, no power at all. And if Sir George Lewis and Mr. Chadwick could not maintain an outlying department in the face of Parliament, how unlikely that an inferior compound of discretion and activity will ever maintain it!

These reasonings show why a changing parliamentary head, a head changing as the ministry changes, is a necessity of good Parliamentary government, and there is happily a natural provision that there will be such heads. Party organization ensures it. In America, where on account of the fixedly recurring presidential election, and the perpetual minor elections, party organization is much more effectually organized than anywhere else, the effect on the offices is tremendous. Every office is filled anew at every presidential change, at least every change which brings in a new party. Not only the greatest posts, as in England, but the minor posts change their occupants. The scale of the financial operations of the Federal government is now so increased that most likely in that department, at least, there must in future remain a permanent element of great efficiency; a revenue of £90,000,000 sterling cannot be collected and expended with a trifling and changing staff. But till now the Americans have tried to get on not only with changing heads to a bureaucracy, as the English, but without any stable bureaucracy at all. They have facilities for trying it which no one else has. All Americans can administer, and the number of them really fit to be in succession lawyers, financiers, or military managers is wonderful; they need not be as afraid of a change of all their officials as European countries must, for the incoming substitutes are sure to be much better there than here; and they do not fear, as we English fear, that the outgoing officials will be left destitute in middle life, with no hope for the future and no recompense for the past, for in America (whatever may be the cause of it) opportunities are numberless, and a man who is ruined by being 'off the rails' in England soon there gets on another line. The Americans will probably to some extent modify their past system of total administrative cataclysms, but their very existence in the only competing form of free government should prepare us for and make us patient with the mild transitions of Parliamentary government.

These arguments will, I think, seem conclusive to almost every one; but, at this moment, many people will meet them thus: they will say, 'You prove what we do not deny, that this system of periodical change is a necessary ingredient in Parliamentary government, but you have not proved what we do deny, that this change is a good thing. Parliamentary government may have that effect, among others, for anything we care: we maintain merely that it is a defect.' In answer, I think it may be shown not, indeed, that this precise change is necessary to a permanently perfect administration, but that some analogous change, some change of the same species, is so.

At this moment, in England, there is a sort of leaning towards bureaucracy—at least, among writers and talkers. There is a seizure of partiality to it. The English people do not easily change their rooted notions, but they have many unrooted notions. Any great European event is sure for a moment to excite a sort of twinge of conversion to something or other. Just now, the triumph of the Prussians—the bureaucratic people, as is believed, *par excellence*—has excited a kind of admiration for bureaucracy, which a few years since we should have thought impossible. I do not presume to criticize the Prussian bureaucracy of my own knowledge; it certainly is not a pleasant institution for foreigners to come across, though agreeableness to travellers is but of very second-rate importance. But it is quite certain that the Prussian bureaucracy, though we, for a moment, half admire it at a distance, does not permanently please the most intelligent and liberal Prussians at home. What are two among the principal aims of the *Fortschritt Partei*—the party of progress—as Mr. Grant Duff, the most accurate and philosophical of our describers, delineates them?

First, 'a liberal system, conscientiously carried out in all the details of the administration, with a view to avoiding the scandals now of frequent occurrence, when an obstinate or bigoted official sets at defiance the liberal initiations of the government, trusting to backstairs influence'.

Second, 'an easy method of bringing to justice guilty officials, who are at present, as in France, in all conflicts with simple citizens, like men armed *cap-à-pie* fighting with undefenceless'. A system against which the most intelligent native liberals bring even with colour of reason such grave objections, is a dangerous model for foreign imitation.

The defects of bureaucracy are, indeed, well known. It is a form of government which has been tried often enough in the world, and it is easy to show what, human nature being what it in the long run is, the defects of a bureaucracy must in the long run be.

It is an inevitable defect, that bureaucrats will care more for routine than for results; or, as Burke put it, 'that they will think the substance of business not to be much more important than the forms of it'. Their whole education and all the habit of their lives make them do so. They are brought young into the particular part of the public service to which they are attached; they are occupied for years in learning its forms—afterwards, for years too, in applying these forms to trifling matters. They are, to use the phrase of an old writer, 'but the tailors of business; they cut the clothes, but they do not find the body'. Men so trained must come to think the routine of business not a means, but an end—to imagine the elaborate machinery of which they form a part, and from which they derive their dignity, to be a grand and achieved result, not a working and changeable instrument. But in a miscellaneous world, there is now one evil and now another. The very means which best helped you yesterday, may very likely be those which most impede you to-morrow—you may want to do a different thing to-morrow, and all your accumulation of means for yesterday's work is but an obstacle to the new work. The Prussian military system is the theme of popular wonder now, yet it sixty years pointed the moral against form. We have all heard the saying that 'Frederic the Great lost the battle of Jena'. It was the system which he had established—a good system for his wants and his times, which, blindly adhered to, and continued into a different age—put to strive with new competitors,—brought his country to ruin. The 'dead and formal' Prussian system was then contrasted with the 'living' French system—the sudden outcome of the new explosive democracy. The system which now exists is the product of the reaction; and the history of its predecessor is a warning what its future history may be too. It is not more celebrated for its day than Frederic's for his, and principle teaches that a bureaucracy, elated by sudden success, and marvelling at its own merit, is the most unimproving and shallow of governments.

Not only does a bureaucracy thus tend to under-government, in point of quality; it tends to over-government, in point of quantity. The trained official hates the rude, untrained public. He thinks that they are stupid, ignorant, reckless—that they cannot tell their own interest—that they should have the leave of the office before they do anything. Protection is the natural inborn creed of every official body; free trade is an extrinsic idea, alien to its notions, and hardly to be assimilated with life; and it is easy to see how an accomplished critic, used to a free and active life, could thus describe the official.

'Every imaginable and real social interest,' says Mr. Laing, 'religion, education, law, police, every branch of public or private business, personal liberty to move from place to place, even from parish to parish within the same jurisdiction; liberty to engage in any branch of trade or industry,

on a small or large scale, all the objects, in short, in
which body, mind, and capital can be employed in
civilized society, were gradually laid hold of for the
employment and support of functionaries, were
centralized in *bureaux*, were superintended, licensed,
inspected, reported upon, and interfered with by
a host of officials scattered over the land, and maintained at the public expense, yet with no conceivable
utility in their duties. They are not, however,
gentlemen at large, enjoying salary without service.
They are under a semi-military discipline. In
Bavaria, for instance, the superior civil functionary
can place his inferior functionary under house-
arrest, for neglect of duty, or other offence against
civil functionary discipline. In Wurtemberg, the
functionary cannot marry without leave from his
superior. Voltaire says, somewhere, that, "the art of
government is to make two-thirds of a nation pay all
it possibly can pay for the benefit of the other
third". This is realized in Germany by the functionary system. The functionaries are not there for
the benefit of the people, but the people for the
benefit of the functionaries. All this machinery of
functionarism, with its numerous ranks and grada-
tions in every district, filled with a staff of clerks and
expectants in every department looking for employment, appointments, or promotions, was intended
to be a new support of the throne in the new social
state of the Continent; a third class, in connexion
with the people by their various official duties of
interference in all public or private affairs, yet
attached by their interests to the kingly power. The
Beamptenstand, or functionary class, was to be the
equivalent to the class of nobility, gentry, capitalists,
and men of larger landed property than the peasant-
proprietors, and was to make up in numbers for the
want of individual weight and influence. In France,

at the expulsion of Louis Philippe, the civil functionaries were stated to amount to 807,030 individuals. This civil army was more than double of the military. In Germany, this class is necessarily more numerous in proportion to the population, the landwehr system imposing many more restrictions than the conscription on the free action of the people, and requiring more officials to manage it, and the semi-feudal jurisdictions and forms of law requiring much more writing and intricate forms of procedure before the courts than the Code Napoleon.'

A bureaucracy is sure to think that its duty is to augment official power, official business, or official members, rather than to leave free the energies of mankind; it overdoes the quantity of government, as well as impairs its quality.

The truth is, that a skilled bureaucracy—a bureaucracy trained from early life to its special avocation—is, though it boasts of an appearance of science, quite inconsistent with the true principles of the art of business. That art has not yet been condensed into precepts, but a great many experiments have been made, and a vast floating vapour of knowledge floats through society. One of the most sure principles is, that success depends on a due mixture of special and nonspecial minds—of minds which attend to the means, and of minds which attend to the end. The success of the great joint-stock banks of London—the most remarkable achievement of recent business—has been an example of the use of this mixture. These banks are managed by a board of persons mostly *not* trained to the business, supplemented by, and annexed to, a body of specially trained officers, who have been bred to banking all their lives. These mixed banks have quite beaten the old banks, composed exclusively of pure bankers; it is found that the board of directors has greater and more flexible knowledge—more insight into the wants of a commercial community—knows when to lend and when not to lend, better than the old bankers, who had never looked at life, except out of the bank windows. Just so the most successful railways in Europe have been conducted—not by engineers or traffic managers—but by capitalists; by men of a certain business culture, if of no other. These capitalists buy and use the services of skilled managers, as the unlearned attorney buys and uses the services of the skilled barrister, and manage far better than any of the different sorts of special men under them. They combine these different specialties—make it clear where the realm of one ends and that of the other begins, and add to it a wide knowledge of large affairs, which no special man can have, and which is only gained by diversified action. But this utility of leading minds used to generalize, and acting upon various materials, is entirely dependent upon their position. They must not be at the bottom—they must not even be half-way up—they must be at the top. A merchant's clerk would be a child at a bank counter; but the merchant himself could, very likely, give good, clear, and useful advice in a bank court. The merchant's clerk would be equally at sea in a railway office, but the merchant himself could give good advice, very likely, at a board of directors. The summits (if I may so say) of the various kinds of business are, like the tops of mountains, much more alike than the parts below—the bare principles are much the same; it is only the rich variegated details of the lower strata that so contrast with one another. But it needs travelling to know that the summits *are* the same. Those who live on one mountain believe that *their* mountain is wholly unlike all others.

The application of this principle to Parliamentary government is very plain; it shows at once that the intrusion from without upon an office of an exterior head of the office, is not an evil, but that, on the contrary, it is essential to the perfection of that office. If it is left to itself, the office will become technical, self-absorbed, self-multiplying. It will be likely to overlook the end in the means; it will fail from narrowness of mind; it will be eager in seeming to do; it will be idle in real doing. An extrinsic chief is the fit corrector of such errors. He can say to the permanent chief, skilled in the forms and pompous with the memories of his office, 'Will you, Sir, explain to me how this regulation conduces to the end in view? According to the natural view of things, the applicant should state the whole of his wishes to one clerk on one paper; you make him say it to five clerks on five papers.' Or, again, 'Does it not appear to you, Sir, that the reason of this formality is extinct? When we were building wood ships, it was quite right to have such precautions against fire; but now that we are building iron ships', &c., &c. If a junior clerk asked these questions, he would be 'pooh-poohed'! It is only the head of an office that can get them answered. It is he, and he only, that brings the rubbish of office to the burning-glass of sense.

The immense importance of such a fresh mind is greatest in a country where business changes most. A dead, inactive, agricultural country may be governed by an unalterable bureau for years and years, and no harm come of it. If a wise man arranged the bureau rightly in the beginning, it may run rightly a long time. But, if the country be a progressive, eager, changing one, soon the bureau will either cramp improvement, or be destroyed itself.

This conception of the use of a Parliamentary head shows how wrong is the obvious notion which regards him as the principal administrator of his office. The late Sir George Lewis used to be fond of explaining this subject. He had every means of knowing. He was bred in the permanent civil service. He was a very successful Chancellor of the Exchequer, a very successful Home Secretary, and he died Minister for War. He used to say, 'It is not the business of a Cabinet Minister to work his department. His business is to see that it is properly worked. If he does much, he is probably doing harm. The permanent staff of the office can do what he chooses to do much better, or if they cannot, they ought to be removed. He is only a bird of passage, and cannot compete with those who are in the office all their lives round.' Sir George Lewis was a perfect Parliamentary head of an office, so far as that head is to be a keen critic and rational corrector of it.

But Sir George Lewis was not perfect: he was not even an average good head in another respect. The use of a fresh mind applied to the official mind is not only a corrective use, it is also an animating use. A public department is very apt to be dead to what is wanting for a great occasion till the occasion is past. The vague public mind will appreciate some signal duty before the precise, occupied administration perceives it. The Duke of Newcastle was of this use at least in the Crimean war. He roused up his department, though when roused it could not act. A perfect parliamentary minister would be one who should add the animating capacity of the Duke of Newcastle to the accumulated sense, the detective instinct, and the *laissez-faire* habit of Sir George Lewis.

As soon as we take the true view of Parliamentary

office we shall perceive that fairly frequent change in the official is an advantage, not a mistake. If his function is to bring a representative of outside sense and outside animation in contact with the inside world, he ought often to be changed. No man is a perfect representative of outside sense. 'There is some one', says the true French saying, 'who is more able than Talleyrand, more able than Napoleon. *C'est tout le monde.*' That many-sided sense finds no microcosm in any single individual. Still less are the critical function and the animating function of a Parliamentary minister likely to be perfectly exercised by one and the same man. Impelling power and restraining wisdom are as opposite as any two things, and are rarely found together. And even if the natural mind of the Parliamentary minister was perfect, long contact with the office would destroy his use. Inevitably he would accept the ways of office, think its thoughts, live its life. The 'dyer's hand would be subdued to what it works in'. If the function of a Parliamentary minister is to be an outsider to his office, we must not choose one who, by habit, thought, and life, is acclimatized to its ways.

There is every reason to expect that a Parliamentary statesman will be a man of quite sufficient intelligence, quite enough various knowledge, quite enough miscellaneous experience, to represent effectually general sense in opposition to bureaucratic sense. Most Cabinet ministers in charge of considerable departments are men of superior ability; I have heard an eminent living statesman of long experience say that in his time he only knew one instance to the contrary. And there is the best protection that it shall be so. A considerable Cabinet minister has to defend his Department in the face of mankind; and though distant observers and sharp writers may depreciate it, this is a very difficult thing. A fool, who has publicly to explain great affairs, who has publicly to answer detective questions, who has publicly to argue against able and quick opponents, must soon be shown to be a fool. The very nature of Parliamentary government answers for the discovery of substantial incompetence.

At any rate, none of the competing forms of government have nearly so effectual a procedure for putting a good untechnical minister to correct and impel the routine ones. There are but four important forms of government in the present state of the world,—the Parliamentary, the Presidential, the Hereditary, and the Dictatorial, or Revolutionary. Of these I have shown that, as now worked in America, the Presidential form of government is incompatible with a skilled bureaucracy. If the whole official class change when a new party goes out or comes in, a good official system is impossible. Even if more officials should be permanent in America than now, still, vast numbers will always be changed. The whole issue is based on a single election—on the choice of President; by that internecine conflict all else is won or lost. The managers of the contest have the greatest possible facility in using what I may call patronage-bribery. Everybody knows that, as a fact, the President can give what places he likes to what persons, and when his friends tell A. B., 'If we win C. D. shall be turned out of Utica Post-office, and you, A. B., shall have it', A. B. believes it, and is justified in doing so. But no individual member of Parliament can promise place effectually. *He* may not be able to give the places. His party may come in, but he will be powerless. In the United States party intensity is aggravated by concentrating an overwhelming importance on a single contest, and the efficiency of promised offices as a means of corruption is augmented, because the victor can give what he likes to whom he likes.

Nor is this the only defect of a Presidential government in reference to the choice of officers. The President has the principal anomaly of a Parliamentary government without having its corrective. At each change of party the President distributes (as here) the principal offices to his principal supporters. But he has an opportunity for singular favouritism. The minister lurks in the office; he need do nothing in public; he need not show for years whether he is a fool or wise. The nation can tell what a Parliamentary member is by the open test of Parliament; but no one, save from actual contact, or by rare position, can tell anything certain of a Presidential minister.

The case of a minister under an hereditary form of government is yet worse. The hereditary king may be weak; may be under the government of women; may appoint a minister from childish motives; may remove one from absurd whims. There is no security that an hereditary king will be competent to choose a good chief minister, and thousands of such kings have chosen millions of bad ministers.

By the Dictatorial, or Revolutionary, sort of government, I mean that very important sort in which the sovereign—the absolute sovereign—is selected by insurrection. In theory, one would have certainly hoped that by this time such a crude elective machinery would have been reduced to a secondary part. But, in fact, the greatest nation (or, perhaps, after the exploits of Bismarck, I should say one of the two greatest nations of the Continent) vacillates between the Revolutionary and the Parliamentary, and now is governed under the revolutionary form. France elects its ruler in the streets of Paris. Flatterers may suggest that the democratic empire will become hereditary, but close observers know that it cannot. The idea of the government is that the Emperor represents the people in capacity, in judgement, in instinct. But no family through generations can have sufficient, or half sufficient, mind to do so. The representative despot must be chosen by fighting, as Napoleon I and Napoleon III were chosen. And such a government is likely, whatever be its other defects, to have a far better and abler administration than any other government. The head of the government must be a man of the most consummate ability. He cannot keep his place, he can hardly keep his life, unless he is. He is sure to be active, because he knows that his power, and perhaps his head, may be lost if he be negligent. The whole frame of his State is strained to keep down revolution. The most difficult of all political problems is to be solved—the people are to be at once thoroughly restrained and thoroughly pleased. The executive must be like a steel shirt of the Middle Ages—extremely hard and extremely flexible. It must give way to attractive novelties which do not hurt; it must resist such as are dangerous; it must maintain old things which are good and fitting; it must alter such as cramp and give pain. The dictator dare not appoint a bad minister if he would. I admit that such a despot is a better selector of administrators than a parliament; that he will know how to mix fresh minds and used minds better; that he is under a stronger motive to combine them well; that here is to be seen the best of all choosers with the keenest motives to choose. But I need not prove in England that the revolutionary selection of rulers obtains administrative efficiency at a price altogether transcending its value; that it shocks credit by its catastrophes; that for intervals it does not protect property or life; that it maintains an undergrowth of fear through all prosperity; that it may take years to find the true capable despot; that the interregna of the incapable are full of all evil; that the fit despot may die as soon as found; that the good administration and all else hang by the thread of his life.

But if, with the exception of this terrible revolutionary government, a Parliamentary government upon principle surpasses all its competitors in administrative efficiency, why is it that our English Government, which is beyond comparison the best of Parliamentary governments, is not celebrated through the world for administrative efficiency? It is noted for many things, why is it not noted for that? Why, according to popular belief, is it rather characterized by the very contrary?

One great reason of the diffused impression is, that the English Government attempts so much. Our military system is that which is most attacked. Objectors say we spend much more on our army than the great military monarchies, and yet with an inferior result. But, then, what we attempt is incalculably more difficult. The continental monarchies have only to defend compact European territories by the many soldiers whom they force to fight; the English try to defend without any compulsion—only by such soldiers as they persuade to serve—territories far surpassing all Europe in magnitude, and situated all over the habitable globe. Our Horse Guards and War Office may not be at all perfect—I believe they are not; but if they had sufficient recruits selected by force of law—if they had, as in Prussia, the absolute command of each man's time for a few years, and the right to call him out afterwards when they liked, we should be much surprised at the sudden ease and quickness with which they did things. I have no doubt too that any accomplished soldier of the Continent would reject as impossible what we after a fashion effect. He would not attempt to defend a vast scattered empire, with many islands, a long frontier line in every continent, and a very tempting bit of plunder at the centre, by mere volunteer recruits, who mostly come from the worst class of the people,—whom the Great Duke called the 'scum of the earth',—who come in uncertain numbers year by year,—who by some political accident may not come in adequate numbers, or at all, in the year we need them most. Our War Office attempts what foreign War Offices (perhaps rightly) would not try at; their officers have means of incalculable force denied to ours, though ours is set to harder tasks.

Again, the English navy undertakes to defend a line of coast and a set of dependencies far surpassing those of any continental power. And the extent of our operations is a singular difficulty just now. It requires us to keep a large stock of ships and arms. But on the other hand, there are most important reasons why we should not keep much. The naval art and the military art are both in a state of transition; the last discovery of to-day is out of date, and superseded by an antagonistic discovery to-morrow. Any large accumulation of vessels or guns is sure to contain much that will be useless, unfitting, antediluvian, when it comes to be tried. There are two cries against the Admiralty which go on side by side: one says, 'We have not ships enough, no "relief" ships, no *navy*, to tell the truth'; the other cry says, 'We have all the wrong ships, all the wrong guns, and nothing but the wrong; in their foolish constructive mania the

Admiralty have been building when they ought to have been waiting; they have heaped a curious museum of exploded inventions, but they have given us nothing serviceable'. The two cries for opposite policies go on together, and blacken our Executive together, though each is a defence of the Executive against the other.

Again, the Home Department in England struggles with difficulties of which abroad they have long got rid. We love independent 'local authorities', little centres of outlying authority. When the metropolitan executive most wishes to act, it cannot act effectually because these lesser bodies hesitate, deliberate, or even disobey. But local independence has no necessary connexion with Parliamentary government. The degree of local freedom desirable in a country varies according to many circumstances, and a Parliamentary government may consist with any degree of it. We certainly ought not to debit Parliamentary government as a general and applicable polity with the particular vices of the guardians of the poor in England, though it is so debited every day.

Again, as our administration has in England this peculiar difficulty, so on the other hand foreign competing administrations have a peculiar advantage. Abroad a man under Government is a superior being; he is higher than the rest of the world; he is envied by almost all of it. This gives the Government the easy pick of the *élite* of the nation. All clever people are eager to be under Government, and are hardly to be satisfied elsewhere. But in England there is no such superiority, and the English have no such feeling. We do not respect a stamp-office clerk, or an exciseman's assistant. A pursy grocer considers he is much above either. Our Government cannot buy for minor clerks the best ability of the nation in the cheap currency of pure honour, and no government is rich enough to buy very much of it in money. Our mercantile opportunities allure away the most ambitious minds. The foreign *bureaux* are filled with a selection from the ablest men of the nation, but only a very few of the best men approach the English offices.

But these are neither the only nor even the principal reasons why our public administration is not so good as, according to principle and to the unimpeded effects of Parliamentary government, it should be. There are two great causes at work, which in their consequences run out into many details, but which in their fundamental nature may be briefly described. The first of these causes is our ignorance. No polity can get out of a nation more than there is in the nation. A free government is essentially a government by persuasion; and as are the people to be persuaded, and as are the persuaders, so will that government be. On many parts of our administration the effect of our extreme ignorance is at once plain. The foreign policy of England has for many years been, according to the judgement now in vogue, inconsequent, fruitless, casual; aiming at no distinct pre-imagined end, based on no steadily pre-conceived principle. I have not room to discuss with how much or how little abatement this decisive censure should be accepted. However, I entirely concede that our recent foreign policy has been open to very grave and serious blame. But would it not have been a miracle if the English people, directing their own policy, and being what they are, had directed a good policy? Are they not above all nations divided from the rest of the world, insular both in situation and in mind, both for good and for evil? Are they not out of the current of common European causes and affairs? Are they not a race contemptuous of others? Are they not a race with no special education or culture as to the modern world, and too often despising such culture? Who could expect such a people to comprehend the new and strange events of foreign places? So far from wondering that the English Parliament has been inefficient in foreign policy, I think it is wonderful, and another sign of the rude, vague imagination that is at the bottom of our people, that we have done so well as we have.

Again, the very conception of the English Constitution, as distinguished from a purely Parliamentary constitution is, that it contains 'dignified' parts— parts, that is, retained, not for intrinsic use, but from their imaginative attraction upon an uncultured and rude population. All such elements tend to diminish simple efficiency. They are like the additional and solely-ornamental wheels introduced into the clocks of the Middle Ages, which tell the then age of the moon or the supreme constellation;— which make little men or birds come out and in theatrically. All such ornamental work is a source of friction and error; it prevents the time being marked accurately; each new wheel is a new source of imperfection. So if authority is given to a person, not on account of his working fitness, but on account of his imaginative efficiency, he will commonly impair good administration. He may do something better than good work of detail, but will spoil good work of detail. The English aristocracy is often of this sort. It has an influence over the people of vast value still, and of infinite value formerly. But no man would select the cadets of an aristocratic house as desirable administrators. They have peculiar disadvantages in the acquisition of business knowledge, business training, and business habits, and they have no peculiar advantages.

Our middle class, too, is very unfit to give us the administrators we ought to have. I cannot now discuss whether all that is said against our education is well grounded; it is called by an excellent judge 'pretentious, insufficient, and unsound'. But I will say that it does not fit men to be men of business as it ought to fit them. Till lately the very simple attainments and habits necessary for a banker's clerk had a scarcity-value. The sort of education which fits a man for the higher posts of practical life is still very rare; there is not even a good agreement as to what it is. Our public officers cannot be as good as the corresponding officers of some foreign nations till our business education is as good as theirs.[1]

But strong as is our ignorance in deteriorating our administration, another cause is stronger still. There are but two foreign administrations probably better than ours, and both these have had something which we have not had. Theirs in both cases were arranged by a man of genius, after careful forethought, and upon a special design. Napoleon built upon a clear stage which the French Revolution bequeathed him. The originality once ascribed to his edifice was indeed untrue; Tocqueville and Lavergne have shown that he did but run up a conspicuous structure in imitation of a latent one before concealed by the medieval complexities of the old régime. But what we are concerned with now is, not Napoleon's originality, but his work. He undoubtedly settled the administration of France upon

---

[1] I am happy to state that this evil is much diminishing. The improvement of school education of the middle class in the last twenty-five years is marvellous.

an effective, consistent, and enduring system; the succeeding governments have but worked the mechanism they inherited from him. Frederick the Great did the same in the new monarchy of Prussia. Both the French system and the Prussian are new machines, made in civilized times to do their appropriate work.

The English offices have never, since they were made, been arranged with any reference to one another; or rather they were never made, but grew as each could. The sort of free-trade which prevailed in public institutions in the English Middle Ages is very curious. Our three courts of law—the Queen's Bench, the Common Pleas, and the Exchequer—for the sake of the fees extended an originally contracted sphere into the entire sphere of litigation. *Boni judicis est ampliare jurisdictionem*, went the old saying; or, in English, 'It is the mark of a good judge to augment the fees of his court', his own income, and the income of his subordinates. The central administration, the Treasury, never asked any account of the moneys the courts thus received; so long as it was not asked to pay anything, it was satisfied. Only last year one of the many remnants of this system cropped up, to the wonder of the public. A clerk in the Patent Office stole some fees, and naturally the men of the nineteenth century thought our principal finance minister, the Chancellor of the Exchequer, would be, as in France, responsible for it. But the English law was different somehow. The Patent Office was under the Lord Chancellor, and the Court of Chancery is one of the multitude of our institutions which owe their existence to fee competition,—and so it was the Lord Chancellor's business to look after the fees, which of course, as an occupied judge, he could not. A certain Act of Parliament did indeed require that the fees of the Patent Office should be paid into the 'Exchequer'; and, again, the 'Chancellor of the Exchequer' was thought to be responsible in the matter, but only by those who did not know. According to our system the Chancellor of the Exchequer is the enemy of the Exchequer; a whole series of enactments try to protect it from him. Until a few months ago there was a very lucrative sinecure called the 'Comptrollership of the Exchequer' designed to guard the Exchequer against its Chancellor; and the last holder, Lord Monteagle, used to say he was the pivot of the English Constitution. I have not room to explain what he meant, and it is not needful; what is to the purpose is that, by an inherited series of historical complexities, a defaulting clerk in an office of no litigation was not under natural authority, the finance minister, but under a far-away judge who had never heard of him.

The whole office of the Lord Chancellor is a heap of anomalies. He is a judge, and it is contrary to obvious principle that any part of administration should be entrusted to a judge; it is of very grave moment that the administration of justice should be kept clear of any sinister temptations. Yet the Lord Chancellor, our chief judge, sits in the Cabinet, and makes party speeches in the Lords. Lord Lyndhurst was a principal Tory politician, and yet he presided in the O'Connell case. Lord Westbury was in chronic wrangle with the bishops, but he gave judgement upon 'Essays and Reviews'. In truth, the Lord Chancellor became a Cabinet Minister, because, being near the person of the sovereign, he was high in court precedence, and not upon a political theory wrong or right.

A friend once told me that an intelligent Italian asked him about the principal English officers, and that he was very puzzled to explain their duties, and especially to explain the relation of their duties to their titles. I do not remember all the cases, but I can recollect that the Italian could not comprehend why the First 'Lord of the Treasury' had as a rule nothing to do with the Treasury, or why the 'Woods and Forests' looked after the sewerage of towns. This conversation was years before the cattle plague, but I should like to have heard the reasons why the Privy Council office had charge of that malady. Of course one could give an historical reason, but I mean an administrative reason—a reason which would show, not how it came to have the duty, but why in future it should keep it.

But the unsystematic and casual arrangement of our public offices is not more striking than their difference of arrangement for the one purpose they have in common. They all, being under the ultimate direction of a Parliamentary official, ought to have the best means of bringing the whole of the higher concerns of the office before that official. When the fresh mind rules, the fresh mind requires to be informed. And most business being rather alike, the machinery for bringing it before the extrinsic chief ought, for the most part, to be similar; at any rate, where it is different, it ought to be different upon reason; and where it is similar, similar upon reason. Yet there are almost no two offices which are exactly alike in the defined relations of the permanent official to the Parliamentary chief. Let us see. The *army and navy* are the most similar in nature, yet there is in the army a permanent outside office, called the Horse Guards, to which there is nothing else like. In the navy, there is a curious anomaly—a Board of Admiralty, also changing with every government, which is to instruct the First Lord in what he does not know.

The relations between the First Lord and the Board have not always been easily intelligible, and those between the War Office and the Horse Guards are in extreme confusion. Even now a Parliamentary paper relating to them has just been presented to the House of Commons, which says the fundamental and ruling document cannot be traced beyond the possession of Sir George Lewis, who was Secretary for War three years since; and the confused details are endless, as they must be in a chronic contention of offices. At the *Board of Trade* there is only the hypothesis of a Board; it has long ceased to exist. Even the President and Vice-President do not regularly meet for the transaction of affairs. The patent of the latter is only to transact business in the absence of the President, and if the two are not intimate, and the President chooses to act himself, the Vice-President sees no papers, and does nothing. At the *Treasury* the shadow of a Board exists, but its members have no power, and are the very officials whom Canning said existed to make a House, to keep a House, and to cheer the ministers. The *India Office* has a fixed 'Council'; but the *Colonial Office*, which rules over our other dependencies and colonies, has not, and never had, the vestige of a council. *Any* of these varied Constitutions may be right, but all of them can scarcely be right.

In truth the real constitution of a permanent office to be ruled by a permanent chief has been discussed only once in England: that case was a peculiar and anomalous one, and the decision then taken was dubious. A new India Office, when the East India Company was abolished, had to be made. The late Mr. James Wilson, a consummate judge of administrative affairs, then maintained that no council ought to be appointed *eo nomine*, but that the true Council of a Cabinet minister was a certain number of highly paid, much occupied, responsible secretaries, whom the minister could consult, either separately or together, as, and when, he chose. Such secretaries, Mr. Wilson maintained, must be able, for no minister will sacrifice his own convenience, and endanger his own reputation by appointing a fool to a post so near himself, and where he can do much harm. A member of a Board may easily be incompetent; if some other members and the chairman are able, the addition of one or two stupid men will not be felt; they will receive their salaries and do nothing. But a permanent under-secretary, charged with a real control over much important business, must be able, or his superior will be blamed, and there will be 'a scrape in Parliament'.

I cannot here discuss, nor am I competent to discuss, the best mode of composing public offices, and of adjusting them to a Parliamentary head. There ought to be on record skilled evidence on the subject before a person without any specific experience can to any purpose think about it. But I may observe that the plan which Mr. Wilson suggested is that followed in the most successful part of our administration, the 'Ways and Means' part. When the Chancellor of the Exchequer prepares a Budget, he requires from the responsible heads of the revenue department their estimates of the public revenue upon the preliminary hypothesis that no change is made, but that last year's taxes will continue; if, afterwards, he thinks of making an alteration, he requires a report on that too. If he has to renew Exchequer bills, or operate anyhow in the City, he takes the opinion, oral or written, of the ablest and most responsible person at the National Debt Office, and the ablest and most responsible at the Treasury. Mr. Gladstone, by far the greatest Chancellor of the Exchequer of this generation, one of the very greatest of any generation, has often gone out of his way to express his obligation to these responsible skilled advisers. The more a man knows himself, the more habituated he is to action in general, the more sure he is to take and to value responsible counsel emanating from ability and suggested by experience. That this principle brings good fruit is certain. We have, by unequivocal admission, the best budget in the world. Why should not the rest of our administration be as good if we did but apply the same method to it?

I leave this to stand as it was originally written since it does not profess to rest on my own knowledge, and only offers a suggestion on good authority. Recent experience seems, however, to show that in all great administrative departments there ought to be some one permanent responsible head through whom the changing Parliamentary chief always acts, from whom he learns everything, and to whom he communicates everything. The daily work of the Exchequer is a trifle compared with that of the Admiralty or the Home Office, and therefore a single principal head is not there so necessary. But the preponderance of evidence at present is that in all offices of very great work some one such head is essential.

NO. VII. ITS SUPPOSED CHECKS AND BALANCES

In a former essay I devoted an elaborate discussion to the comparison of the royal and unroyal form of Parliamentary Government. I showed that at the formation of a ministry, and during the continuance of a ministry, a really sagacious monarch might be of rare use. I ascertained that it was a mistake to fancy that at such times a constitutional monarch had no role and no duties. But I proved likewise that the temper, the disposition, and the faculties then needful to fit a constitutional monarch for usefulness were very rare, at least as rare as the faculties of a great absolute monarch, and that a common man in that place is apt to do at least as much harm as good—perhaps more harm. But in that essay I could not discuss fully the functions of a king at the conclusion of an administration, for then the most peculiar parts of the English government—the power to dissolve the House of Commons, and the power to create new peers—come into play, and until the nature of the House of Lords and the nature of the House of Commons had been explained, I had no premises for an argument as to the characteristic action of the king upon them. We have since considered the functions of the two houses, and also the effects of changes of ministry on our administrative system; we are now, therefore, in a position to discuss the functions of a king at the end of an administration.

I may seem over formal in this matter, but I am very formal on purpose. It appears to me that the functions of our executive in dissolving the Commons and augmenting the Peers are among the most important, and the least appreciated, parts of our whole government, and that hundreds of errors have been made in copying the English constitution from not comprehending them.

Hobbes told us long ago, and everybody now understands that there must be a supreme authority, a conclusive power, in every state on every point somewhere. The idea of government involves it—when that idea is properly understood. But there are two classes of governments. In one the supreme determining power is upon all points the same; in the other, that ultimate power is different upon different points—now resides in one part of the constitution, and now in another. The Americans thought that they were imitating the English in making their constitution upon the last principle—in having one ultimate authority for one sort of matter, and another for another sort. But in truth, the English constitution is the type of the opposite species; it has only one authority for all sorts of matters. To gain a living conception of the difference let us see what the Americans did.

First, they altogether retained what, in part, they could not help, the sovereignty of the separate states. A fundamental article of the Federal constitution says that the powers not 'delegated' to the central government are 'reserved to the states respectively'. And the whole recent history of the Union—perhaps all its history—has been more determined by that enactment than by any other single cause. The sovereignty of the principal matters of state has rested not with the highest government, but with the subordinate government. The Federal government could not touch slavery—the 'domestic institution' which divided the Union into two halves, unlike one another in morals, politics, and social condition, and at last set them

to fight. This determining political fact was not
in the jurisdiction of the highest government in
the country, where you might expect its highest
wisdom, nor in the central government, where you
might look for impartiality, but in local governments, where petty interests were sure to be considered, and where only inferior abilities were likely
to be employed. The capital fact was reserved for
the minor jurisdictions. Again there has been only
one matter comparable to slavery in the United
States, and that has been vitally affected by the
State governments also. Their ultra-democracy is
not a result of Federal legislation, but of State
legislation. The Federal constitution deputed one
of the main items of its structure to the subordinate
governments. One of its clauses provides that the
suffrages for the Federal House of Representatives
shall be, in each State, the same as for the most
numerous branch of the legislature of that State;
and as each State fixes the suffrage for its own legislatures, the States altogether fix the suffrage for the
Federal Lower Chamber. By another clause of the
Federal constitution the States fix the electoral
qualification for voting at a Presidential election.
The primary element in a free government—the
determination how many people shall have a share
in it—in America depends not on the government
but on certain subordinate local, and sometimes, as
in the South now, hostile bodies.

Doubtless the framers of the constitution had not
much choice in the matter. The wisest of them were
anxious to get as much power for the central
government, and to leave as little to the local
governments as they could. But a cry was got
up that this wisdom would create a tyranny and
impair freedom, and with that help, local jealousy
triumphed easily. All Federal government is, in

truth, a case in which what I have called the dignified elements of government do not coincide with the serviceable elements. At the beginning of every league the separate States are the old governments which attract and keep the love and loyalty of the people; the Federal government is a useful thing, but new and unattractive. It must concede much to the State governments, for it is indebted to them for motive power: they are the governments which the people voluntarily obey. When the State governments are not thus loved, they vanish as the little Italian and the little German potentates vanished; no federation is needed; a single central government rules all.

But the division of the sovereign authority in the American constitution is far more complex than this. The part of that authority left to the Federal government is itself divided and subdivided. The greatest instance is the most obvious. The Congress rules the law, but the President rules the administration. One means of unity the constitution does give; the President can veto laws he does not like. But when two-thirds of both houses are unanimous (as has lately happened), they can overrule the President and make the laws without him; so here there are three separate repositories of the legislative power in different cases; first, Congress and the President when they agree; next, the President when he effectually exerts his power; then the requisite two-thirds of Congress when they overrule the President. And the President need not be over-active in carrying out a law he does not approve of. He may indeed be impeached for gross neglect; but between criminal non-feasance and zealous activity there are infinite degrees. Mr. Johnson does not carry out the Freedman's Bureau Bill as Mr. Lincoln, who approved of it, would have carried it out. The American constitution has a special contrivance for varying the supreme legislative authority in different cases, and dividing the administrative authority from it in all cases.

But the administrative power itself is not left thus simple and undivided. One most important part of administration is international policy, and the supreme authority here is not in the President, still less in the House of Representatives, but in the Senate. The President can only make treaties, 'provided two-thirds of Senators present' concur. The sovereignty therefore for the greatest international questions is in a different part of the State altogether from any common administrative or legislative question. It is put in a place by itself.

Again, the Congress declares war, but they would find it very difficult, according to the recent construction of their laws, to compel the President to make a peace. The authors of the constitution doubtless intended that Congress should be able to control the American executive as our Parliament controls ours. They placed the granting of supplies in the House of Representatives exclusively. But they forgot to look after 'paper-money'; and now it has been held that the President has power to emit such money without consulting Congress at all. The first part of the late war was so carried on by Mr. Lincoln; he relied not on the grants of Congress, but on the prerogative of emission. It sounds a joke, but it is true nevertheless, that this power to issue greenbacks is decided to belong to the President as commander-in-chief of the army; it is part of what was called the 'war power'. In truth, money was wanted in the late war, and the administration got it in the readiest way; and the nation, glad not to be more taxed, wholly approved of it. But the fact remains that the President has now, by precedent and decision, a mighty power to continue a war without the consent of Congress, and perhaps against its wish. Against the united will of the American *people* a President would of course be impotent; such is the genius of the place and nation that he would never think of it. But when the nation was (as of late) divided into two parties, one cleaving to the President, the other to the Congress, the now unquestionable power of the President to issue paper-money may give him the power to continue the war though Parliament (as we should speak) may enjoin the war to cease.

And lastly, the whole region of the very highest questions is withdrawn from the ordinary authorities of the State, and reserved for special authorities. The 'constitution' cannot be altered by any authorities within the constitution, but only by authorities without it. Every alteration of it, however urgent or however trifling, must be sanctioned by a complicated proportion of States or legislatures. The consequence is that the most obvious evils cannot be quickly remedied; that the most absurd fictions must be framed to evade the plain sense of mischievous clauses; that a clumsy working and curious technicality mark the politics of a rough-and-ready people. The practical arguments and the legal disquisitions in America are often like those of trustees carrying out a misdrawn will—the sense of what they mean is good, but it can never be worked out fully or defended simply, so hampered is it by the old words of an old testament.

These instances (and others might be added) prove, as history proves too, what was the principal thought of the American constitution-makers. They shrank from placing sovereign power anywhere. They feared that it would generate tyranny; George III had been a tyrant to them, and come what might, they would not make a George III. Accredited theories said that the English Constitution divided the sovereign authority, and in imitation the Americans split up theirs.

The result is seen now. At the critical moment of their history there is no ready, deciding power. The South, after a great rebellion, lies at the feet of its conquerors; its conquerors have to settle what to do with it.[1] They must decide the conditions upon which the Secessionists shall again become fellow citizens, shall again vote, again be represented, again perhaps govern. The most difficult of problems is how to change late foes into free friends. The safety of their great public debt, and with that debt their future credit and their whole power in future wars, may depend on their not giving too much power to those who must see in the debt the cost of their own subjugation, and who must have an inclination towards the repudiation of it, now that their own debt,—the cost of their defence,— has been repudiated. A race, too, formerly enslaved, is now at the mercy of men who hate and despise it, and those who set it free are bound to give it a fair chance for new life. The slave was formerly protected by his chains; he was an article of value; but now he belongs to himself, no one but himself has an interest in his life; and he is at the mercy of the 'mean whites', whose labour he depreciates, and who regard him with a loathing hatred. The greatest moral duty ever set before a government, and the most fearful political problem ever set before a government, are now set before the American. But there is no decision, and no possibility of a decision. The President wants one course,

---

[1] This was written just after the close of the civil war, but I do not know that the great problem stated in it has as yet been adequately solved.

and has power to prevent any other; the Congress wants another course, and has power to prevent any other. The splitting of sovereignty into many parts amounts to there being no sovereign.

The Americans of 1787 thought they were copying the English Constitution, but they were contriving a contrast to it. Just as the American is the type of *composite* governments, in which the supreme power is divided between many bodies and functionaries, so the English is the type of *simple* constitutions, in which the ultimate power upon all questions is in the hands of the same persons.

The ultimate authority in the English Constitution is a newly-elected House of Commons. No matter whether the question upon which it decides be administrative or legislative; no matter whether it concerns high matters of the essential constitution or small matters of daily detail; no matter whether it be a question of making a war or continuing a war; no matter whether it be the imposing a tax or the issuing a paper currency; no matter whether it be a question relating to India, or Ireland, or London, —a new House of Commons can despotically and finally resolve.

The House of Commons may, as was explained, assent in minor matters to the revision of the House of Lords, and submit in matters about which it cares little to the suspensive veto of the House of Lords; but when sure of the popular assent, and when freshly elected, it is absolute,—it can rule as it likes and decide as it likes. And it can take the best security that it does not decide in vain. It can ensure that its decrees shall be executed, for it, and it alone, appoints the executive; it can inflict the most severe of all penalties on neglect, for it can remove the executive. It can choose, to effect its wishes, those who wish the same; and so its will is sure to be done. A stipulated majority of both Houses of the American Congress can overrule by stated enactment their executive; but the popular branch of our legislature can make and unmake ours.

The English constitution, in a word, is framed on the principle of choosing a single sovereign authority, and making it good: the American, upon the principle of having many sovereign authorities, and hoping that their multitude may atone for their inferiority. The Americans now extol their institutions, and so defraud themselves of their due praise. But if they had not a genius for politics; if they had not a moderation in action singularly curious where superficial speech is so violent; if they had not a regard for law, such as no great people have yet evinced, and infinitely surpassing ours,—the multiplicity of authorities in the American Constitution would long ago have brought it to a bad end. Sensible shareholders, I have heard a shrewd attorney say, can work *any* deed of settlement; and so the men of Massachusetts could, I believe, work *any* Constitution.[1] But political philosophy must analyse political history; it must distinguish what is due to the excellence of the people, and what to the excellence of the laws; it must carefully calculate the exact effect of each part of the constitution, though thus it may destroy many an idol of the multitude, and detect the secret of utility where but few imagined it to lie.

How important singleness and unity are in political action no one, I imagine, can doubt. We may distinguish and define its parts; but policy is a unit and a whole. It acts by laws—by adminis-

---

[1] Of course I am not speaking here of the South and South-East, as they now are. How any free government is to exist in societies where so many bad elements are so much perturbed, I cannot imagine.

trators; it requires now one, now the other; unless it can easily move both it will be impeded soon; unless it has an absolute command of both its work will be imperfect. The interlaced character of human affairs requires a single determining energy; a distinct force for each artificial compartment will make but a motley patchwork, if it live long enough to make anything. The excellence of the British Constitution is that it has achieved this unity; that in it the sovereign power is single, possible, and good.

The success is primarily due to the peculiar provision of the English Constitution, which places the choice of the executive in the 'people's house'; but it could not have been thoroughly achieved except for two parts, which I venture to call the 'safety-valve' of the constitution, and the 'regulator'.

The safety-valve is the peculiar provision of the constitution, of which I spoke at great length in my essay on the House of Lords. The head of the executive can overcome the resistance of the second chamber by choosing new members of that chamber; if he do not find a majority, he can make a majority. This is a safety-valve of the truest kind. It enables the popular will—the will of which the executive is the exponent, the will of which it is the appointee— to carry out within the constitution desires and conceptions which one branch of the constitution dislikes and resists. It lets forth a dangerous accumulation of inhibited power, which might sweep this constitution before it, as like accumulations have often swept away like constitutions.

The regulator, as I venture to call it, of our single sovereignty is the power of dissolving the otherwise sovereign chamber confided to the chief executive. The defects of the popular branch of a legislature as a sovereign have been expounded at length in a previous essay. Briefly, they may be summed up in three accusations.

First. Caprice is the commonest and most formidable vice of a choosing chamber. Wherever in our colonies Parliamentary government is unsuccessful, or is alleged to be unsuccessful, this is the vice which first impairs it. The assembly cannot be induced to maintain any administration; it shifts its selection now from one minister to another minister, and in consequence there is no government at all.

Secondly. The very remedy for such caprice entails another evil. The only mode by which a cohesive majority and a lasting administration can be upheld in a Parliamentary government, is party organization; but that organization itself tends to aggravate party violence and party animosity. It is, in substance, subjecting the whole nation to the rule of a section of the nation, selected because of its speciality. Parliamentary government is, in its essence, a sectarian government, and is possible only when sects are cohesive.

Thirdly. A parliament, like every other sort of sovereign, has peculiar feelings, peculiar prejudices, peculiar interests; and it may pursue these in opposition to the desires, and even in opposition to the well-being, of the nation. It has its selfishness as well as its caprice and its parties.

The mode in which the regulating wheel of our constitution produces its effect is plain. It does not impair the authority of Parliaments as a species, but it impairs the power of the individual Parliament. It enables a particular person outside parliament to say, 'You Members of Parliament are not doing your duty. You are gratifying caprice at the cost of the nation. You are indulging party spirit at the cost of the nation. You are helping yourself at the cost of the nation. I will see whether the nation approves what you are doing or not; I will appeal from Parliament No. 1 to Parliament No. 2.'

By far the best way to appreciate this peculiar provision of our constitution is to trace it in action, —to see, as we saw before of the other powers of English royalty, how far it is dependent on the existence of an hereditary king, and how far it can be exercised by a premier whom Parliament elects. When we examine the nature of the particular person required to exercise the power, a vivid idea of that power is itself brought home to us.

First. As to the caprice of parliament in the choice of a premier, who is the best person to check it? Clearly the premier himself. He is the person most interested in maintaining his administration, and therefore the most likely person to use efficiently and dexterously the power by which it is to be maintained. The intervention of an extrinsic king occasions a difficulty. A capricious Parliament may always hope that his caprice may coincide with theirs. In the days when George III assailed his governments, the premier was habitually deprived of his due authority. Intrigues were encouraged because it was always dubious whether the king-hated minister would be permitted to appeal from the intriguers, and always a chance that the conspiring monarch might appoint one of the conspirators to be premier in his room. The caprice of Parliament is better checked when the faculty of dissolution is entrusted to its appointee, than when it is set apart in an outlying and an alien authority.

But, on the contrary, the party zeal and the self-seeking of Parliament are best checked by an authority which has no connexion with Parliament or dependence upon it—supposing that such authority is morally and intellectually equal to the performance of the entrusted function. The Prime Minister obviously being the nominee of a party majority is likely to share its feeling, and is sure to be obliged to *say* that he shares it. The actual contact with affairs is indeed likely to purify him from many prejudices, to tame him of many fanaticisms, to beat out of him many errors. The present Conservative Government contains more than one member who regards his party as intellectually benighted; who either never speaks their peculiar dialect, or who speaks it condescendingly, and with an 'aside'; who respects their accumulated prejudices as the 'potential energies' on which he subsists, but who despises them while he lives by them. Years ago Mr. Disraeli called Sir Robert Peel's Ministry—the last Conservative Ministry that had real power—'an organized hypocrisy', so much did the ideas of its 'head' differ from the sensations of its 'tail'. Probably he now comprehends—if he did not always—that the air of Downing Street brings certain ideas to those who live there, and that the hard, compact prejudices of opposition are soon melted and mitigated in the great Gulf Stream of affairs. Lord Palmerston, too, was a typical example of a leader lulling rather than arousing, assuaging rather than acerbating, the minds of his followers. But though the composing effect of close difficulties will commonly make a premier cease to be an immoderate partisan, yet a partisan to some extent he must be, and a violent one he may be; and in that case he is not a good person to check the party. When the leading sect (so to speak) in Parliament is doing what the nation do not like, an instant appeal ought to be registered, and Parliament ought to be dissolved. But a zealot of a premier will not appeal; he will follow his formulae; he will believe he is doing good service when, perhaps, he is but pushing to unpopular consequences the narrow maxims of an inchoate theory. At such a minute a constitutional king—such as Leopold the First was, and as Prince Albert might have been—is invaluable; he can and will prevent Parliament from hurting the nation.

Again, too, on the selfishness of Parliament an extrinsic check is clearly more efficient than an intrinsic. A premier who is made by Parliament may share the bad impulses of those who chose him; or, at any rate, he may have made 'capital' out of them—he may have seemed to share them. The self-interests, the jobbing propensities of the assembly are sure indeed to be of very secondary interest to him. What he will care most for is the permanence, is the interest—whether corrupt or uncorrupt—of his own ministry. He will be disinclined to anything coarsely unpopular. In the order of nature, a new assembly must come before long, and he will be indisposed to shock the feelings of the electors from whom that assembly must emanate. But though the interest of the minister is inconsistent with appalling jobbery, he will be inclined to mitigated jobbery. He will temporize; he will try to give a seemly dress to unseemly matters; to do as much harm as will content the assembly, and yet not so much harm as will offend the nation. He will not shrink from becoming a *particeps criminis*; he will but endeavour to dilute the crime. The intervention of an extrinsic, impartial, and capable authority—if such can be found—will undoubtedly restrain the covetousness as well as the factiousness of a choosing assembly.

But can such a head be found? In one case I think it has been found. Our colonial governors are precisely *Dei ex machinâ*. They are always intelligent, for they have to live by a difficult trade; they are nearly sure to be impartial, for they come from the ends of the earth; they are sure not to participate in the selfish desires of any colonial class or body, for long before those desires can have attained fruition they will have passed to the other side of the world, be busy with other faces and other minds, be almost out of hearing what happens in a region they have half forgotten. A colonial governor is a super-parliamentary authority, animated by a wisdom which is probably in quantity considerable, and is different from that of the local Parliament, even if not above it. But even in this case the advantage of this extrinsic authority is purchased at a heavy price—a price which must not be made light of, because it is often worth paying. A colonial governor is a ruler who has no permanent interest in the colony he governs; who perhaps had to look for it in the map when he was sent thither; who takes years before he really understands its parties and its controversies; who, though without prejudice himself, is apt to be a slave to the prejudices of local people near him; who inevitably, and almost laudably, governs not in the interest of the colony, which he may mistake, but in his own interest, which he sees and is sure of. The first desire of a colonial governor is not to get into a 'scrape', not to do anything which may give trouble to his superiors—the Colonial Office—at home, which may cause an untimely and dubious recall, which may hurt his after career. He is sure to leave upon the colony the feeling that they have a ruler who only half knows them, and does not so much as half care for them. We hardly appreciate this common feeling in our colonies, because *we* appoint *their* sovereign; but we should understand it in an instant if, by a political metamorphosis, the choice were turned the other way—if *they* appointed *our* sovereign. We should then say at once, 'How

is it possible a man from New Zealand can understand England? how is it possible that a man longing
to get back to the antipodes can care for England?
how can we trust one who lives by the fluctuating
favour of a distant authority? how can we heartily
obey one who is but a foreigner with the accident
of an identical language?'

I dwell on the evils which impair the advantage
of colonial governorship because that is the most
favoured case of super-parliamentary royalty, and
because from looking at it we can bring freshly
home to our minds what the real difficulties of that
institution are. We are so familiar with it, that we
do not understand it. We are like people who have
known a man all their lives, and yet are quite surprised when he displays some obvious characteristic
which casual observers have detected at a glance.
I have known a man who did not know what colour
his sister's eyes were, though he had seen her every
day for twenty years; or rather, he did not know
because he had so seen her: so true is the philosophical maxim that we neglect the constant element
in our thoughts, though it is probably the most
important, and attend almost only to the varying
elements—the differentiating elements (as men now
speak)—though they are apt to be less potent. But
when we perceive by the roundabout example of
a colonial governor how difficult the task of a constitutional king is in the exercise of the function of
dissolving parliament, we at once see how unlikely
it is that an hereditary monarch will be possessed
of the requisite faculties.

An hereditary king is but an ordinary person,
upon an average, at best; he is nearly sure to be
badly educated for business; he is very little likely
to have a taste for business; he is solicited from
youth by every temptation to pleasure; he probably

passed the whole of his youth in the vicious situation of the heir-apparent, who can do nothing because he has no appointed work, and who will be considered almost to outstep his function if he undertake optional work. For the most part, a constitutional king is a *damaged* common man; not forced to business by necessity as a despot often is, but yet spoiled for business by most of the temptations which spoil a despot. History, too, seems to show that hereditary royal families gather from the repeated influence of their corrupting situation some dark taint in the blood, some transmitted and growing poison which hurts their judgements, darkens all their sorrow, and is a cloud on half their pleasure. It has been said, not truly, but with a possible approximation to truth, 'That in 1802 every hereditary monarch was insane'. Is it likely that this sort of monarchs will be able to catch the exact moment when, in opposition to the wishes of a triumphant ministry, they ought to dissolve Parliament? To do so with efficiency they must be able to perceive that the Parliament is wrong, and that the nation knows it is wrong. Now to know that Parliament is wrong, a man must be, if not a great statesman, yet a considerable statesman—a statesman of some sort. He must have great natural vigour, for no less will comprehend the hard principles of national policy. He must have incessant industry, for no less will keep him abreast with the involved detail to which those principles relate, and the miscellaneous occasions to which they must be applied. A man made common by nature, and made worse by life, is not likely to have either; he is nearly sure not to be *both* clever and industrious. And a monarch in the recesses of a palace, listening to a charmed flattery, unbiased by the miscellaneous world, who has always been hedged in by rank, is likely to be but a poor judge of public opinion. He may have an inborn tact for finding it out; but his life will never teach it him, and will probably enfeeble it in him.

But there is a still worse case, a case which the life of George III—which is a sort of museum of the defects of a constitutional king—suggests at once. The Parliament may be wiser than the people, and yet the king may be of the same mind with the people. During the last years of the American war, the Premier, Lord North, upon whom the first responsibility rested, was averse to continuing it, and knew it could not succeed. Parliament was much of the same mind; if Lord North had been able to come down to Parliament with a peace in his hand, Parliament would probably have rejoiced, and the nation under the guidance of Parliament, though saddened by its losses, probably would have been satisfied. The opinion of that day was more like the American opinion of the present day than like our present opinion. It was much slower in its formation than our opinion now, and obeyed much more easily sudden impulses from the central administration. If Lord North had been able to throw the undivided energy and the undistracted authority of the Executive Government into the excellent work of making a peace and carrying a peace, years of bloodshed might have been spared, and an entail of enmity cut off that has not yet run out. But there was a power behind the Prime Minister; George III was madly eager to continue the war, and the nation —not seeing how hopeless the strife was, not comprehending the lasting antipathy which their obstinacy was creating—ignorant, dull, and helpless— was ready to go on too. Even if Lord North had wished to make peace, and had persuaded Parliament accordingly, all his work would have been useless; a superior power could and would have appealed from a wise and pacific Parliament to a sullen and warlike nation. The check which our constitution finds for the special vices of our Parliament was misused to curb its wisdom.

The more we study the nature of Cabinet Government, the more we shall shrink from exposing at a vital instant its delicate machinery to a blow from a casual, incompetent, and perhaps semi-insane outsider. The preponderant probability is that on a great occasion the Premier and Parliament will really be wiser than the king. The Premier is sure to be able, and is sure to be most anxious to decide well; if he fail to decide, he loses his place, though through all blunders the king keeps his; the judgement of the man, naturally very discerning, is sharpened by a heavy penalty, from which the judgement of the man, by nature much less intelligent, is exempt. Parliament, too, is for the most part a sound, careful, and practical body of men. Principle shows that the power of dismissing a Government with which Parliament is satisfied, and of dissolving that Parliament upon an appeal to the people, is not a power which a common hereditary monarch will in the long run be able beneficially to exercise.

Accordingly this power has almost, if not quite, dropped out of the reality of our constitution. Nothing, perhaps, would more surprise the English people than if the Queen by a *coup d'état* and on a sudden destroyed a ministry firm in the allegiance and secure of a majority in Parliament. That power indisputably, in theory, belongs to her; but it has passed so far away from the minds of men, that it would terrify them, if she used it, like a volcanic eruption from Primrose Hill. The last analogy to it is not one to be coveted as a precedent. In 1835

William IV dismissed an administration which, though disorganized by the loss of its leader in the Commons, was an existing Government, had a premier in the Lords ready to go on, and a leader in the Commons willing to begin. The King fancied that public opinion was leaving the Whigs and going over to the Tories, and he thought he should accelerate the transition by ejecting the former. But the event showed that he misjudged. His *perception* indeed was right; the English people were wavering in their allegiance to the Whigs, who had no leader that touched the popular heart, none in whom Liberalism could personify itself and become a passion—who besides were a body long used to opposition, and therefore making blunders in office—who were borne to power by a popular impulse which they only half comprehended, and perhaps less than half shared. But the King's *policy* was wrong; he impeded the re-action instead of aiding it. He forced on a premature Tory Government, which was as unsuccessful as all wise people perceived that it must be. The popular distaste to the Whigs was as yet but incipient, inefficient; and the intervention of the Crown was advantageous to them, because it looked inconsistent with the liberties of the people. And in so far as William IV was right in detecting an incipient change of opinion, he did but detect an erroneous change. What was desirable was the prolongation of Liberal rule. The commencing dissatisfaction did but relate to the personal demerits of the Whig leaders, and other temporary adjuncts of free principles, and not to those principles intrinsically. So that the last precedent for a royal onslaught on a ministry ended thus:—in opposing the right principles, in aiding the wrong principles, in hurting the party it was meant to help. After such a warning, it is likely that our monarchs will pursue the policy which a long course of quiet precedent at present directs— they will leave a Ministry trusted by Parliament to the judgement of Parliament.

Indeed, the dangers arising from a party spirit in Parliament exceeding that of the nation, and of a selfishness in Parliament contradicting the true interest of the nation, are not great dangers in a country where the mind of the nation is steadily political, and where its control over its representatives is constant. A steady opposition to a formed public opinion is hardly possible in our House of Commons, so incessant is the national attention to politics, and so keen the fear in the mind of each member that he may lose his valued seat. These dangers belong to early and scattered communities, where there are no interesting political questions, where the distances are great, where no vigilant opinion passes judgement on parliamentary excesses, where few care to have seats in the chamber, and where many of those few are from their characters and their antecedents better not there than there. The one great vice of parliamentary government in an adult political nation, is the caprice of Parliament in the choice of a ministry. A nation can hardly control it here; and it is not good that, except within wide limits, it should control it. The Parliamentary judgement of the merits or demerits of an administration very generally depends on matters which the Parliament, being close at hand, distinctly sees, and which the distant nation does not see. But where personality enters, capriciousness begins. It is easy to imagine a House of Commons which is discontented with all statesmen, which is contented with none, which is made up of little parties, which votes in small knots, which will adhere steadily to no leader, which gives every leader a chance and a hope. Such Parliaments require the imminent check of possible dissolution; but that check is (as has been shown) better in the premier than in the sovereign; and by the late practice of our constitution, its use is yearly ebbing from the sovereign and yearly centring in the premier. The Queen can hardly now refuse a defeated minister the chance of a dissolution, any more than she can dissolve in the time of an undefeated one, and without his consent.

We shall find the case much the same with the safety-valve, as I have called it, of our constitution. A good, capable, hereditary monarch would exercise it better than a premier, but a premier could manage it well enough; and a monarch capable of doing better will be born only once in a century, whereas monarchs likely to do worse will be born every day.

There are two modes in which the power of our executive to create Peers—to nominate, that is, additional members of our upper and revising chamber—now acts: one constant, habitual, though not adequately noticed by the popular mind as it goes on; and the other possible and terrific, scarcely ever really exercised, but always by its reserved magic maintaining a great and a restraining influence. The Crown creates Peers, a few year by year, and thus modifies continually the characteristic feeling of the House of Lords. I have heard people say, who ought to know, that the *English* peerage (the only one upon which unhappily the power of new creation now acts) is now more Whig than Tory. Thirty years ago the majority was indisputably the other way. Owing to very curious circumstances English parties have not alternated in power as a good deal of speculation predicted they would, and a good deal of current language assumes they have.

The Whig Party were in office some seventy years (with very small breaks), from the death of Queen Anne to the coalition between Lord North and Mr. Fox; then the Tories (with only such breaks) were in power for nearly fifty years, till 1832; and since, the Whig Party has always, with very trifling intervals, been predominant. Consequently, each continuously-governing party has had the means of modifying the upper house to suit its views. The profuse Tory creations of half a century had made the House of Lords bigotedly Tory before the first Reform Act, but it is wonderfully mitigated now. The Irish Peers and the Scotch Peers—being nominated by an almost unaltered constituency, and representing the feelings of the majority of that constituency only (no minority having any voice)—present an unchangeable Tory element. But the element in which change is permitted has been changed. Whether the English Peerage be or be not predominantly now Tory, it is certainly not Tory after the fashion of the Toryism of 1832. The Whig additions have indeed sprung from a class commonly rather adjoining upon Toryism than much inclining to Radicalism. It is not from men of large wealth that a very great impetus to organic change should be expected. The additions to the Peers have matched nicely enough with the old Peers, and therefore they have effected more easily a greater and more permeating modification. The addition of a contrasting mass would have excited the old leaven, but the delicate infusion of ingredients similar in genus, though different in species, has modified the new compound without irritating the old original.

This ordinary and common use of the peer-creating power is always in the hands of the premier, and depends for its characteristic use on being there.

He, as the head of the predominant party, is the proper person to modify gradually the permanent chamber which, perhaps, was at starting hostile to him; and, at any rate, can be best harmonized with the public opinion he represents by the additions he makes. Hardly any contrived constitution possesses a machinery for modifying its secondary house so delicate, so flexible, and so constant. If the power of creating life peers had been added, the mitigating influence of the responsible executive upon the House of Lords would have been as good as such a thing can be.

The catastrophic creation of Peers for the purpose of swamping the upper house is utterly different. If an able and impartial exterior king is at hand, this power is best in that king. It is a power only to be used on great occasions, when the object is immense, and the party strife unmitigated. This is the conclusive, the swaying power of the moment, and of course, therefore, it had better be in the hands of a power both capable and impartial, than of a premier who must in some degree be a partisan. The value of a discreet, calm, wise monarch, if such should happen to be reigning at the acute crisis of a nation's destiny, is priceless. He may prevent years of tumult, save bloodshed and civil war, lay up a store of grateful fame to himself, prevent the accumulated intestine hatred of each party to its opposite. But the question comes back, Will there be such a monarch just then? What is the chance of having him just then? What will be the use of the monarch whom the accidents of inheritance, such as we know them to be, must upon an average bring us just then?

The answer to these questions is not satisfactory, if we take it from the little experience we have had in this rare matter. There have been but two cases at all approaching to a catastrophic creation of Peers —to a creation which would suddenly change the majority of the Lords—in English history. One was in Queen Anne's time. The majority of peers in Queen Anne's time were Whig, and by profuse and quick creations Harley's Ministry changed it to a Tory majority. So great was the popular effect, that in the next reign one of the most contested ministerial proposals was a proposal to take the power of indefinite peer-creation from the Crown, and to make the number of Lords fixed, as that of the Commons is fixed. But the sovereign had little to do with the matter. Queen Anne was one of the smallest people ever set in a great place. Swift bitterly and justly said 'she had not a store of amity by her for more than one friend at a time', and just then her affection was concentrated on a waiting-maid. Her waiting-maid told her to make peers, and she made them. But of large thought and comprehensive statesmanship she was as destitute as Mrs. Masham. She supported a bad ministry by the most extreme of measures, and she did it on caprice. The case of William IV is still more instructive. He was a very conscientious king, but at the same time an exceedingly weak king. His correspondence with Lord Grey on this subject fills more than half a large volume, or rather his secretary's correspondence, for he kept a very clever man to write what he thought, or at least what those about him thought. It is a strange instance of high-placed weakness and conscientious vacillation. After endless letters the king consents to make a *reasonable* number of peers if required to pass the second reading of the Reform Bill, but owing to desertion of the 'Waverers' from the Tories, the second reading is carried without it by nine, and then the king refuses to make peers, or at least

enough peers when a vital amendment is carried by
Lord Lyndhurst, which would have destroyed, and
was meant to destroy, the Bill. In consequence,
there was a tremendous crisis, and nearly a Revolution. A more striking example of well-meaning
imbecility is scarcely to be found in history. No one
who reads it carefully will doubt that the discretionary power of making peers would have been far
better in Lord Grey's hands than in the king's. It
was the uncertainty whether the king would exercise
it, and how far he would exercise it, that mainly
animated the opposition. In fact, you may place
power in weak hands at a revolution, but you
cannot keep it in weak hands. It runs out of them
into strong ones. An ordinary hereditary sovereign
—a William IV, or a George IV—is unfit to
exercise the peer-creating power when most wanted.
A half-insane king, like George III, would be
worse. He might use it by unaccountable impulse
when not required, and refuse to use it out of sullen
madness when required.

The existence of a fancied check on the premier
is in truth an evil, because it prevents the enforce-
ment of a real check. It would be easy to provide
by law that an extraordinary number of Peers—say
more than ten annually—should not be created
except on a vote of some large majority, suppose
three-fourths of the lower house. This would ensure
that the premier should not use the reserve force of
the constitution as if it were an ordinary force; that
he should not use it except when the whole nation
fixedly wished it; that it should be kept for a revolution, not expended on administration; and it would
ensure that he should then have it to use. Queen
Anne's case and William IV's case prove that
neither object is certainly attained by entrusting this
critical and extreme force to the chance idiosyn-

cracies and habitual mediocrity of an hereditary sovereign.

It may be asked why I argue at such length a question in appearance so removed from practice, and in one point of view so irrelevant to my subject. No one proposes to remove Queen Victoria; if any one is in a safe place on earth, she is in a safe place. In these very essays it has been shown that the mass of our people would obey no one else, that the reverence she excites is the potential energy—as science now speaks—out of which all minor forces are made, and from which lesser functions take their efficiency. But looking not to the present hour and this single country, but to the world at large and coming times, no question can be more practical.

What grows upon the world is a certain matter-of-factness. The test of each century, more than of the century before, is the test of results. New countries are arising all over the world where there are no fixed sources of reverence; which have to make them; which have to create institutions which must generate loyalty by conspicuous utility. This matter-of-factness is the growth even in Europe of the two greatest and newest intellectual agencies of our time. One of these is business. We see so much of the material fruits of commerce, that we forget its mental fruits. It begets a mind desirous of things, careless of ideas, not acquainted with the niceties of words. In all labour there should be profit, is its motto. It is not only true that we have 'left swords for ledgers', but war itself is made as much by the ledger as by the sword. The soldier—that is, the great soldier—of to-day is not a romantic animal, dashing at forlorn hopes, animated by frantic senti-ment, full of fancies as to a lady-love or a sovereign; but a quiet, grave man, busied in charts, exact in sums, master of the art of tactics, occupied in trivial detail; thinking, as the Duke of Wellington was said to do, *most* of the shoes of his soldiers; despising all manner of *éclat* and eloquence; perhaps, like Count Moltke, 'silent in seven languages'. We have reached a 'climate' of opinion where figures rule, where our very supporter of Divine right, as we deemed him, our Count Bismarck, amputates kings right and left, applies the test of results to each, and lets none live who are not to do something. There has in truth been a great change during the last five hundred years in the predominant occupations of the ruling part of mankind; formerly they passed their time either in exciting action or inanimate repose. A feudal baron had nothing between war and the chase—keenly animating things both—and what was called 'inglorious ease'. Modern life is scanty in excitements, but incessant in quiet action. Its perpetual commerce is creating a 'stock-taking' habit—the habit of asking each man, thing, and institution, 'Well, what have you done since I saw you last?'

Our physical science, which is becoming the dominant culture of thousands, and which is beginning to permeate our common literature to an extent which few watch enough, quite tends the same way. The two peculiarities are its homeliness and its inquisitiveness: its value for the most 'stupid' facts, as one used to call them, and its incessant wish for verification—to be sure, by tiresome seeing and hearing, that they are facts. The old excitement of thought has half died out, or rather it is diffused in quiet pleasure over a life, instead of being concentrated in intense and eager spasms. An old philosopher—a Descartes, suppose—fancied that out of primitive truths, which he could by ardent excogitation know, he might by pure deduction evolve the entire universe. Intense self-examination, and

intense reason would, he thought, make out everything. The soul, 'itself by itself', could tell all it
wanted if it would be true to its sublimer isolation.
The greatest enjoyment possible to man was that
which this philosophy promises its votaries—the
pleasure of being always right, and always reasoning
—without ever being bound to look at anything. But
our most ambitious schemes of philosophy now start
quite differently. Mr. Darwin begins:—

'When on board H.M.S. *Beagle*, as naturalist, I
was much struck with certain facts in the distribution of the organic beings inhabiting South America,
and in the geological relations of the present to the
past inhabitants of that continent. These facts, as
will be seen in the latter chapters of this volume,
seemed to throw some light on the origin of species
—that mystery of mysteries, as it has been called
by one of our greatest philosophers. On my return
home, it occurred to me, in 1837, that something
might perhaps be made out on this question by
patiently accumulating and reflecting on all sorts of
facts which could possibly have any bearing on it.
After five years' work I allowed myself to speculate
on the subject, and drew up some short notes; these
I enlarged in 1844 into a sketch of the conclusions
which then seemed to me probable: from that
period to the present day I have steadily pursued
the same object. I hope that I may be excused for
entering on these personal details, as I give them
to show that I have not been hasty in coming to
a decision.'

If he hopes finally to solve his great problem, it
is by careful experiments in pigeon fancying, and
other sorts of artificial variety making. His hero is
not a self-enclosed, excited philosopher, but 'that
most skilful breeder, Sir John Sebright, who used
to say, with respect to pigeons, that he would

produce any given feathers in three years, but it would take him six years to obtain a head and a beak'. I am not saying that the new thought is better than the old; it is no business of mine to say anything about that; I only wish to bring home to the mind, as nothing but instances can bring it home, how matter-of-fact, how petty, as it would at first sight look, even our most ambitious science has become.

In the new communities which our emigrating habit now constantly creates, this prosaic turn of mind is intensified. In the American mind and in the colonial mind there is, as contrasted with the old English mind, a *literalness*, a tendency to say, 'The facts are so-and-so, whatever may be thought or fancied about them'. We used before the civil war to say that the Americans worshipped the almighty dollar; we now know that they can scatter money almost recklessly when they will. But what we meant was half right—they worship visible value; obvious, undeniable, intrusive result. And in Australia and New Zealand the same turn comes uppermost. It grows from the struggle with the wilderness. Physical difficulty is the enemy of early communities, and an incessant conflict with it for generations leaves a mark of reality on the mind— a painful mark almost to us, used to impalpable fears and the half-fanciful dangers of an old and complicated society. The 'new Englands' of all latitudes are bare-minded (if I may so say) as compared with the 'old'.

When, therefore, the new communities of the colonized world have to choose a government, they must choose one in which *all* the institutions are of an obvious evident utility. We catch the Americans smiling at our Queen with her secret mystery, and our Prince of Wales with his happy inaction. It is impossible, in fact, to convince their prosaic minds that constitutional royalty is a rational government, that it is suited to a new age and an unbroken country, that those who start afresh can start with it. The princelings who run about the world with excellent intentions, but an entire ignorance of business, are to them a locomotive advertisement that this sort of government is European in its limitations and medieval in its origin; that though it has yet a great part to play in the old states, it has no place or part in new states. The *réalisme impitoyable* which good critics find in a most characteristic part of the literature of the nineteenth century, is to be found also in its politics. An ostentatious utility must characterize its creations.

The deepest interest, therefore, attaches to the problem of this essay. If hereditary royalty had been essential to parliamentary government, we might well have despaired of that government. But accurate investigation shows that this royalty is not essential; that, upon an average, it is not even in a high degree useful; that though a king with high courage and fine discretion,—a king with a genius for the place,—is always useful, and at rare moments priceless, yet that a common king, a king such as birth brings, is of no use at difficult crises, while in the common course of things his aid is neither likely nor required—he will do nothing, and he need do nothing. But we happily find that a new country need not fall back into the fatal division of powers incidental to a presidential government; it may, if other conditions serve, obtain the ready, well-placed, identical sort of sovereignty which belongs to the English constitution, under the unroyal form of Parliamentary government.

NO. VIII. THE PREREQUISITES OF CABINET GOVERNMENT, AND THE PECULIAR FORM WHICH THEY HAVE ASSUMED IN ENGLAND

CABINET GOVERNMENT is rare because its prerequisites are many. It requires the co-existence of several national characteristics which are not often found together in the world, and which should be perceived more distinctly than they often are. It is fancied that the possession of a certain intelligence, and a few simple virtues, are the sole requisites. These mental and moral qualities are necessary, but much else is necessary also. A cabinet government is the government of a committee elected by the legislature, and there are therefore a double set of conditions to it: first, those which are essential to all elective governments as such; and second, those which are requisite to this particular elective government. There are prerequisites for the genus, and additional ones for the species.

The first prerequisite of elective government is the *mutual confidence* of the electors. We are so accustomed to submit to be ruled by elected ministers, that we are apt to fancy all mankind would readily be so too. Knowledge and civilization have at least made this progress, that we instinctively, without argument, almost without consciousness, allow a certain number of specified persons to choose our rulers for us. It seems to us the simplest thing in the world. But it is one of the gravest things.

The peculiar marks of semi-barbarous people are diffused distrust and indiscriminate suspicion. People, in all but the most favoured times and places, are rooted to the places where they were born, think the thoughts of those places, can endure no other thoughts. The next parish even is suspected. Its inhabitants have different usages, almost imperceptibly different, but yet different; they speak a varying accent; they use a few peculiar words; tradition says that their faith is dubious. And if the next parish is a little suspected, the next county is much more suspected. Here is a definite beginning of new maxims, new thoughts, new ways: the immemorial boundary-mark begins in feeling a strange world. And if the next county is dubious, a remote county is untrustworthy. 'Vagrants come from thence' men know, and they know nothing else. The inhabitants of the north speak a dialect different from the dialect of the south: they have other laws, another aristocracy, another life. In ages when distant territories are blanks in the mind, when neighbourhood is a sentiment, when locality is a passion, concerted co-operation between remote regions is impossible even on trivial matters. Neither would rely enough upon the good faith, good sense, and good judgement of the other. Neither could enough calculate on the other.

And if such co-operation is not to be expected in trivial matters, it is not to be thought of in the most vital matter of government—the choice of the executive ruler. To fancy that Northumberland in the thirteenth century would have consented to ally itself with Somersetshire for the choice of a chief magistrate is absurd; it would scarcely have allied itself to choose a hangman. Even now, if it were palpably explained, neither district would like it. But no one says at a county election, 'The object of this present meeting is to choose our delegate to what the Americans call the "Electoral College", to the assembly which names our first magistrate—

our substitute for their president. Representatives from this county will meet representatives from other counties, from cities and boroughs, and proceed to choose our rulers.' Such bald exposition would have been impossible in old times; it would be considered queer, eccentric, if it were used now. Happily, the process of election is so indirect and hidden, and the introduction of that process was so gradual and latent, that we scarcely perceive the immense political trust we repose in each other. The best mercantile credit seems to those who give it, natural, simple, obvious; they do not argue about it, or think about it. The best political credit is analogous; we trust our countrymen without remembering that we trust them.

A second and very rare condition of an elective government is a *calm* national mind—a tone of mind sufficiently stable to bear the necessary excitement of conspicuous revolutions. No barbarous, no semi-civilized nation has ever possessed this. The mass of uneducated men could not now in England be told 'go to, choose your rulers'; they would go wild; their imaginations would fancy unreal dangers, and the attempt at election would issue in some forcible usurpation. The incalculable advantage of august institutions in a free state is, that they prevent this collapse. The excitement of choosing our rulers is prevented by the apparent existence of an unchosen ruler. The poorer and more ignorant classes—those who would most feel excitement, who would most be misled by excitement—really believe that the Queen governs. You could not explain to them the recondite difference between 'reigning' and 'governing'; the words necessary to express it do not exist in their dialect; the ideas necessary to comprehend it do not exist in their minds. The separation of principal power from principal station is a refinement which they could not even conceive. They fancy they are governed by an hereditary queen, a queen by the grace of God, when they are really governed by a cabinet and a parliament—men like themselves, chosen by themselves. The conspicuous dignity awakens the sentiment of reverence, and men, often very undignified, seize the occasion to govern by means of it.

Lastly. The third condition of all elective government is what I may call *rationality*, by which I mean a power involving intelligence, but yet distinct from it. A whole people electing its rulers must be able to form a distinct conception of distant objects. Mostly, the 'divinity' that surrounds a king altogether prevents anything like a steady conception of him. You fancy that the object of your loyalty is as much elevated above you by intrinsic nature as he is by extrinsic position; you deify him in sentiment, as once men deified him in doctrine. This illusion has been and still is of incalculable benefit to the human race. It prevents, indeed, men from choosing their rulers; you cannot invest with that loyal illusion a man who was yesterday what you are, who to-morrow may be so again, whom you chose to be what he is. But though this superstition prevents the election of rulers, it renders possible the existence of unelected rulers. Untaught people fancy that their king, crowned with the holy crown, anointed with the oil of Rheims, descended of the House of Plantagenet, is a different sort of being from any one not descended of the Royal House—not crowned—not anointed. They believe that there is *one* man whom by mystic right they should obey; and therefore they do obey him. It is only in later times, when the world is wider, its experience larger, and its thought colder, that the plain rule of a palpably chosen ruler is even possible.

These conditions narrowly restrict elective government. But the prerequisites of a cabinet government are rarer still; it demands not only the conditions I have mentioned, but the possibility likewise of a good legislature—a legislature competent to elect a sufficient administration.

Now a competent legislature is very rare. *Any* permanent legislature at all, any constantly acting mechanism for enacting and repealing laws, is, though it seems to us so natural, quite contrary to the inveterate conceptions of mankind. The great majority of nations conceive of their law, either as something Divinely given, and therefore unalterable, or as a fundamental habit, inherited from the past to be transmitted to the future. The English Parliament, of which the prominent functions are now legislative, was not all so once. It was rather a *preservative* body. The custom of the realm—the aboriginal transmitted law—the law which was in the breast of the judges, could not be altered without the consent of parliament, and therefore everybody felt sure it would not be altered except in grave, peculiar, and anomalous cases. The *valued* use of parliament was not half so much to alter the law, as to prevent the laws being altered. And such too was its real use. In early societies it matters much more that the law should be fixed than that it should be good. Any law which the people of ignorant times enact is sure to involve many misconceptions, and to cause many evils. Perfection in legislation is not to be looked for, and is not, indeed, much wanted in a rude, painful, confined life. But such an age covets fixity. That men should enjoy the fruits of their labour, that the law of property should be known, that the law of marriage should be known, that the whole course of life should be kept in a calculable track, is the *summum bonum* of early ages,

I

the first desire of semi-civilized mankind. In that age men do not want to have their laws adapted, but to have their laws steady. The passions are so powerful, force so eager, the social bond so weak, that the august spectacle of an all but unalterable law is necessary to preserve society. In the early stages of human society all change is thought an evil. And *most* change is an evil. The conditions of life are so simple and so unvarying that any decent sort of rules suffice, so long as men know what they are. Custom is the first check on tyranny; that fixed routine of social life at which modern innovations chafe, and by which modern improvement is impeded, is the primitive check on base power. The perception of political expediency has then hardly begun; the sense of abstract justice is weak and vague; and a rigid adherence to the fixed mould of transmitted usage is essential to an unmarred, unspoiled, unbroken life.

In such an age a legislature continuously sitting, always making laws, always repealing laws, would have been both an anomaly and a nuisance. But in the present state of the civilized part of the world such difficulties are obsolete. There is a diffused desire in civilized communities for an *adjusting* legislation; for a legislation which should adapt the inherited laws to the new wants of a world which now changes every day. It has ceased to be necessary to maintain bad laws, because it is necessary to have some laws. Civilization is robust enough to bear the incision of legal improvements. But taking history at large, the rarity of cabinets is mostly due to the greater rarity of continuous legislatures.

Other conditions, however, limit even at the present day the area of a cabinet government. It must be possible to have not only a legislature, but to have a competent legislature—a legislature willing to elect and willing to maintain an efficient executive. And this is no easy matter. It is indeed true that we need not trouble ourselves to look for that elaborate and complicated organization which partially exists in the House of Commons, and which is more fully and freely expanded in plans for improving the House of Commons. We are not now concerned with perfection or excellence; we seek only for simple fitness and bare competency.

The conditions of fitness are two. First, you must get a good legislature; and next, you must keep it good. And these are by no means so nearly connected as might be thought at first sight. To keep a legislature efficient, it must have a sufficient supply of substantial business. If you employ the best set of men to do nearly nothing, they will quarrel with each other about that nothing. Where great questions end, little parties begin. And a very happy community, with few new laws to make, few old bad laws to repeal, and but simple foreign relations to adjust, has great difficulty in employing a legislature. There is nothing for it to enact, and nothing for it to settle. Accordingly, there is great danger that the legislature, being debarred from all other kind of business, may take to quarrelling about its elective business; that controversies as to ministries may occupy all its time, and yet that time be perniciously employed; that a constant succession of feeble administrations, unable to govern and unfit to govern, may be substituted for the proper result of cabinet government,—a sufficient body of men long enough in power to evince their sufficiency. The exact amount of non-elective business necessary for a parliament which is to elect the executive cannot, of course, be formally stated. There are no numbers and no statistics in the theory of constitutions. All we can say is, that a parliament with little business, which is to be as efficient as a parliament with much business, must be in all other respects much better. An indifferent parliament may be much improved by the steadying effect of grave affairs; but a parliament which has no such affairs must be intrinsically excellent, or it will fail utterly.

But the difficulty of keeping a good legislature, is evidently secondary to the difficulty of first getting it. There are two kinds of nations which can elect a good parliament. The first is a nation in which the mass of the people are intelligent, and in which they are comfortable. Where there is no honest poverty, where education is diffused, and political intelligence is common, it is easy for the mass of the people to elect a fair legislature. The ideal is roughly realized in the North American colonies of England, and in the whole free States of the Union. In these countries there is no such thing as honest poverty; physical comfort, such as the poor cannot imagine here, is there easily attainable by healthy industry. Education is diffused much, and is fast spreading. Ignorant emigrants from the Old World often prize the intellectual advantages of which they are themselves destitute, and are annoyed at their inferiority in a place where rudimentary culture is so common. The greatest difficulty of such new communities is commonly geographical. The population is mostly scattered; and where population is sparse, discussion is difficult. But in a country very large, as we reckon in Europe, a people really intelligent, really educated, really comfortable, would soon form a good opinion. No one can doubt that the New England States, if they were a separate community, would have an education, a political capacity, and an intelligence such as the numerical majority of no people, equally numerous, has ever possessed. In a state of this sort, where all the community is fit to choose a sufficient legislature, it is possible, it is almost easy, to create that legislature. If the New England States possessed a cabinet government as a separate nation, they would be as renowned in the world for political sagacity as they now are for diffused happiness.

The structure of these communities is indeed based on the principle of equality, and it is impossible that *any* such community can wholly satisfy the severe requirements of a political theorist. In every old community its primitive and guiding assumption is at war with truth. By its theory all people are entitled to the same political power, and they can only be so entitled on the ground that in politics they are equally wise. But at the outset of an agricultural colony this postulate is as near the truth as politics want. There are in such communities no large properties, no great capitals, no refined classes —every one is comfortable and homely, and no one is at all more. Equality is not artificially established in a new colony; it establishes itself. There is a story that among the first settlers in Western Australia, some, who were rich, took out labourers at their own expense, and also carriages to ride in. But soon they had to try if they could live in the carriages. Before the masters' houses were built, the labourers had gone off—they were building houses and cultivating land for themselves, and the masters were left to sit in their carriages. Whether this exact thing happened I do not know, but this sort of thing has happened a thousand times. There have been a whole series of attempts to transplant to the colonies a graduated English society. But they have always failed at the first step. The rude classes at the bottom felt that they were equal to or better than the delicate classes at the top; they shifted for themselves, and left the 'gentlefolks' to shift for themselves; the base of the elaborate pyramid spread abroad, and the apex tumbled in and perished. In the early ages of an agricultural colony, whether you have political democracy or not, social democracy you must have, for nature makes it, and not you. But in time, wealth grows and inequality begins. A and his children are industrious, and prosper; B and his children are idle, and fail. If manufactures on a considerable scale are established—and most young communities strive even by protection to establish them—the tendency to inequality is intensified. The capitalist becomes a unit with much, and his labourers a crowd with little. After generations of education, too, there arise varieties of culture—there will be an upper thousand, or ten thousand, of highly cultivated people in the midst of a great nation of moderately educated people. In theory it is desirable that this highest class of wealth and leisure should have an influence far out of proportion to its mere number: a perfect constitution would find for it a delicate expedient to make its fine thought tell upon the surrounding cruder thought. But as the world goes, when the whole of the population is as instructed and as intelligent as in the case I am supposing, we need not care much about this. Great communities have scarcely ever—never save for transient moments—been ruled by their highest thought. And if we can get them ruled by a decent capable thought, we may be well enough contented with our work. We have done more than could be expected, though not all which could be desired. At any rate, an isocratic polity—a polity where every one votes, and where every one votes alike—is, in a community of sound education and diffused intelligence, a conceivable case of cabinet government. It satisfies the essential condition; there is a people able to elect a parliament able to choose.

But suppose the mass of the people are not able to elect—and this is the case with the numerical majority of all but the rarest nations—how is a cabinet government to be then possible? It is only possible in what I may venture to call *deferential* nations. It has been thought strange, but there *are* nations in which the numerous unwiser part wishes to be ruled by the less numerous wiser part. The numerical majority—whether by custom or by choice, is immaterial is ready, is eager to delegate its power of choosing its ruler to a certain select minority. It abdicates in favour of its *élite*, and consents to obey whoever that *élite* may confide in. It acknowledges as its secondary electors—as the choosers of its government—an educated minority, at once competent and unresisted; it has a kind of loyalty to some superior persons who are fit to choose a good government, and whom no other class opposes. A nation in such a happy state as this has obvious advantages for constructing a cabinet government. It has the best people to elect a legislature, and therefore it may fairly be expected to choose a good legislature—a legislature competent to select a good administration.

England is the type of deferential countries, and the manner in which it is so, and has become so, is extremely curious. The middle classes—the ordinary majority of educated men—are in the present day the despotic power in England. 'Public opinion', nowadays, 'is the opinion of the bald-headed man at the back of the omnibus.' It is *not* the opinion of the aristocratical classes as such; or of the most educated or refined classes as such; it is simply the opinion of the ordinary mass of educated, but still commonplace, mankind. If you look at the mass of the constituencies, you will see that they are not very interesting people; and perhaps if you look behind the scenes and see the people who manipulate and work the constituencies, you will find that these are yet more uninteresting. The English constitution in its palpable form is this—the mass of the people yield obedience to a select few; and when you see this select few, you perceive that though not of the lowest class, nor of an unrespectable class, they are yet of a heavy sensible class—the last people in the world to whom, if they were drawn up in a row, an immense nation would ever give an exclusive preference.

In fact, the mass of the English people yield a deference rather to something else than to their rulers. They defer to what we may call the *theatrical show* of society. A certain state passes before them; a certain pomp of great men; a certain spectacle of beautiful women; a wonderful scene of wealth and enjoyment is displayed, and they are coerced by it. Their imagination is bowed down; they feel they are not equal to the life which is revealed to them. Courts and aristocracies have the great quality which rules the multitude, though philosophers can see nothing in it—visibility. Courtiers can do what others cannot. A common man may as well try to rival the actors on the stage in their acting, as the aristocracy in *their* acting. The higher world, as it looks from without, is a stage on which the actors walk their parts much better than the spectators can. This play is played in every district. Every rustic feels that his house is not like my lord's house; his life like my lord's life; his wife like my lady. The climax of the play is the Queen: nobody supposes that their house is like the court; their life like her life; her orders like their orders. There is in England a certain charmed spectacle which imposes on the many, and guides their fancies as it will. As a rustic on coming to London finds himself in the presence of a great show and vast exhibition of inconceivable mechanical things, so by the structure of our society he finds himself face to face with a great exhibition of political things which he could not have imagined, which he could not make—to which he feels in himself scarcely anything analogous.

Philosophers may deride this superstition, but its results are inestimable. By the spectacle of this august society, countless ignorant men and women are induced to obey the few nominal electors—the £10 borough renters, and the £50 county renters—who have nothing imposing about them, nothing which would attract the eye or fascinate the fancy. What impresses men is not mind, but the result of mind. And the greatest of these results is this wonderful spectacle of society, which is ever new, and yet ever the same; in which accidents pass and essence remains; in which one generation dies and another succeeds, as if they were birds in a cage, or animals in a menagerie; of which it seems almost more than a metaphor to treat the parts as limbs of a perpetual living thing, so silently do they seem to change, so wonderfully and so perfectly does the conspicuous life of the new year take the place of the conspicuous life of last year. The apparent rulers of the English nation are like the most imposing personages of a splendid procession: it is by them the mob are influenced; it is they whom the spectators cheer. The real rulers are secreted in second-rate carriages; no one cares for them or asks about them, but they are obeyed implicitly and unconsciously by reason of the splendour of those who eclipsed and preceded them.

It is quite true that this imaginative sentiment is supported by a sensation of political satisfaction. It cannot be said that the mass of the English people are well off. There are whole classes who have not a conception of what the higher orders call comfort; who have not the prerequisites of moral existence; who cannot lead the life that becomes a man. But the most miserable of these classes do not impute their misery to politics. If a political agitator were to lecture to the peasants of Dorsetshire, and try to excite political dissatisfaction, it is much more likely that he would be pelted than that he would succeed. Of parliament these miserable creatures know scarcely anything; of the cabinet they never heard. But they would say that, 'for all they have heard, the Queen is very good'; and rebelling against the structure of society is to their minds rebelling against the Queen, who rules that society, in whom all its most impressive part—the part that they know—culminates. The mass of the English people are politically contented as well as politically deferential.

A deferential community, even though its lowest classes are not intelligent, is far more suited to a cabinet government than any kind of democratic country, because it is more suited to political excellence. The highest classes can rule in it; and the highest classes must, as such, have more political ability than the lower classes. A life of labour, an incomplete education, a monotonous occupation, a career in which the hands are used much and the judgement is used little, cannot create as much flexible thought, as much applicable intelligence, as a life of leisure, a long culture, a varied experience, an existence by which the judgement is incessantly exercised, and by which it may be incessantly improved. A country of respectful poor, though far less happy than where there are no poor to be respectful, is nevertheless far more fitted for the best government. You can use the best classes of the respectful country; you can only use the worst where every man thinks he is as good as every other.

It is evident that no difficulty can be greater than that of founding a deferential nation. Respect is traditional; it is given not to what is proved to be good, but to what is known to be old. Certain classes in certain nations retain by common acceptance a marked political preference, because they have always possessed it, and because they inherit a sort of pomp which seems to make them worthy of it. But in a new colony, in a community where merit *may* be equal, and where there *cannot* be traditional marks of merit and fitness, it is obvious that a political deference can be yielded to higher culture, only upon proof, first of its existence, and next of its political value. But it is nearly impossible to give such a proof so as to satisfy persons of less culture. In a future and better age of the world it may be effected; but in this age the requisite premises scarcely exist; if the discussion be effectually open, if the debate be fairly begun, it is hardly possible to obtain a rational, an argumentative acquiescence in the rule of the cultivated few. As yet the few rule by their hold, not over the reason of the multitude, but over their imaginations and their habits; over their fancies as to distant things they do not know at all, over their customs as to near things which they know very well.

A deferential community in which the bulk of the people are ignorant, is therefore in a state of what is called in mechanics unstable equilibrium. If the equilibrium is once disturbed there is no tendency to return to it, but rather to depart from it. A cone balanced on its point is in unstable equilibrium, for if you push it ever so little it will depart farther and farther from its position and fall to the earth. So in communities where the masses are ignorant but respectful, if you once permit the ignorant class to begin to rule you may bid farewell to deference for ever. Their demagogues will inculcate, their newspapers will recount, that the rule of the existing dynasty (the people) is better than the rule of the fallen dynasty (the aristocracy). A people very rarely hears two sides of a subject in which it is much interested; the popular organs take up the side which is acceptable, and none but the popular organs in fact reach the people. A people *never* hears censure of itself. No one will tell it that the educated minority whom it dethroned governed better or more wisely than it governs. A democracy will never, save after an awful catastrophe, return what has once been conceded to it, for to do so would be to admit an inferiority in itself, of which, except by some almost unbearable misfortune, it could never be convinced.

NO. IX. ITS HISTORY, AND THE EFFECTS OF THAT HISTORY.— CONCLUSION

A VOLUME might seem wanted to say anything worth saying [1] on the History of the English Constitution, and a great and new volume might still be written on it, if a competent writer took it in hand. The subject has never been treated by any one combining the lights of the newest research and the lights of the most matured philosophy. Since the masterly book of Hallam was written, both political thought and historical knowledge have gained much, and we might have a treatise applying our strengthened calculus to our augmented facts. I do not pretend that I could write such a book, but there are a few salient particulars which may be fitly brought together, both because of their past interest and of their present importance.

There is a certain common polity, or germ of polity, which we find in all the rude nations that have attained civilization. These nations seem to begin in what I may call a consultative and tentative

---

[1] Since the first edition of this book was published several valuable works have appeared, which, on many points, throw much light on our early constitutional history, especially Mr. Stubbs's *Select Charters and other Illustrations of English Constitutional History, from the Earliest Times to the Reign of Edward the First*, Mr. Freeman's lecture on *The Growth of the English Constitution*, and the chapter on the Anglo-Saxon Constitution in his *History of the Norman Conquest*: but we have not yet a great and authoritative work on the whole subject such as I wished for when I wrote the passage in the text, and as it is most desirable that we should have.

absolutism. The king of early days, in vigorous nations, was not absolute as despots now are; there was then no standing army to repress rebellion, no organized *espionage* to spy out discontent, no skilled bureaucracy to smooth the ruts of obedient life. The early king was indeed consecrated by a religious sanction; he was essentially a man apart, a man above others, divinely anointed, or even God-begotten. But in nations capable of freedom this religious domination was never despotic. There was indeed no legal limit: the very words could not be translated into the dialect of those times. The notion of law as we have it—of a rule imposed by human authority, capable of being altered by that authority when it likes, and in fact, so altered habitually—could not be conveyed to early nations, who regarded law half as an invincible prescription, and half as a Divine revelation. Law 'came out of the king's mouth'; he gave it as Solomon gave judgement,—embedded in the particular case, and upon the authority of Heaven as well as his own. A Divine limit to the Divine revealer was impossible, and there was no other source of law. But though there was no legal limit, there was a practical limit to subjection in (what may be called) the pagan part of human nature,—the inseparable obstinacy of freemen. They *never* would do exactly what they were told.

To early royalty, as Homer describes it in Greece and as we may well imagine it elsewhere, there were always two adjuncts: one, the 'old men', the men of weight, the council, the βουλή, of which the king asked advice, from the debates in which the king tried to learn what he could do and what he ought to do. Besides this there was the ἀγορά, the purely listening assembly, as some have called it, but the *tentative* assembly, as I think it might best be called.

The king came down to his assembled people in form to announce his will, but in reality, speaking in very modern words, to 'feel his way'. He was sacred, no doubt; and popular, very likely; still he was half like a popular premier speaking to a high-spirited chamber; there were limits to his authority and power—limits which he would discover by trying whether eager cheers received his mandate, or only hollow murmurs and a thinking silence.

This polity is a good one for its era and its place, but there is a fatal defect in it. The reverential associations upon which the government is built are transmitted according to one law, and the capacity needful to work the government is transmitted according to another law. The popular homage clings to the line of god-descended kings; it is transmitted by inheritance. But very soon that line comes to a child or an idiot, or one by some defect or other incapable. Then we find everywhere the truth of the old saying, that liberty thrives under weak princes; then the listening assembly begins not only to murmur, but to speak; then the grave council begins not so much to suggest as to inculcate, not so much to advise as to enjoin.

Mr. Grote has told at length how out of these appendages of the original kingdom the free States of Greece derived their origin, and how they gradually grew—the oligarchical States expanding the council, and the democratical expanding the assembly. The history has as many varieties in detail as there were Greek cities, but the essense is the same everywhere. The political characteristic of the early Greeks, and of the early Romans, too, is that out of the *tentacula* of a monarchy they developed the organs of a republic.

English history has been in substance the same, though its form is different, and its growth far slower and longer. The scale was larger, and the elements more various. A Greek city soon got rid of its kings, for the political sacredness of the monarch would not bear the daily inspection and constant criticism of an eager and talking multitude. Everywhere in Greece the slave population—the most ignorant, and therefore the most unsusceptible of intellectual influences—was struck out of the account. But England began as a kingdom of considerable size, inhabited by distinct races, none of them fit for prosaic criticism, and all subject to the superstition of royalty. In early England, too, royalty was much more than a superstition. A very strong executive was needed to keep down a divided, an armed, and an impatient country; and therefore the problem of political development was delicate. A formed free government in a homogeneous nation may have a strong executive; but during the transition state, while the republic is in course of development and the monarchy in course of decay, the executive is of necessity weak. The polity is divided, and its action feeble and failing. The different orders of English people have progressed, too, at different rates. The change in the state of the higher classes since the Middle Ages is enormous, and it is all improvement; but the lower have varied little, and many argue that in some important respects they have got worse, even if in others they have got better. The development of the English Constitution was of necessity slow, because a quick one would have destroyed the executive and killed the State, and because the most numerous classes, who changed very little, were not prepared for any catastrophic change in our institutions.

I cannot presume to speak of the time before the conquest, and the exact nature even of all Anglo-Norman institutions is perhaps dubious: at least, in nearly all cases there have been many controversies. Political zeal, whether Whig or Tory, has wanted to find a model in the past; and the whole state of society being confused, the precedents altering with the caprice of men and the chance of events, ingenious advocacy has had a happy field. But all that I need speak of is quite plain. There was a great 'council' of the realm, to which the king summoned the most considerable persons in England, the persons he most wanted to advise him, and the persons whose tempers he was most anxious to ascertain. Exactly who came to it at first is obscure and unimportant. I need not distinguish between the 'magnum concilium in Parliament' and the 'magnum concilium out of Parliament'. Gradually the principal assemblies summoned by the English sovereign took the precise and definite form of Lords and Commons, as in their outside we now see them. But their real nature was very different. The Parliament of to-day is a ruling body; the medieval Parliament was, if I may so say, an *expressive* body. Its function was to tell the executive—the king—what the nation wished he should do; to some extent, to guide him by new wisdom, and, to a very great extent, to guide him by new facts. These facts were their own feelings, which were the feelings of the people, because they were part and parcel of the people. From thence the king learned, or had the means to learn, what the nation would endure, and what it would not endure; —what he might do, and what he might not do. If he much mistook this, there was a rebellion.

There are, as is well known, three great periods in the English Constitution. The first of these is the ante-Tudor period. The English Parliament then seemed to be gaining extraordinary strength and power. The title to the crown was uncertain; some monarchs were imbecile. Many ambitious men wanted to 'take the people into partnership'. Certain precedents of that time were cited with grave authority centuries after, when the time of freedom had really arrived. But the causes of this rapid growth soon produced an even more sudden decline. Confusion fostered it, and confusion destroyed it. The structure of society then was feudal; the towns were only an adjunct and a make-weight. The principal popular force was an aristo-cratic force, acting with the co-operation of the gentry and yeomanry, and resting on the loyal fealty of sworn retainers. The head of this force, on whom its efficiency depended, was the high nobility. But the high nobility killed itself out. The great barons who adhered to the 'Red Rose' or the 'White Rose', or who fluctuated from one to the other, became poorer, fewer, and less potent every year. When the great struggle ended at Bosworth, a large part of the greatest combatants were gone. The restless, aspiring, rich barons, who made the civil war, were broken by it. Henry VII attained a kingdom in which there was a Parliament to advise, but scarcely a Parliament to control.

The consultative government of the ante-Tudor period had little resemblance to some of the modern governments which French philosophers call by that name. The French Empire, I believe, calls itself so. But its assemblies are symmetrical 'shams'. They are elected by a universal suffrage, by the ballot, and in districts once marked out with an eye to equality, and still retaining a look of equality. But our English parliaments were *un*symmetrical realities. They were elected anyhow; the sheriff had a considerable licence in sending writs to boroughs, that is, he could in part pick its constituencies; and in each borough there was a rush and scramble for the franchise, so that the strongest local party got it, whether few or many. But in England at that time there was a great and distinct desire to know the opinion of the nation, because there was a real and close necessity. The nation was wanted to do something—to assist the sovereign in some war, to pay some old debt, to contribute its force and aid in the critical conjuncture of the time. It would not have suited the ante-Tudor kings to have had a fictitious assembly; they would have lost their sole *feeler*, their only instrument for discovering national opinion. Nor could they have manufactured such an assembly if they wished. The instrument in that behalf is the centralized executive, and there was then no *préfet* by whom the opinion of a rural locality could be made to order, and adjusted to suit the wishes of the capital. Looking at the mode of election, a theorist would say that these parliaments were but 'chance' collections of influential Englishmen. There would be many corrections and limitations to add to that statement if it were wanted to make it accurate, but the statement itself hits exactly the principal excellence of those parliaments. If not 'chance' collections of Englishmen, they were 'undesigned' collections; no administrations made them or could make them. They were bona fide counsellors, whose opinion might be wise or unwise, but was anyhow of paramount importance, because their co-operation was wanted for what was in hand.

Legislation as a positive power was very secondary in those old parliaments. I believe no statute at all, as far as we know, was passed in the reign of Richard I, and all the ante-Tudor acts together would look meagre enough to a modern Parliamentary agent who had to live by them. But the negative action of parliament upon the law was essential to its whole idea, and ran through every part of its use. That the king could not change what was then the almost sacred *datum* of the common law, without seeing whether his nation liked it or not, was an essential part of the 'tentative' system. The king had to feel his way in this exceptional, singular act, as those ages deemed original legislation, as well as in lesser acts. The legislation was his at last; he enacted after consulting his Lords and Commons; his was the sacred mouth which gave holy firmness to the enactment; but he only dared alter the rule regulating the common life of his people after consulting those people; he would not have been obeyed if he had not, by a rude age which did not fear civil war as we fear it now. Many most important enactments of that period (and the fact is most characteristic) are declaratory acts. They do not profess to enjoin by inherent authority what the law shall in future be, but to state and mark what the law is; they are declarations of immemorial custom, not precepts of new duties. Even in the 'Great Charter' the notion of new enactments was secondary, it was a great mixture of old and new; it was a sort of compact defining what was doubtful in floating custom, and was re-enacted over and over again, as boundaries are perambulated once a year, and rights and claims tending to desuetude thereby made patent and cleared of new obstructions. In truth, such great 'charters' were rather treaties between different orders and factions, confirming ancient rights, or what claimed to be such, than laws in our ordinary sense. They were the 'deeds of arrangement' of medieval society affirmed and re-affirmed from time to time, and the principal controversy was, of course, between the king and nation—the king trying to see how far the nation would let him go, and the nation murmuring and recalcitrating, and seeing how many acts of administration they could prevent, and how many of its claims they could resist.

Sir James Mackintosh says that Magna Charta 'converted the right of taxation into the shield of liberty', but it did nothing of the sort. The liberty existed before, and the right to be taxed was an efflorescence and instance of it, not a substratum or a cause. The necessity of consulting the great council of the realm before taxation, the principle that the declaration of grievances by the Parliament was to precede the grant of supplies to the sovereign, are but conspicuous instances of the primitive doctrine of the ante-Tudor period, that the king must consult the great council of the realm before he did anything, since he always wanted help. The right of self-taxation was justly inserted in the 'great treaty'; but it would have been a dead letter, save for the armed force and aristocratic organization which compelled the king to make a treaty; it was a result, not a basis—an example, not a cause.

The civil wars of many years killed out the old councils (if I might so say): that is, destroyed three parts of the greater nobility who were its most potent members, tired the small nobility and the gentry, and overthrew the aristocratic organization on which all previous effectual resistance to the sovereign had been based.

The second period of the British Constitution begins with the accession of the House of Tudor, and goes down to 1688; it is in substance the history of the growth, development, and gradually acquired supremacy of the new great council. I have no room and no occasion to narrate again the familiar history of the many steps by which the slavish Parliament of Henry VIII grew into the murmuring Parliament of Queen Elizabeth, the mutinous Parliament of James I, and the rebellious Parliament of Charles I. The steps were many, but the energy was one—the growth of the English middle-class, using that word in its most inclusive sense, and its animation under the influence of Protestantism. No one, I think, can doubt that Lord Macaulay is right in saying that political causes would not alone have then provoked such a resistance to the sovereign, unless propelled by religious theory. Of course the English people went to and fro from Catholicism to Protestantism, and from Protestantism to Catholicism (not to mention that the Protestantism was of several shades and sects), just as the first Tudor kings and queens wished. But that was in the pre-Puritan era. The mass of Englishmen were in an undecided state, just as Hooper tells us his father was—'Not believing in Protestantism, yet not disinclined to it'. Gradually, however, a strong Evangelic spirit (as we should now speak) and a still stronger anti-Papal spirit entered into the middle sort of Englishmen, and added to that force, fibre, and substance which they have never wanted, an ideal warmth and fervour which they have almost always wanted. Hence the saying that Cromwell founded the English Constitution. Of course, in seeming, Cromwell's work died with him; his dynasty was rejected, his republic cast aside; but the spirit which culminated in him never sank again, never ceased to be a potent, though often a latent and volcanic, force in the country. Charles II said that he would never go again on his travels for anything or anybody; and he well knew that though the men whom he met at Worcester might be dead, still the spirit which warmed them was alive and young in others.

But the Cromwellian republic and the strict Puritan creed were utterly hateful to most Englishmen. They were, if I may venture on saying so, like the 'Rouge' element in France and elsewhere—the sole revolutionary force in the entire State, and were hated as such. That force could do little of itself; indeed, its bare appearance tended to frighten and alienate the moderate and dull as well as the refined and reasoning classes. Alone it was impotent against the solid clay of the English apathetic nature. But give this fiery element a body of decent-looking earth; give it an excuse for breaking out on an occasion, when the decent, the cultivated, and aristocratic classes could join with it, and they could conquer by means of it, and it could be disguised in their covering.

Such an excuse was found in 1688. James II, by incredible and pertinacious folly, irritated not only the classes which had fought *against* his father, but also those who had fought *for* his father. He offended the Anglican classes as well as the Puritan classes; all the Whig nobles and half the Tory nobles, as well as the dissenting bourgeois. The rule of Parliament was established by the concurrence of the usual supporters of royalty with the usual opponents of it. But the result was long weak. Our revolution has been called the minimum of a revolution, because in law, at least, it only changed the dynasty, but exactly on that account it was the greatest shock to the common multitude, who see the dynasty but see nothing else. The support of the main aristocracy held together the bulk of the deferential classes, but it held them together imperfectly, uneasily, and unwillingly. Huge masses of crude prejudice swayed hither and thither for many years. If an able Stuart had with credible sincerity professed Protestantism, probably he might have overturned the House of Hanover. So strong was inbred reverence for hereditary right, that until the accession of George III the English government was always subject to the unceasing attrition of a competitive sovereign.

This was the result of what I insist on tediously, but what is most necessary to insist on, for it is a cardinal particular in the whole topic. Many of the English people—the higher and more educated portion—had come to comprehend the nature of constitutional government, but the mass did not comprehend it. They looked to the sovereign as the government, and to the sovereign only. These were carried forward by the magic of the aristocracy, and principally by the influence of the great Whig families with their adjuncts. Without that aid reason or liberty would never have held them.

Though the rule of Parliament was definitely established in 1688, yet the mode of exercising that rule has since changed. At first Parliament did not know how to exercise it; the organization of parties and the appointment of cabinets by parties grew up in the manner Macaulay has described so well. Up to the latest period the sovereign was supposed, to a most mischievous extent, to interfere in the choice of the persons to be Ministers. When George III finally became insane, in 1810, every one believed that George IV, on assuming power as Prince Regent, would turn out Mr. Perceval's government and empower Lord Grey or Lord Grenville, the Whig leaders, to form another. The Tory ministry was carrying on a successful war—a war of existence —against Napoleon; but in the people's mind, the necessity at such an occasion for an unchanged government did not outweigh the fancy that George IV was a Whig. And a Whig, it is true, he had been before the French Revolution, when he lived an indescribable life in St. James's Street with Mr. Fox. But Lord Grey and Lord Grenville were rigid men, and had no immoral sort of influence. What liberalism of opinion the Regent ever had was frightened out of him (as of other people) by the Reign of Terror. He felt, according to the saying of another monarch, that 'he lived by being a royalist'. It soon appeared that he was most anxious to retain Mr. Perceval, and that he was most eager to quarrel with the Whig Lords. As we all know, he kept the ministry whom he found in office; but that it should have been thought he could then change them, is a significant example how exceedingly modern our notions of the despotic action of Parliament in fact are.

By the steps of the struggle thus rudely mentioned (and by others which I have no room to speak of, nor need I), the change which in the Greek cities was effected both in appearance and in fact, has been effected in England, though in reality only, and not in outside. Here, too, the appendages of a monarchy have been converted into the essence of a republic; only here, because of a more numerous heterogeneous political population, it is needful to keep the ancient show while we secretly interpolate the new reality.

This long and curious history has left its trace on almost every part of our present political condition; its effects lie at the root of many of our most important controversies; and because these effects are not rightly perceived, many of these controversies are misconceived.

One of the most curious peculiarities of the English people is its dislike of the executive government. We are not in this respect 'un vrai peuple moderne', like the Americans. The Americans conceive of their executive as one of their appointed agents; when it intervenes in common life, it does so, they consider, in virtue of the mandate of the sovereign people, and there is no invasion or dereliction of freedom in that people interfering with itself. The French, the Swiss, and all nations who breathe the full atmosphere of the nineteenth century, think so too. The material necessities of this age require a strong executive; a nation destitute of it cannot be clean, or healthy, or vigorous like a nation possessing it. By definition, a nation calling itself free should have no jealousy of the executive, for freedom means that the nation, the political part of the nation, wields the executive. But our history has reversed the English feeling: our freedom is the result of centuries of resistance, more or less legal, or more or less illegal, more or less audacious, or more or less timid, to the executive Government. We have, accordingly, inherited the traditions of conflict, and preserve them in the fullness of victory. We look on State action, not as our own action, but as alien action; as an imposed tyranny from without, not as the consummated result of our own organized wishes. I remember at the Census of 1851 hearing a very sensible old lady say that 'the liberties of England were at an end'; if Government might be thus inquisitorial, if they might ask who slept in your house, or what your age was, what, she argued, might they not ask and what might they not do?

The natural impulse of the English people is to resist authority. The introduction of effectual policemen was not liked; I know people, old people I admit, who to this day consider them an infringement of freedom, and an imitation of the *gendarmes* of France. If the original policemen had been started with the present helmets, the result might have been dubious; there might have been a cry of military tyranny, and the inbred insubordination of the English people might have prevailed over the very modern love of *perfect* peace and order. The old notion that the Government is an extrinsic agency still rules our imaginations, though it is no longer true, and though in calm and intellectual moments we well know it is not. Nor is it merely our history which produces this effect; we might get over that; but the results of that history co-operate. Our double Government so acts: when we want to point the antipathy to the executive, we refer to the jealousy of the Crown, so deeply embedded in the very substance of constitutional authority; so many people are loth to admit the Queen, in spite of law and fact, to be the people's appointee and agent, that it is a good rhetorical emphasis to speak of her prerogative as something *non*-popular, and therefore to be distrusted. By the very nature of our Government our executive cannot be liked and trusted as the Swiss or the American is liked and trusted.

Out of the same history and the same results proceed our tolerance of those 'local authorities' which so puzzle many foreigners. In the struggle with the Crown these local centres served as props and fulcrums. In the early parliaments it was the local bodies who sent members to parliament, the counties, and the boroughs; and in that way, and because of *their* free life, the parliament was free too. If active, real bodies had not sent the representatives, they would have been powerless. This is very much the reason why our old rights of suffrage were so various; the Government let whatever people happened to be the strongest in each town choose the members. They applied to the electing bodies the test of 'natural selection'; whatever set of people were locally strong enough to elect, did so. Afterwards, in the civil war, many of the corporations, like that of London, were important bases of resistance. The case of London is typical and remarkable. Probably, if there is any body more than another which an educated Englishman nowadays regards with little favour, it is the Corporation of London. He connects it with hereditary abuses perfectly preserved, with large revenues imperfectly accounted for, with a system which stops the principal city government at an old archway, with the perpetuation of a hundred detestable parishes, with the maintenance of a horde of luxurious and useless bodies. For the want of all which makes Paris nice and splendid we justly reproach the Corporation of London; for the existence of much of what makes London mean and squalid we justly reproach it too. Yet the Corporation of London was for centuries a bulwark of English liberty. The conscious support of the near and organized capital gave the Long Parliament a vigour and vitality which they could have found nowhere else. Their leading patriots took refuge in the City, and the nearest approach to an English 'sitting in permanence' is the committee at Guildhall, where all members 'that came were to have voices'. Down to George III's time the City was a useful centre of popular judgement. Here, as elsewhere, we have built into our polity pieces of the scaffolding by which it was erected.

De Tocqueville indeed used to maintain that in this matter the English were not merely historically excusable, but likewise politically judicious. He founded what may be called the *culte* of corporations. And it was natural that in France, where there is scarcely any power of self-organization in the people, where the *préfet* must be asked upon every subject, and take the initiative in every movement, a solitary thinker should be repelled from the exaggerations of which he knew the evil, to the contrary exaggeration of which he did not. But in a country like England, where business is in the air, where we can organize a vigilance committee on every abuse and an executive committee for every remedy —as a matter of political instruction, which was De Tocqueville's point—we need not care how much power is delegated to outlying bodies, and how much is kept for the central body. We have had the instruction municipalities could give us: we have been through all that. Now we are quite grown up, and can put away childish things.

The same causes account for the innumerable anomalies of our polity. I own that I do not entirely sympathize with the horror of these anomalies which haunts some of our best critics. It is natural that those who by special and admirable culture have come to look at all things upon the artistic side, should start back from these queer peculiarities. But it is natural also that persons used to analyse political institutions should look at these anomalies with a little tenderness and a little interest. They *may* have something to teach us. Political philosophy is still more imperfect; it has been framed from observations taken upon regular specimens of politics and States; as to these its teaching is most valuable. But we must ever remember that its *data* are imperfect. The lessons are good where its primitive assumptions hold, but may be false where those assumptions fail. A philosophical politician regards a political anomaly as a scientific physician regards a rare disease—it is to him an 'interesting case'. There may still be instruction here, though we have worked out the lessons of common cases. I cannot, therefore, join in the full cry against anomalies; in my judgement it may quickly overrun the scent, and so miss what we should be glad to find.

Subject to this saving remark, however, I not only

admit, but maintain, that our constitution is full of curious oddities, which are impeding and mischievous, and ought to be struck out. Our law very often reminds one of those outskirts of cities where you cannot for a long time tell how the streets come to wind about in so capricious and serpent-like a manner. At last it strikes you that they grew up, house by house, on the devious tracks of the old green lanes; and if you follow on to the existing fields, you may often find the change half complete. Just so the lines of our constitution were framed in old eras of sparse population, few wants, and simple habits; and we adhere in seeming to their shape, though civilization has come with its dangers, complications, and enjoyments. These anomalies, in a hundred instances, mark the old boundaries of a constitutional struggle. The casual line was traced according to the strength of deceased combatants; succeeding generations fought elsewhere; and the hesitating line of a half-drawn battle was left to stand for a perpetual limit.

I do not count as an anomaly the existence of our double government, with all its infinite accidents, though half the superficial peculiarities that are often complained of arise out of it. The co-existence of a Queen's seeming prerogative and a Downing Street's real government is just suited to such a country as this, in such an age as ours.[1]

[1] So well is our real Government concealed, that if you tell a cabman to drive to 'Downing Street' he most likely will never have heard of it, and will not in the least know where to take you. It is only a 'disguised republic' which is suited to such a being as the Englishman in such a century as the nineteenth.

INTRODUCTION

TO

THE SECOND EDITION

THERE is a great difficulty in the way of a writer who
attempts to sketch a living Constitution—a Constitution that is in actual work and power. The difficulty is that the object is in constant change. An
historical writer does not feel this difficulty: he deals
only with the past; he can say definitely, the Constitution worked in such and such a manner in the
year at which he begins, and in a manner in such and
such respects different in the year at which he ends;
he begins with a definite point of time and ends with
one also. But a contemporary writer who tries to
paint what is before him is puzzled and perplexed;
what he sees is changing daily. He must paint it as
it stood at some one time, or else he will be putting
side by side in his representations things which
never were contemporaneous in reality. The difficulty is the greater because a writer who deals with
a living government naturally compares it with the
most important other living governments, and these
are changing too; what he illustrates are altered in
one way, and his sources of illustration are altered
probably in a different way. This difficulty has been
constantly in my way in preparing a second edition
of this book. It describes the English Constitution
as it stood in the years 1865 and 1866. Roughly
speaking, it describes its working as it was in the
time of Lord Palmerston; and since that time there
have been many changes, some of spirit and some
of detail. In so short a period there have rarely been

more changes. If I had given a sketch of the Palmerston time as a sketch of the present time, it would have been in many points untrue; and if I had tried to change the sketch of seven years since into a sketch of the present time, I should probably have blurred the picture and have given something equally unlike both.

The best plan in such a case is, I think, to keep the original sketch in all essentials as it was at first written, and to describe shortly such changes either in the Constitution itself, or in the Constitutions compared with it, as seem material. There are in this book various expressions which allude to persons who were living and to events which were happening when it first appeared; and I have carefully preserved these. They will serve to warn the reader what time he is reading about, and to prevent his mistaking the date at which the likeness was attempted to be taken. I proceed to speak of the changes which have taken place either in the Constitution itself or in the competing institutions which illustrate it.

It is too soon as yet to attempt to estimate the effect of the Reform Act of 1867. The people enfranchised under it do not yet know their own power: a single election, so far from teaching us how they will use that power, has not been even enough to explain to them that they have such power. The Reform Act of 1832 did not for many years disclose its real consequences; a writer in 1836, whether he approved or disapproved of them, whether he thought too little of or whether he exaggerated them, would have been sure to be mistaken in them. A new Constitution does not produce its full effect as long as all its subjects were reared under an old Constitution, as long as its statesmen were trained by that old Constitution. It is not really tested till it comes to be worked by statesmen and among a people neither of whom are guided by a different experience.

In one respect we are indeed particularly likely to be mistaken as to the effect of the last Reform Bill. Undeniably there has lately been a great change in our politics. It is commonly said that 'there is not a brick of the Palmerston House standing'. The change since 1865 is a change not in one point but in a thousand points; it is a change not of particular details but of pervading spirit. We are now quarrelling as to the minor details of an Education Act; in Lord Palmerston's time no such Act could have passed. In Lord Palmerston's time Sir George Grey said that the disestablishment of the Irish Church would be an 'act of Revolution': it has now been disestablished by great majorities, with Sir George Grey himself assenting. A new world has arisen which is not as the old world; and we naturally ascribe the change to the Reform Act. But this is a complete mistake. If there had been no Reform Act at all there would, nevertheless, have been a great change in English politics. There has been a change of the sort which, above all, generates other changes—a change of generation. Generally one generation in politics succeeds another almost silently; at every moment men of all ages between thirty and seventy have considerable influence; each year removes many old men, makes all others older, brings in many new. The transition is so gradual that we hardly perceive it. The board of directors of the political company has a few slight changes every year, and therefore the shareholders are conscious of no abrupt change. But sometimes there *is* an abrupt change. It occasionally happens that several ruling directors who are about the same age live on for many years, manage the company all through those years, and then go off the scene almost together. In that case the affairs of the company are apt to alter much, for good or for evil: sometimes it becomes more successful, sometimes it is ruined, but it hardly ever stays as it was. Something like this happened before 1865. All through the period between 1832 and 1865, the pre-32 statesmen—if I may so call them—Lord Derby, Lord Russell, Lord Palmerston retained great power. Lord Palmerston to the last retained great prohibitive power. Though in some ways always young, he had not a particle of sympathy with the younger generation; he brought forward no young men; he obstructed all that young men wished. In consequence, at his death a new generation all at once started into life: the pre-32 all at once died out. Most of the new politicians were men who might well have been Lord Palmerston's grandchildren. He came into Parliament in 1806, they entered it after 1856. Such an enormous change in the age of the workers necessarily caused a great change in the kind of work attempted and the way in which it was done. What we call the 'spirit' of politics is more surely changed by a change of generation in the men than by any other change whatever. Even if there had been no Reform Act, this single cause would have effected grave alterations.

The mere settlement of the Reform question made a great change too. If it could have been settled by any other change, or even without any change, the instant effect of the settlement would still have been immense. New questions would have appeared at once. A political country is like an American forest: you have only to cut down the old trees, and immediately new trees come up to replace them; the seeds were waiting in the ground, and they began to grow as soon as the withdrawal of the old ones brought in light and air. These new questions of themselves would have made a new atmosphere, new parties, new debates.

Of course I am not arguing that so important an innovation as the Reform Act of 1867 will not have very great effects. It must, in all likelihood, have many great ones. I am only saying that as yet we do not know what those effects are; that the great evident change since 1865 is certainly not strictly due to it; probably is not even in a principal measure due to it; that we have still to conjecture what it will cause and what it will not cause.

The principal question arises most naturally from a main doctrine of these essays. I have said that cabinet government is possible in England because England was a deferential country. I meant that the nominal constituency was not the real constituency; that the mass of the 'ten-pound' householders did not really form their own opinions, and did not exact of their representatives an obedience to those opinions; that they were in fact guided in their judgement by the better educated classes; that they preferred representatives from those classes, and gave those representatives much licence. If a hundred small shopkeepers had by miracle been added to any of the '32 Parliaments, they would have felt outcasts there. Nothing could be more unlike those Parliaments than the average mass of the constituency from which it was chosen.

I do not of course mean that the ten-pound householders were great admirers of intellect or good judges of refinement. We all know that, for the most part, they were not so at all: very few Englishmen are. They were not influenced by ideas, but by facts; not by things palpable, but by things impalpable. Not to put too fine a point upon it, they were influenced by rank and wealth. No doubt the better sort of them believed that those who were superior to them in these indisputable respects were superior also in the more intangible qualities of sense and knowledge. But the mass of the old electors did not analyse very much: they liked to have one of their 'betters' to represent them; if he was rich, they respected him much; and if he was a lord, they liked him the better. The issue put before these electors was which of two rich people will you choose? And each of those rich people was put forward by great parties whose notions were the notions of the rich—whose plans were their plans. The electors only selected one or two wealthy men to carry out the schemes of one or two wealthy associations.

So fully was this so, that the class to whom the great body of the ten-pound householders belonged—the lower middle class—was above all classes the one most hardly treated in the imposition of the taxes. A small shopkeeper or a clerk who just, and only just, was rich enough to pay income tax, was perhaps the only severely-taxed man in the country. He paid the rates, the tea, sugar, tobacco, malt, and spirit taxes, as well as the income tax, but his means were exceedingly small. Curiously enough the class which in theory was omnipotent was the only class financially ill-treated. Throughout the history of our former Parliaments the constituency could no more have originated the policy which those Parliaments selected than they could have made the solar system.

As I have endeavoured to show in this volume, the deference of the old electors to their betters was the only way in which our old system could be maintained. No doubt countries can be imagined in which the mass of the electors would be thoroughly competent to form good opinions; approximations to that state happily exist. But such was not the state of the minor English shopkeepers. They were just competent to make a selection between two sets of superior ideas; or rather—for the conceptions of such people are more personal than abstract—between two opposing parties, each professing a creed of such ideas. But they could do no more. Their own notions, if they had been cross-examined upon them, would have been found always most confused and often most foolish. They were competent to decide an issue selected by the higher classes, but they were incompetent to do more.

The grave question now is, How far will this peculiar old system continue and how far will it be altered? I am afraid I must put aside at once the idea that it will be altered entirely and altered for the better. I cannot expect that the new class of voters will be at all more able to form sound opinions on complex questions than the old voters. There was indeed an idea—a very prevalent idea when the first edition of this book was published—that there then was an unrepresented class of skilled artisans who could form superior opinions on national matters, and ought to have the means of expressing them. We used to frame elaborate schemes to give them such means. But the Reform Act of 1867 did not stop at skilled labour; it enfranchised unskilled labour too. And no one will contend that the ordinary working-man who has no special skill, and who is only rated because he has a house, can judge much of intellectual matters. The messenger in an office is not more intelligent than the clerks, not better educated but worse: and yet the messenger is probably a very superior specimen of the newly enfranchised classes. The average can only earn very scanty wages by coarse labour. They have no time to improve themselves, for they are labouring the whole day through; and their early education was so small that in most cases it is dubious whether, even if they had much time, they could use it to good purpose. We have not enfranchised a class less needing to be guided by their betters than the old class; on the contrary, the new class need it more than the old. The real question is, Will they submit to it, will they defer in the same way to wealth and rank, and to the higher qualities of which these are the rough symbols and the common accompaniments?

There is a peculiar difficulty in answering this question. Generally, the debates upon the passing of an Act contain much valuable instruction as to what may be expected of it. But the debates on the Reform Act of 1867 hardly tell anything. They are taken up with technicalities as to the ratepayers and the compound householder. Nobody in the country knew what was being done. I happened at the time to visit a purely agricultural and conservative county, and I asked the local Tories, 'Do you understand this Reform Bill? Do you know that your Conservative Government has brought in a Bill far more Radical than any former Bill, and that it is very likely to be passed?' The answer I got was, 'What stuff you talk! How can it be a Radical Reform Bill? Why *Bright* opposes it!' There was no answering that in a way which a 'common jury' could understand. The Bill was supported by *The Times* and opposed by Mr. Bright; and therefore the mass of the Conservatives and of common moderate people, without distinction of party, had no conception of the effect. They said it was 'London nonsense' if you tried to explain it to them. The nation indeed generally looks to the discussions in Parliament to enlighten it as to the effect of Bills. But in this case neither party, as a party, could speak out. Many, perhaps most of the intelligent Conservatives, were fearful of the consequences of the proposal; but as it was made by the heads of their own party, they did not like to oppose it, and the discipline of party carried them with it. On the other side, many, probably most of the intelligent Liberals, were in consternation at the Bill; they had been in the habit for years of proposing Reform Bills; they knew the points of difference between each Bill, and perceived that this was by far the most sweeping which had ever been proposed by any Ministry. But they were almost all unwilling to say so. They would have offended a large section in their constituencies if they had resisted a Tory Bill because it was too democratic; the extreme partisans of democracy would have said, 'The enemies of the people have confidence enough in the people to entrust them with this power, but you, a "Liberal", and a professed friend of the people, have not that confidence; if that is so, we will never vote for you again'. Many Radical members who had been asking for years for household suffrage were much more surprised than pleased at the near chance of obtaining it; they had asked for it as bargainers ask for the highest possible price, but they never expected to get it. Altogether the Liberals, or at least the extreme Liberals, were much like a man who has been pushing hard against an opposing door till, on a sudden, the door opens, the resistance ceases, and he is thrown violently forward. Persons in such an unpleasant predicament can scarcely criticize effectually, and certainly the Liberals did not so criticize. We have had no such previous discussions as should guide our expectations from the Reform Bill, nor such as under ordinary circumstances we should have had.

Nor does the experience of the last election much help us. The circumstances were too exceptional.

In the first place, Mr. Gladstone's personal popularity was such as has not been seen since the time of Mr. Pitt, and such as may never be seen again. Certainly it will very rarely be seen. A bad speaker is said to have been asked how he got on as a candidate. 'Oh,' he answered, 'when I do not know what to say, I say "Gladstone", and then they are sure to cheer, and I have time to think.' In fact, that popularity acted as a guide both to constituencies and to members. The candidates only said they would vote with Mr. Gladstone, and the constituencies only chose those who said so. Even the minority could only be described as anti-Gladstone, just as the majority could only be described as pro-Gladstone. The remains, too, of the old electoral organization were exceedingly powerful; the old voters voted as they had been told, and the new voters mostly voted with them. In extremely few cases was there any new and contrary organization. At the last election the trial of the new system hardly began, and, as far as it did begin, it was favoured by a peculiar guidance.

In the meantime our statesmen have the greatest opportunities they have had for many years, and likewise the greatest duty. They have to guide the new voters in the exercise of the franchise; to guide them quietly, and without saying what they are doing, but still to guide them. The leading statesmen in a free country have great momentary power. They settle the conversation of mankind. It is they who, by a great speech or two, determine what shall be said and what shall be written for long after. They, in conjunction with their counsellors, settle the programme of their party—the 'platform', as the Americans call it, on which they and those associated with them are to take their stand for the political campaign. It is by that programme, by

a comparison of the programmes of different statesmen, that the world forms its judgement. The
common ordinary mind is quite unfit to fix for itself
what political question it shall attend to; it is as
much as it can do to judge decently of the questions
which drift down to it, and are brought before it;
it almost never settles its topics; it can only decide
upon the issues of those topics. And in settling what
these questions shall be, statesmen have now especially a great responsibility. If they raise questions
which will excite the lower orders of mankind; if
they raise questions on which those orders are likely
to be wrong; if they raise questions on which the
interest of those orders is not identical with, or is
antagonistic to, the whole interest of the state, they
will have done the greatest harm they can do. The
future of this country depends on the happy working
of a delicate experiment, and they will have done all
they could to vitiate that experiment. Just when it
is desirable that ignorant men, new to politics,
should have good issues, and only good issues, put
before them, these statesmen will have suggested
bad issues. They will have suggested topics which
will bind the poor as a class together; topics which
will excite them against the rich; topics the discussion of which in the only form in which that
discussion reaches their ear will be to make them
think that some new law can make them comfortable
—that it is the present law which makes them uncomfortable—that Government has at its disposal
an inexhaustible fund out of which it can give to
those who now want without also creating elsewhere
other and greater wants. If the first work of the poor
voters is to try to create a 'poor man's paradise',
as poor men are apt to fancy that Paradise, and as
they are apt to think they can create it, the great
political trial now beginning will simply fail. The

wide gift of the elective franchise will be a great calamity to the whole nation, and to those who gain it as great a calamity as to any.

I do not of course mean that statesmen can choose with absolute freedom what topics they will deal with, and what they will not. I am, of course, aware that they choose under stringent conditions. In excited states of the public mind they have scarcely a discretion at all; the tendency of the public perturbation determines what shall and what shall not be dealt with. But, upon the other hand, in quiet times statesmen have great power; when there is no fire lighted they can settle what fire shall be lit. And as the new suffrage is happily to be tried in a quiet time, the responsibility of our statesmen is great because their power is great too.

And the mode in which the questions dealt with are discussed is almost as important as the selection of these questions. It is for our principal statesmen to lead the public, and not to let the public lead them. No doubt when statesmen live by public favour, as ours do, this is a hard saying, and it requires to be carefully limited. I do not mean that our statesmen should assume a pedantic and *doctrinaire* tone with the English people; if there is anything which English people thoroughly detest, it is that tone exactly. And they are right in detesting it; if a man cannot give guidance and communicate instruction formally without telling his audience 'I am better than you; I have studied this as you have not', then he is not fit for a guide or an instructor. A statesman who should show that *gaucherie* would exhibit a defect of imagination, and expose an incapacity for dealing with men which would be a great hindrance to him in his calling. But much argument is not required to guide the public, still less a formal exposition of that argument. What is mostly needed is the manly utterance of clear conclusions; if a statesman gives these in a felicitous way (and if with a few light and humorous illustrations, so much the better), he has done his part. He will have given the text, the scribes in the newspapers will write the sermon. A statesman ought to show his own nature, and talk in a palpable way what is to him important truth. And so he will both guide and benefit the nation. But if, especially at a time when great ignorance has an unusual power in public affairs, he chooses to accept and reiterate the decisions of that ignorance, he is only the hireling of the nation, and does little save hurt it.

I shall be told that this is very obvious, and that everybody knows that 2 and 2 make 4, and that there is no use in inculcating it. But I answer that the lesson is not observed in fact; people do not do their political sums so. Of all our political dangers, the greatest I conceive is that they will neglect the lesson. In plain English, what I fear is that both our political parties will bid for the support of the working-man; that both of them will promise to do as he likes if he will only tell them what it is; that, as he now holds the casting-vote in our affairs, both parties will beg and pray him to give that vote to them. I can conceive of nothing more corrupting or worse for a set of poor ignorant people than that two combinations of well-taught and rich men should constantly offer to defer to their decision, and compete for the office of executing it. *Vox populi* will be *Vox diaboli* if it is worked in that manner.

And, on the other hand, my imagination conjures up a contrary danger. I can conceive that questions *being* raised which, if continually agitated, would combine the working-men as a class together, the higher orders might have to consider whether they would concede the measure that would settle such questions, or whether they would risk the effect of the working-men's combination.

No doubt the question cannot be easily discussed in the abstract; much must depend on the nature of the measures in each particular case; on the evil they would cause if conceded; on the attractiveness of their idea to the working-classes if refused. But in all cases it must be remembered that a political combination of the lower classes, as such and for their own objects, is an evil of the first magnitude; that a permanent combination of them would make them (now that so many of them have the suffrage) supreme in the country; and that their supremacy, in the state they now are, means the supremacy of ignorance over instruction and of numbers over knowledge. So long as they are not taught to act together, there is a chance of this being averted, and it can only be averted by the greatest wisdom and the greatest foresight in the higher classes. They must avoid, not only every evil, but every appearance of evil; while they have still the power they must remove, not only every actual grievance, but, where it is possible, every seeming grievance too; they must willingly concede every claim which they can safely concede, in order that they may not have to concede unwillingly some claim which would impair the safety of the country.

This advice, too, will be said to be obvious; but I have the greatest fear that, when the time comes, it will be cast aside as timid and cowardly. So strong are the combative propensities of man, that he would rather fight a losing battle than not fight at all. It is most difficult to persuade people that by fighting they may strengthen the enemy, yet that would be so here; since a losing battle—especially a long and well-fought one—would have thoroughly taught the lower orders to combine, and would have left the higher orders face to face with an irritated, organized, and superior voting power. The courage which strengthens an enemy, and which so loses, not only the present battle, but many after battles, is a heavy curse to men and nations.

In one minor respect, indeed, I think we may see with distinctness the effect of the Reform Bill of 1867. I think it has completed one change which the Act of 1832 began; it has completed the change which that Act made in the relation of the House of Lords to the House of Commons. As I have endeavoured in this book to explain, the literary theory of the English Constitution is on this point quite wrong as usual. According to that theory, the two Houses are two branches of the Legislature, perfectly equal and perfectly distinct. But before the Act of 1832 they were not so distinct; there was a very large and a very strong common element. By their commanding influence in many boroughs and counties the Lords nominated a considerable part of the Commons; the majority of the other part were the richer gentry—men in most respects like the Lords, and sympathizing with the Lords. Under the Constitution as it then was the two Houses were not in their essence distinct; they were in their essence similar; they were, in the main, not Houses of contrasted origin, but Houses of like origin. The predominant part of both was taken from the same class —from the English gentry, titled and untitled. By the Act of 1832 this was much altered. The aristocracy and the gentry lost their predominance in the House of Commons; that predominance passed to the middle class. The two Houses then became distinct, but then they ceased to be co-equal. The Duke of Wellington, in a most remarkable paper, has explained what pains he took to induce the Lords to submit to their new position, and to submit, time after time, their will to the will of the Commons.

The Reform Act of 1867 has, I think, unmistakably completed the effect which the Act of 1832 began, but left unfinished. The middle-class element has gained greatly by the second change, and the aristocratic element has lost greatly. If you examine carefully the lists of members, especially of the most prominent members, of either side of the House, you will not find that they are in general aristocratic names. Considering the power and position of the titled aristocracy, you will perhaps be astonished at the small degree in which it contributes to the active part of our governing Assembly. The spirit of our present House of Commons is plutocratic, not aristocratic; its most prominent statesmen are not men of ancient descent or of great hereditary estate; they are men mostly of substantial means, but they are mostly, too, connected more or less closely with the new trading wealth. The spirit of the two Assemblies has become far more contrasted than it ever was.

The full effect of the Reform Act of 1832 was indeed postponed by the cause which I mentioned just now. The statesmen who worked the system which was put up had themselves been educated under the system which was pulled down. Strangely enough, their predominant guidance lasted as long as the system which they created. Lord Palmerston, Lord Russell, Lord Derby, died or else lost their influence within a year or two of 1867. The complete consequences of the Act of 1832 upon the House of Lords could not be seen while the Commons were subject to such aristocratic guidance. Much of the change which might have been expected from the Act of 1832 was held in suspense, and did not begin till that measure had been followed by another of similar and greater power.

The work which the Duke of Wellington in part performed has now, therefore, to be completed also He met the half difficulty; we have to surmount the whole one. We have to frame such tacit rules, to establish such ruling but unenacted customs, as will make the House of Lords yield to the Commons when and as often as our new Constitution requires that it should yield. I shall be asked, How often is that, and what is the test by which you know it?

I answer that the House of Lords must yield whenever the opinion of the Commons is also the opinion of the nation, and when it is clear that the nation has made up its mind. Whether or not the nation has made up its mind is a question to be decided by all the circumstances of the case, and in the common way in which all practical questions are decided. There are some people who lay down a sort of mechanical test: they say the House of Lords should be at liberty to reject a measure passed by the Commons once or more, and then if the Commons sent it up again and again, infer that the nation is determined. But no important practical question in real life can be uniformly settled by a fixed and formal rule in this way. This rule would prove that the Lords might have rejected the Reform Act of 1832. Whenever the nation was both excited and determined, such a rule would be an acute and dangerous political poison. It would teach the House of Lords that it might shut its eyes to all the facts of real life, and decide simply by an abstract formula. If in 1832 the Lords had so acted, there would have been a revolution. Undoubtedly there is a general truth in the rule. Whether a Bill has come up once only, or whether it has come up several times, is one important fact in judging whether the nation is determined to have that measure enacted; it is an indication, but it is only one of the indications. There are others equally decisive. The unanimous voice of the people may be so strong, and may be conveyed through so many organs, that it may be assumed to be lasting.

Englishmen are so very miscellaneous, that that which has *really* convinced a great and varied majority of them for the present may fairly be assumed to be likely to continue permanently to convince them. One sort might easily fall into a temporary and erroneous fanaticism, but all sorts simultaneously are very unlikely to do so.

I should venture so far as to lay down for an approximate rule, that the House of Lords ought, on a first-class subject, to be slow—very slow—in rejecting a Bill passed even once by a large majority of the House of Commons. I would not of course lay this down as an unvarying rule: as I have said, I have for practical purposes no belief in unvarying rules. Majorities may be either genuine or fictitious, and if they are not genuine, if they do not embody the opinion of the representative as well as the opinion of the constituency, no one would wish to have any attention paid to them. But if the opinion of the nation be strong and be universal, if it be really believed by members of Parliament, as well as by those who send them to Parliament, in my judgement the Lords should yield at once, and should not resist it.

My main reason is one which has not been much urged. As a theoretical writer I can venture to say, what no elected member of Parliament, Conservative or Liberal, can venture to say, that I am exceedingly afraid of the ignorant multitude of the new constituencies. I wish to have as great and as compact a power as possible to resist it. But a dis-

sension between the Lords and Commons divides
that resisting power; as I have explained, the House
of Commons still mainly represents the plutocracy,
the Lords represent the aristocracy. The main
interest of both these classes is now identical, which
is to prevent or to mitigate the rule of uneducated
members. But to prevent it effectually, they must
not quarrel among themselves; they must not bid
one against the other for the aid of their common
opponent. And this is precisely the effect of a
division between Lords and Commons. The two
great bodies of the educated rich go to the constituencies to decide between them, and the majority
of the constituencies now consist of the uneducated
poor. This cannot be for the advantage of any one.

In doing so besides the aristocracy forfeit their
natural position—that by which they would gain
most power, and in which they would do most good.
They ought to be the heads of the plutocracy. In
all countries new wealth is ready to worship old
wealth, if old wealth will only let it, and I need not
say that in England new wealth is eager in its worship. Satirist after satirist has told us how quick,
how willing, how anxious are the newly-made rich to
associate with the ancient rich. Rank probably in
no country whatever has so much 'market' value as
it has in England just now. Of course there have
been many countries in which certain old families,
whether rich or poor, were worshipped by whole
populations with a more intense and poetic homage;
but I doubt if there has ever been any in which all
old families and all titled families received more
ready observance from those who were their equals,
perhaps their superiors, in wealth, their equals in
culture, and their inferiors only in descent and rank.
The possessors of the 'material' distinctions of life,
as a political economist would class them, rush to

worship those who possess the *im*material distinctions. Nothing can be more politically useful than such homage, if it be skilfully used; no folly can be idler than to repel and reject it.

The worship is the more politically important because it is the worship of the political superior for the political inferior. At an election the non-titled are much more powerful than the titled. Certain individual peers have, from their great possessions, great electioneering influence, but, as a whole, the House of Peers is not a principal electioneering force. It has so many poor men inside it, and so many rich men outside it, that its electioneering value is impaired. Besides it is in the nature of the curious influence of rank to work much more on men singly than on men collectively; it is an influence which most men—at least most Englishmen—feel very much, but of which most Englishmen are somewhat ashamed. Accordingly, when any number of men are collected together, each of whom worships rank in his heart, the whole body will patiently hear—in many cases will cheer and approve—some rather strong speeches against rank. Each man is a little afraid that his 'sneaking kindness for a lord', as Mr. Gladstone put it, be found out; he is not sure how far that weakness is shared by those around him. And thus Englishmen easily find themselves committed to anti-aristocratic sentiments which are the direct opposite of their real feeling, and their collective action may be bitterly hostile to rank while the secret sentiment of each separately is especially favourable to rank. In 1832 the close boroughs, which were largely held by peers, and were still more largely supposed to be held by them, were swept away with a tumult of delight; and in another similar time of great excitement, the Lords themselves, if they deserve it, might pass away. The democratic passions gain by fomenting a diffused excitement, and by massing men in concourses; the aristocratic sentiments gain by calm and quiet, and act most on men by themselves, in their families, and when female influence is not absent. The overt electioneering power of the Lords does not at all equal its real social power. The English plutocracy, as is often said of something yet coarser, must be 'humoured not drove'; they may easily be impelled against the aristocracy, though they respect it very much; and as they are much stronger than the aristocracy, they might, if angered, even destroy it; though in order to destroy it, they must help to arouse a wild excitement among the ignorant poor, which, if once roused, may not be easily calmed, and which may be fatal to far more than its beginners intend.

This is the explanation of the anomaly which puzzles many clever Lords. They think, if they do not say, 'Why are we pinned up here? Why are we not in the Commons where we could have so much more power? Why is this nominal rank given us, at the price of substantial influence? If we prefer real weight to unreal prestige, why may we not have it?' The reply is, that the whole body of the Lords have an incalculably greater influence over society while there is still a House of Lords, than they would have if the House of Lords were abolished; and that though one or two clever young peers might do better in the Commons, the whole order of peers, young and old, clever and not clever, is much better where it is. The selfish instinct of the mass of peers on this point is a keener and more exact judge of the real world than the fine intelligence of one or two of them.

If the House of Peers ever goes, it will go in a storm, and the storm will not leave all else as it is.

It will not destroy the House of Peers and leave the rich young peers, with their wealth and their titles, to sit in the Commons. It would probably sweep all titles before it—at least all legal titles—and somehow or other it would break up the curious system by which the estates of great families all go to the eldest son. That system is a very artificial one; you may make a fine argument for it, but you cannot make a loud argument, an argument which would reach and rule the multitude. The thing looks like injustice, and in a time of popular passion it would not stand. Much short of the compulsory equal division of the Code Napoleon, stringent clauses might be provided to obstruct and prevent these great aggregations of property. Few things certainly are less likely than a violent tempest like this to destroy large and hereditary estates. But then, too, few things are less likely than an outbreak to destroy the House of Lords—my point is, that a catastrophe which levels one will not spare the other.

I conceive, therefore, that the great power of the House of Lords should be exercised very timidly and very cautiously. For the sake of keeping the headship of the plutocracy, and through that of the nation, they should not offend the plutocracy; the points upon which they have to yield are mostly very minor ones, and they should yield many great points rather than risk the bottom of their power. They should give large donations out of income, if by so doing they keep, as they would keep, their capital intact. The Duke of Wellington guided the House of Lords in this manner for years, and nothing could prosper better for them or for the country, and the Lords have only to go back to the good path in which he directed them.

The events of 1870 caused much discussion upon life peerages, and we have gained this great step, that whereas the former leader of the Tory Party in the Lords—Lord Lyndhurst—defeated the last proposal to make life peers, Lord Derby, when leader of that party, desired to create them. As I have given in this book what seemed to me good reasons for making them, I need not repeat those reasons here, I need only say how the notion stands in my judgement now.

I cannot look on life peerages in the way in which some of their strongest advocates regard them; I cannot think of them as a mode in which a permanent opposition or a contrast between the Houses of Lords and Commons is to be remedied. To be effectual in that way, life peerages must be very numerous. Now the House of Lords will never consent to a very numerous life peerage without a storm; they must be in terror to do it, or they will not do it. And if the storm blows strongly enough to do so much, in all likelihood it will blow strongly enough to do much more. If the revolution is powerful enough and eager enough to make an immense number of life peers, probably it will sweep away the hereditary principle in the Upper Chamber entirely. Of course one may fancy it to be otherwise; we may conceive of a political storm just going to a life peerage limit, and then stopping suddenly. But in politics we must not trouble ourselves with exceedingly exceptional accidents: it is quite difficult enough to count on and provide for the regular and plain probabilities. To speak mathematically, we may easily miss the permanent course of the political curve if we engross our minds with its cusps and conjugate points.

Nor, on the other hand, can I sympathize with the objection to life peerages which some of the Radical Party take and feel. They think it will strengthen the Lords, and so make them better able to oppose the Commons; they think, if they do not say, 'The House of Lords is our enemy and that of all Liberals; happily the mass of it is not intellectual; a few clever men are born there which we cannot help, but we will not "vaccinate" it with genius; we will not put in a set of clever men for their lives who may as likely as not turn against us'. This objection assumes that clever peers are just as likely to oppose the Commons as stupid peers. But this I deny. Most clever men who are in such a good place as the House of Lords plainly is, will be very unwilling to lose it if they can help it; at the clear call of a great duty they might lose it, but only at such a call. And it does not take a clever man to see that systematic opposition of the Commons is the only thing which can endanger the Lords, or which will make an individual peer cease to be a peer. The greater you make the *sense* of the Lords, the more they will see that their plain interest is to make friends of the plutocracy, and to be the chiefs of it, and not to wish to oppose the Commons where that plutocracy rules.

It is true that a completely new House of Lords, mainly composed of men of ability, selected because they were able, might very likely attempt to make ability the predominant power in the state, and to rival, if not conquer, the House of Commons, where the standard of intelligence is not much above the common English average. But in the present English world such a House of Lords would soon lose all influence. People would say, 'it was too clever by half', and in an Englishman's mouth that means a very severe censure. The English people would think it grossly anomalous if their elected assembly of rich men were thwarted by a nominated assembly of talkers and writers. Sensible men of substantial means are what we wish to be ruled by, and a peer-age of genius would not compare with it in power.

It is true, too, that at present some of the cleverest peers are not so ready as some others to agree with the Commons. But it is not unnatural that persons of high rank and of great ability should be unwilling to bend to persons of lower rank, and of certainly not greater ability. A few of such peers (for they are very few) might say, 'We had rather not have our peerage if we are to buy it at the price of yielding'. But a life peer who had fought his way up to the peers, would never think so. Young men who are born to rank may risk it, not middle-aged or old men who have earned their rank. A moderate number of life peers would almost always counsel moderation to the Lords, and would almost always be right in counselling it.

Recent discussions have also brought into curious prominence another part of the Constitution. I said in this book that it would very much surprise people if they were only told how many things the Queen could do without consulting Parliament, and it certainly has so proved, for when the Queen abolished Purchase in the Army by an act of prerogative (after the Lords had rejected the Bill for doing so), there was a great and general astonishment.

But this is nothing to what the Queen can by law do without consulting Parliament. Not to mention other things, she could disband the army (by law she cannot engage more than a certain number of men, but she is not obliged to engage any men); she could dismiss all the officers, from the General Commanding-in-Chief downwards; she could dismiss all the sailors too; she could sell off all our ships of war and all our naval stores; she could make a peace by the sacrifice of Cornwall, and begin a war for the conquest of Brittany. She could make every citizen in the United Kingdom, male or female, a peer; she could make every parish in the United

Kingdom a 'university'; she could dismiss most of the civil servants; she could pardon all offenders. In a word, the Queen could by prerogative upset all the action of civil government within the government, could disgrace the nation by a bad war or peace, and could, by disbanding our forces, whether land or sea, leave us defenceless against foreign nations. Why do we not fear that she would do this, or any approach to it?

Because there are two checks—one ancient and coarse, the other modern and delicate. The first is the check of impeachment. Any Minister who advised the Queen so to use her prerogative as to endanger the safety of the realm, might be impeached for high treason, and would be so. Such a Minister would, in our technical law, be said to have levied, or aided to levy, 'war against the Queen'. This counsel to her so to use her prerogative would by the Judge be declared to be an act of violence against herself, and in that peculiar but effectual way the offender could be condemned and executed. Against all gross excesses of the prerogative this is a sufficient protection. But it would be no protection against minor mistakes; any error of judgement committed bona fide, and only entailing consequences which one person might say were good, and another say were bad, could not be so punished. It would be possible to impeach any Minister who disbanded the Queen's army, and it would be done for certain. But suppose a Minister were to reduce the army or the navy much below the contemplated strength—suppose he were only to spend upon them one-third of the amount which Parliament had permitted him to spend—suppose a Minister of Lord Palmerston's principles were suddenly and while in office converted to the principles of Mr. Bright and Mr. Cobden, and were to act on those principles, he could not be impeached. The law of treason neither could nor ought to be enforced against an act which was an error of judgement, not of intention—which was in good faith intended not to impair the well-being of the State, but to promote and augment it. Against such misuses of the prerogative our remedy is a change of Ministry. And in general this works very well. Every Minister looks long before he incurs that penalty, and no one incurs it wantonly. But, nevertheless, there are two defects in it. The first is that it may not be a remedy at all; it may be only a punishment. A Minister may risk his dismissal; he may do some act difficult to undo, and then all which may be left will be to remove and censure him. And the second is that it is only one House of Parliament which has much to say to this remedy, such as it is: the House of Commons only can remove a Minister by a vote of censure. Most of the Ministries for thirty years have never possessed the confidence of the Lords, and in such cases a vote of censure by the Lords could therefore have but little weight; it would be simply the particular expression of a general political disapproval. It would be like a vote of censure on a Liberal Government by the Carlton, or on a Tory Government by the Reform Club. And in no case has an adverse vote by the Lords the same decisive effect as a vote of the Commons; the Lower House is the ruling and the choosing House, and if a Government really possesses that, it thoroughly possesses nine-tenths of what it requires. The support of the Lords is an aid and a luxury; that of the Commons is a strict and indispensable necessary.

These difficulties are particularly raised by questions of foreign policy. On most domestic subjects, either custom or legislation have limited the use of the prerogative. The mode of governing the country, according to the existing laws, is mostly worn into a rut, and most Administrations move in it because it is easier to move there than anywhere else. Most political crises—the decisive votes, which determine the fate of Government—are generally either on questions of foreign policy or of new laws; and the questions of foreign policy come out generally in this way, that the Government has already done something, and that it is for the one part of the Legislature alone—for the House of Commons, and not for the House of Lords—to say whether they have or have not forfeited their place by the treaty they have made.

I think every one must admit that this is not an arrangement which seems right on the face of it. Treaties are quite as important as most laws, and to require the elaborate assent of representative assemblies to every word of the law, and not to consult them even as to the essence of the treaty, is prima facie ludicrous. In the older forms of the English Constitution, this may have been quite right; the power was then really lodged in the Crown, and because Parliament met very seldom, and for other reasons, it was then necessary that, on a multitude of points, the Crown should have much more power than is amply sufficient for it at present. But now the real power is not in the Sovereign, it is in the Prime Minister and in the Cabinet—that is in the hands of a committee appointed by Parliament, and of the chairman of that committee. Now, beforehand, no one would have ventured to suggest that a committee of Parliament on Foreign relations should be able to commit the country to the greatest international obligations without consulting either Parliament or the country. No other select committee has any comparable power; and considering how carefully we have fettered and limited the powers of all other subordinate authorities, our allowing so much discretionary power on matters peculiarly dangerous and peculiarly delicate to rest in the sole charge of one secret committee is exceedingly strange. No doubt it may be beneficial; many seeming anomalies are so, but at first sight it does not look right.

I confess that I should see no advantage in it if our two Chambers were sufficiently homogeneous and sufficiently harmonious. On the contrary, if those two Chambers were as they ought to be, I should believe it to be a great defect. If the Administration had in both Houses a majority—not a mechanical majority ready to accept anything, but a fair and reasonable one, predisposed to think the Government right, but not ready to find it to be so in the face of facts and in opposition to whatever might occur; if a good Government were thus placed, I should think it decidedly better that the agreements of the Administration with foreign powers should be submitted to Parliament. They would then receive that which is best for all arrangements of business, an understanding and sympathizing criticism, but still a criticism. The majority of the Legislature being well disposed to the Government, would not 'find' against it except it had really committed some big and plain mistake. But if the Government had made such a mistake, certainly the majority of the Legislature would find against it. In a country fit for Parliamentary institutions, the partisanship of members of the Legislature never comes in manifest opposition to the plain interest of the nation; if it did, the nation being (as are all nations capable of Parliamentary institutions) constantly attentive to public affairs, would inflict on them the maximum Parliamentary penalty at the next election, and at many future elections. It would break their career. No English majority dare vote for an exceedingly bad treaty; it would rather desert its own leader than ensure its own ruin. And an English minority, inheriting a long experience of Parliamentary affairs, would not be exceedingly ready to reject a treaty made with a foreign Government. The leaders of an English Opposition are very conversant with the schoolboy maxim, 'Two can play at that fun'. They know that the next time they are in office the same sort of sharp practice may be used against them, and therefore they will not use it. So strong is this predisposition, that not long since a subordinate member of the Opposition declared that the 'front benches' of the two sides of the House—that is, the leaders of the Government and the leaders of the Opposition—were in constant tacit league to suppress the objections of independent members. And what he said is often quite true. There are often seeming objections which are not real objections, at least, which are, in the particular cases, outweighed by counter-considerations; and these 'independent members' having no real responsibility, not being likely to be hurt themselves if they make a mistake, are sure to blurt out, and to want to act upon. But the responsible heads of the party who may have to decide similar things, or even the same things, themselves will not permit it. They refuse, out of interest as well as out of patriotism, to engage the country in a permanent foreign scrape, to secure for themselves and their party a momentary home advantage. Accordingly, a Government which negotiated a treaty would feel that its treaty would be subject certainly to a scrutiny, but still to a candid and a lenient scrutiny; that it would go before judges, of whom the majority were favourable, and among whom the most influential part of the minority were in this case much opposed to excessive antagonism. And this seems to be the best position in which negotiators can be placed, namely, that they should be sure to have to account to considerate and fair persons, but not to have to account to inconsiderate and unfair ones.

At present the Government which negotiates a treaty can hardly be said to be accountable to any one. It is sure to be subjected to vague censure. Benjamin Franklin said, 'I have never known a peace made, even the most advantageous, that was not censured as inadequate, and the makers condemned as injudicious or corrupt. "Blessed are the peace-makers" is, I suppose, to be understood in the other world, for in this they are frequently cursed.' And this is very often the view taken now in England of treaties. There being nothing practical in the Opposition—nothing likely to hamper them hereafter, the leaders of Opposition are nearly sure to suggest every objection. The thing is done and cannot be undone, and the most natural wish of the Opposition leaders is to prove that if they had been in office, and it therefore had been theirs to do it, they could have done it much better. On the other hand, it is quite possible that there may be no real criticism on a treaty at all; or the treaty has been made by the Government, and as it cannot be unmade by any one, the Opposition may not think it worth while to say much about it. The Government, therefore, is never certain of any criticism; on the contrary, it has a good chance of escaping criticism; but if there be any criticism the Government must expect it to be bitter, sharp, and captious —made as an irresponsible objector would make it, and not as a responsible statesman, who may have to deal with a difficulty if he make it, and therefore will be cautious how he says anything which may make it.

This is what happens in common cases; and in

the uncommon—the ninety-ninth case in a hundred
—in which the Opposition hoped to turn out the
Government because of the alleged badness of the
treaty they have made, the criticism is sure to be of
the most undesirable character, and to say what is
most offensive to foreign nations. All the practised
acumen of anti-Government writers and speakers is
sure to be engaged in proving that England has been
imposed upon—that, as was said in one case, 'The
moral and the intellectual qualities have been divided;
that *our* negotiation had the moral, and the negotiation on the other side the intellectual', and so on.
The whole pitch of party malice is then expended,
because there is nothing to check the party in opposition. The treaty has been made, and though it
may be censured, and the party which made it
ousted, yet the difficulty it was meant to cure is
cured, and the opposing party, if it takes office, will
not have that difficulty to deal with.

In abstract theory these defects in our present
practice would seem exceedingly great, but in practice they are not so. English statesmen and English
parties have really a great patriotism, they can rarely
be persuaded even by their passions or their interest
to do anything contrary to the real interest of England, or anything which would lower England in the
eyes of foreign nations. And they would seriously
hurt themselves if they did. But still these are the
real tendencies of our present practice, and these are
only prevented by qualities in the nation and
qualities in our statesmen, which will just as much
exist if we change our practice.

It certainly would be in many ways advantageous
to change it. If we require that in some form the
assent of Parliament shall be given to such treaties,
we should have a real discussion prior to the making
of such treaties. We should have the reasons for the

treaty plainly stated, and also the reasons against it. At present, as we have seen, the discussion is unreal. The thing is done and cannot be altered; and what is said often ought not to be said because it is captious, and what is not said ought as often to be said because it is material. We should have a manlier and plainer way of dealing with foreign policy, if Ministers were obliged to explain clearly their foreign contracts before they were valid, just as they have to explain their domestic proposals before they can become laws.

The objections to this are, as far as I know, three, and three only.

1st. That it would not be always desirable for Ministers to state clearly the motives which induced them to agree to foreign compacts. 'Treaties', it is said, 'are in one great respect different from laws, they concern not only the Government which binds, the nation so bound, but a third party too—a foreign country—and the feelings of that country are to be considered as well as our own. And that foreign country will, probably, in the present state of the world be a despotic one, where discussion is not practised, where it is not understood, where the expressions of different speakers are not accurately weighed, where undue offence may easily be given.' This objection might be easily avoided by requiring that the discussion upon treaties in Parliament like that discussion in the American Senate should be 'in secret session', and that no report should be published of it. But I should, for my own part, be rather disposed to risk a public debate. Despotic nations now cannot understand England; it is to them an anomaly 'chartered by Providence'; they have been time out of mind puzzled by its institutions, vexed at its statesmen, and angry at its newspapers. A little more of such perplexity and such vexation does not seem to me a great evil. And if it be meant as it often is meant, that the whole truth as to treaties cannot be spoken out, I answer, that neither can the whole truth as to laws. All important laws affect large 'vested interests'; they touch great sources of political strength; and these great interests require to be treated as delicately, and with as nice a manipulation of language, as the feelings of any foreign country. A Parliamentary Minister is a man trained by elaborate practice not to blurt out crude things, and an English Parliament is an assembly which particularly dislikes anything *gauche* or anything imprudent. They would still more dislike it if it hurt themselves and the country as well as the speaker.

I am, too, disposed to deny entirely that there can be any treaty for which adequate reasons cannot be given to the English people, which the English people ought to make. A great deal of the reticence of diplomacy had, I think history shows, much better be spoken out. The worst families are those in which the members never really speak their minds to one another; they maintain an atmosphere of unreality, and every one always lives in an atmosphere of suppressed ill-feeling. It is the same with nations. The parties concerned would almost always be better for hearing the substantial reasons which induced the negotiators to make the treaty, and the negotiators would do their work much better, for half the ambiguities in treaties are caused by the negotiators not liking the fact or not taking the pains to put their own meaning distinctly before their own minds. And they would be obliged to make it plain if they had to defend it and argue on it before a great assembly.

Secondly, it may be objected to the change suggested that Parliament is not always sitting, and that if treaties required its assent, it might have to be sometimes summoned out of season, or the treaties would have to be delayed. And this is as far as it goes a just objection, but I do not imagine that it goes far. The great bulk of treaties could wait a little without harm, and in the very few cases when urgent haste is necessary, an Autumn session of Parliament could well be justified, for the occasion must be of grave and critical importance.

Thirdly, it may be said that if we required the consent of both Houses of Parliament to foreign treaties before they were valid we should much augment the power of the House of Lords. And this is also, I think, a just objection as far as it goes. The House of Lords, as it cannot turn out the Ministry for making treaties, has in no case a decisive weight in foreign policy, though its debates on them are often excellent; and there is a real danger at present in giving it such weight. They are not under the same guidance as the House of Commons. In the House of Commons, of necessity, the Ministry has a majority, and the majority will agree to the treaties the leaders have made if they fairly can. They will not be anxious to disagree with them. But the majority of the House of Lords may always be, and has lately been generally, an opposition majority, and therefore the treaty may be submitted to critics exactly pledged to opposite views. It might be like submitting the design of an architect known to hold 'medieval principles' to a committee wedded to 'classical principles'.

Still, upon the whole, I think the augmentation of the power of the Peers might be risked without real fear of serious harm. Our present practice, as has been explained, only works because of the good sense of those by whom it is worked, and the new practice would have to rely on a similar good sense and practicality too. The House of Lords must deal with the assent to treaties as they do with the assent to laws; they must defer to the voice of the country and the authority of the Commons even in cases where their own judgement might guide them otherwise. In very vital treaties probably, being Englishmen, they would be of the same mind as the rest of Englishmen. If in such cases they showed a reluctance to act as the people wished, they would have the same lesson taught them as on vital and exciting questions of domestic legislation, and the case is not so likely to happen, for on these internal and organic questions the interest and the feeling of the Peers is often presumably opposed to that of other classes—they may be anxious not to relinquish the very power which other classes are anxious to acquire; but in foreign policy there is no similar antagonism of interest—a peer and a non-peer have presumably in that matter the same interest and the same wishes.

Probably, if it were considered to be desirable to give to Parliament a more direct control over questions of foreign policy than it possesses now, the better way would be not to require a formal vote to the treaty clause by clause. This would entail too much time, and would lead to unnecessary changes in minor details. It would be enough to let the treaty be laid upon the table of both Houses, say for fourteen days, and to acquire validity unless objected to by one House or other before that interval had expired.

II

This is all which I think I need say on the domestic events which have changed, or suggested changes, in the English Constitution since this book was written. But there are also some foreign events which have illustrated it, and of these I should like to say a few words.

Naturally, the most striking of these illustrative changes comes from France. Since 1789 France has always been trying political experiments, from which others may profit much, though as yet she herself has profited little. She is now trying one singularly illustrative of the English Constitution. When the first edition of this book was published I had great difficulty in persuading many people that it was possible for a non-monarchical state, for the real chief of the practical Executive—the Premier as we should call him—to be nominated and to be removable by the vote of the National Assembly. The United States and its copies were the only present and familiar republics, and in these the system was exactly opposite. The Executive was there appointed by the people as the Legislative was too. No conspicuous example of any other sort of Republic then existed. But now France has given an example—M. Thiers is (with one exception) just the *chef du pouvoir exécutif* that I endeavoured more than once in this book to describe. He is appointed by and is removable by the Assembly. He comes down and speaks in it just as our Premier does; he is responsible for managing it just as our Premier is. No one can any longer doubt the possibility of a republic in which the Executive and the Legislative authorities were united and fixed; no one can assert such union to be the incommunicable attribute of a Constitutional Monarchy.

But, unfortunately, we can as yet only infer from this experiment that such a constitution is possible; we cannot as yet say whether it will be bad or good. The circumstances are very peculiar, and that in three ways. First, the trial of a specially Parliamentary Republic, of a Republic where Parliament appoints the Minister, is made in a nation which has, to say the least of it, no peculiar aptitude for Parliamentary Government; which has possibly a peculiar inaptitude for it. In the last but one of these essays I have tried to describe one of the mental conditions of Parliamentary Government, which I call 'rationality', by which I do not mean reasoning power, but rather the power of hearing the reasons of others, of comparing them quietly with one's own reasons, and then being guided by the result. But a French Assembly is not easy to reason with. Every Assembly is divided into parties and into sections of parties, and in France each party, almost every section of a party, begins not to clamour but to scream, and to scream as only Frenchmen can, as soon as it hears anything which it particularly dislikes. With an Assembly in this temper, real discussion is impossible, and Parliamentary Government is impossible too, because the Parliament can neither choose men nor measures. The French Assemblies under the Restored Monarchy seem to have been quieter, probably because being elected from a limited constituency they did not contain so many sections of opinion; they had fewer irritants and fewer species of irritability. But the Assemblies of the '48 Republic were disorderly in the extreme. I saw the last myself, and can certify that steady discussion upon a critical point was not possible in it. There was not an audience willing to hear. The Assembly now sitting at Versailles is undoubtedly also, at times, most tumultuous, and a Parliamentary Government in which it governs must be under a peculiar difficulty because as a sovereign it is unstable, capricious, and unruly.

The difficulty is the greater because there is no check, or little, from the French nation upon the Assembly The French, as a nation, do not care for or appreciate Parliamentary Government. I have endeavoured to explain how difficult it is for inexperienced mankind to take to such a government; how much more natural, that is, how much more easy, to uneducated men is loyalty to a monarch. A nation which does not expect good from a Parliament cannot check or punish a Parliament. France expects, I fear, too little from her Parliaments ever to get what she ought. Now that the suffrage is universal, the average intellect and the average culture of the constituent bodies are excessively low; and even such mind and culture as there is has long been enslaved to authority: the French peasant cares more for standing well with his present *préfet* than for anything else whatever; he is far too ignorant to check and watch his Parliament and far too timid to think of doing either, if the executive authority nearest to him did not like it. The experiment of a strictly Parliamentary Republic—of a Republic where the Parliament appoints the Executive—is being tried in France at an extreme disadvantage, because in France a Parliament is unusually likely to be bad, and unusually likely also to be free enough to show its badness.

Secondly, the present polity of France is not a copy of the whole effective part of the British Constitution, but only of a part of it. By our Constitution nominally the Queen, but really the Prime Minister, has the power of dissolving the Assembly. But M. Thiers has no such power; and therefore, under ordinary circumstances, I believe, the policy would soon become unmanageable. The result would be, as I have tried to explain, that the Assembly would be always changing its Ministry, that having no reason to fear the penalty which that change so often brings in England, they would be ready to make it once a month. Caprice is the characteristic vice of miscellaneous Assemblies, and without some check their selection would be unceasingly mutable. This peculiar danger of the present Constitution of France has, however, been prevented by its peculiar circumstances. The Assembly have not been inclined to remove M. Thiers, because in their lamentable present position they could not replace M. Thiers. He has a monopoly of the necessary reputation. It is the Empire—the Empire which he always opposed—that has done him this kindness. For twenty years no great political reputation could arise in France. The Emperor governed, and no one member could show a capacity for government. M. Rouher, though of vast real ability, was in the popular idea only the Emperor's agent; and even had it been otherwise, M. Rouher, the one great man of Imperialism, could not have been selected as a head of the Government, at a moment of the greatest reaction against the Empire. Of the chiefs before the twenty years' silence, of the eminent men known to be able to handle Parliaments and to govern Parliaments, M. Thiers was the only one still physically able to begin again to do so. The miracle is, that at seventy-four even he should still be able. As no other great chief of the Parliament régime existed, M. Thiers is not only the best choice, but the only choice. If he were taken away, it would be most difficult to make any other choice, and that difficulty keeps him where he is. At every crisis the Assembly feels that after M. Thiers 'the deluge', and he lives upon that feeling. A change of the President, though legally simple, is in practice all but impossible; because all know that such a change might be a change, not only of the President, but of much more too: that very probably it might be a change of the polity—that it might bring in a Monarchy or an Empire.

Lastly, by a natural consequence of the position, M. Thiers does not govern as a Parliamentary Premier governs. He is not, he boasts that he is not, the head of a party. On the contrary, being the one person essential to all parties, he selects Ministers from all parties, he constructs a cabinet in which no one Minister agrees with any other in anything, and with all the members of which he himself frequently disagrees. The selection is quite in his hand. Ordinarily a Parliamentary Premier cannot choose; he is brought in by a party, he is maintained in office by a party; and that party requires that as they aid him, he shall aid them; that as they give him the very best thing in the State, he shall give them the next best things. But M. Thiers is under no such restriction. He can choose as he likes, and does choose. Neither in the selection of his Cabinet nor in the management of the Chamber, is M. Thiers guided as a similar person in common circumstances would have to be guided. He is the exception of a moment; he is not the example of a lasting condition.

For these reasons, though we may use the present Constitution of France as a useful aid to our imaginations, in conceiving of a purely Parliamentary republic, of a monarchy *minus* the monarch, we must not think of it as much more. It is too singular in its nature and too peculiar in its accidents to be a guide to anything except itself.

In this essay I have made many remarks on the American constitution, in comparison with the English; and as to the American constitution we have had a whole world of experience since I first wrote. My great object was to contrast the office of President as an executive officer and to compare it with that of a Prime Minister; and I devoted much space to showing that in one principal respect the

English system is by far the best. The English Premier being appointed by the selection, and being removable at the pleasure, of the preponderant Legislative Assembly, is sure to be able to rely on that assembly. If he wants legislation to aid his policy he can obtain that legislation; he can carry out that policy. But the American President has no similar security. He is elected in one way, at one time, and Congress (no matter which House) is elected in another way, at another time. The two have nothing to bind them together, and in matter of fact, they continually disagree.

This was written in the time of Mr. Lincoln, when Congress, the President, and all the North were united as one man in the war against the South. There was then no patent instance of mere disunion. But between the time when the essays were first written in the 'Fortnightly', and their subsequent junction into a book, Mr. Lincoln was assassinated, and Mr. Johnson, the Vice-President, became President, and so continued for nearly four years. At such a time the characteristic evils of the Presidential system were shown most conspicuously. The President and the Assembly, so far from being (as it is essential to good government that they should be) on terms of close union, were not on terms of common courtesy. So far from being capable of a continuous and concerted co-operation they were all the while trying to thwart one another. He had one plan for the pacification of the South and they another: they would have nothing to say to his plans, and he vetoed their plans as long as the Constitution permitted, and when they were, in spite of him, carried, he, as far as he could (and this was very much), embarrassed them in action. The quarrel in most countries would have gone beyond the law, and come to blows; even in America, the most law-loving of countries, it went as far as possible within the law. Mr. Johnson described the most popular branch of the legislature—the House of Representatives—as a body 'hanging on the verge of government'; and that House impeached him criminally, in the hope that in that way they might get rid of him civilly. Nothing could be so conclusive against the American Constitution, as a Constitution, as that incident. A hostile legislature and a hostile executive were so tied together, that the legislature tried, and tried in vain, to rid itself of the executive by accusing it of illegal practices. The legislature was so afraid of the President's legal power, that it unfairly accused him of acting beyond the law. And the blame thus cast on the American Constitution is so much praise to be given to the American political character. Few nations, perhaps scarcely any nation, could have borne such a trial so easily and so perfectly.

This was the most striking instance of disunion between the President and the Congress that has ever yet occurred, and which probably will ever occur. Probably for very many years the United States will have great and painful reason to remember, that at the moment of all their history, when it was most important to them to collect and concentrate all the strength and wisdom of their policy on the pacification of the South, that policy was divided by a strife in the last degree unseemly and degrading. But it will be for a competent historian hereafter to trace out this accurately and in detail; the time is yet too recent, and I cannot pretend that I know enough to do so. I cannot venture myself to draw the full lessons from these events; I can only predict that when they are drawn, those lessons will be most important and most interesting.

There is, however, one series of events which have

happened in America since the beginning of the civil war, and since the first publication of these essays, on which I should wish to say something in detail— I mean the financial events. These lie within the scope of my peculiar studies, and it is comparatively easy to judge of them, since whatever may be the case with refined statistical reasoning, the great results of money matters speak to and interest all mankind. And every incident in this part of American financial history exemplifies the contrast between a Parliamentary and a Presidential Government.

The distinguishing quality of Parliamentary Government is, that in each stage of a public transaction there is a discussion; that the public assist at this discussion; that it can, through Parliament, turn out an administration which is not doing as it likes, and can put in an administration which will do as it likes. But the characteristic of a Presidential Government is, in a multitude of cases, that there is no such discussion; that when there is a discussion the fate of Government does not turn upon it, and, therefore, the people do not attend to it; that upon the whole the administration itself is pretty much doing as it likes, and neglecting as it likes, subject always to the check that it must not too much offend the mass of the nation. The nation commonly does not attend, but if by gigantic blunders you make it attend, it will remember it and turn you out when its time comes; it will show you that your power is short, and so on the instant weaken that power; it will make your present life in office unbearable and uncomfortable by the hundred modes in which a free people can, without ceasing, act upon the rulers which it elected yesterday, and will have to reject or re-elect to-morrow.

In finance the most striking effect in America has, on the first view of it, certainly been good. It has enabled the Government to obtain and to keep a vast surplus of revenue over expenditure. Even before the civil war it did this—from 1837 to 1857. Mr. Wells tells us that, strange as it may seem, 'There was not a single year in which the unexpended balance in the National Treasury—derived from various sources—at the end of the year, was not in excess of the total expenditure of the preceding year; while in not a few years the unexpended balance was absolutely greater than the sum of the entire expenditure of the twelve months preceding'. But this history before the war is nothing to what has happened since. The following are the surpluses of revenue over expenditure since the end of the civil war:

Year ending June 30.				Surplus. £
1866	.	.	.	5,593,000
1867	.	.	.	21,586,000
1868	.	.	.	4,242,000
1869	.	.	.	7,418,000
1870	.	.	.	18,627,000
1871	.	.	.	16,712,000

No one who knows anything of the working of Parliamentary Government will for a moment imagine that any Parliament would have allowed any executive to keep a surplus of this magnitude. In England, after the French war, the Government of that day, which had brought it to a happy end, which had the glory of Waterloo, which was in consequence exceedingly strong, which had besides elements of strength from close boroughs and Treasury influence such as certainly no Government has ever had since, and such perhaps as no Government ever had before—that Government proposed to keep a moderate surplus and to apply it to the reduction of the debt, but even this the English Parliament would not endure. The administration with all its power derived both from good and evil had to yield; the income tax was abolished, with it went the surplus, and with the surplus all chance of any considerable reduction of the debt for that time. In truth, taxation is so painful that in a sensitive community which has strong organs of expression and action, the maintenance of a great surplus is excessively difficult. The opposition will always say that it is unnecessary, is uncalled for, is injudicious; the cry will be echoed in every constituency; there will be a series of large meetings in the great cities; even in the smaller constituencies there will mostly be smaller meetings; every member of Parliament will be pressed upon by those who elect him; upon this point there will be no distinction between town and country, the country gentleman and the farmer disliking high taxes as much as any in the towns. To maintain a great surplus by heavy taxes to pay off debt has never yet in this country been possible, and to maintain a surplus of the American magnitude would be plainly impossible.

Some part of the difference between England and America arises undoubtedly not from political causes but from economical. America is not a country sensitive to taxes; no great country has perhaps ever been so unsensitive in this respect; certainly she is far less sensitive than England. In reality America is too rich, daily industry there is too common, too skilful, and too productive, for her to care much for fiscal burdens. She is applying all the resources of science and skill and trained labour, which have been in long ages painfully acquired in old countries, to develop with great speed the richest soil and the richest mines of new countries; and the result is untold wealth. Even under a Parliamentary Govern-

ment such a community could and would bear
taxation much more easily than Englishmen ever
would.

But difference of physical character in this respect
is of little moment in comparison with difference of
political constitution. If America was under a Parliamentary Government, she would soon be convinced that in maintaining this great surplus and in
paying this high taxation she would be doing herself
great harm. She is not performing a great duty, but
perpetrating a great injustice. She is injuring posterity by crippling and displacing industry, far more
than she is aiding it by reducing the taxes it will have
to pay. In the first place, the maintenance of the
present high taxation compels the retention of many
taxes which are contrary to the maxims of free
trade. Enormous customs duties are necessary, and
it would be all but impossible to impose equal excise
duties even if the Americans desired it. In consequence, besides what the Americans pay to the
Government, they are paying a great deal to some
of their own citizens, and so are rearing a set of
industries which never ought to have existed, which
are bad speculations at present because other industries would have paid better, and which may cause
a great loss out of pocket hereafter when the debt
is paid off and the fostering tax withdrawn. Then
probably industry will return to its natural channel,
the artificial trade will be first depressed, then discon-
tinued, and the fixed capital employed in the trade
will all be depreciated and much of it be worthless.
Secondly, all taxes on trade and manufacture are
injurious in various ways to them. You cannot put
on a great series of such duties without cramping
trade in a hundred ways and without diminishing
their productiveness exceedingly. America is now
working in heavy fetters, and it would probably be

better for her to lighten those fetters even though a generation or two should have to pay rather higher taxes. Those generations would really benefit, because they would be so much richer that the slightly increased cost of government would never be perceived. At any rate, under a Parliamentary Government this doctrine would have been incessantly inculcated; a whole party would have made it their business to preach it, would have made incessant small motions in Parliament about it, which is the way to popularize their view. And in the end I do not doubt that they would have prevailed. They would have had to teach a lesson both pleasant and true, and such lessons are soon learned. On the whole, therefore, the result of the comparison is that a Presidential Government makes it much easier than the Parliamentary to maintain a great surplus of income over expenditure, but that it does not give the same facility for examining whether it is good or not good to maintain a surplus, and, therefore, that it works blindly, maintaining surpluses when they do extreme harm just as much as when they are very beneficial.

In this point the contrast of Presidential with Parliamentary Government is mixed; one of the defects of Parliamentary Government probably is the difficulty under it of maintaining a surplus revenue to discharge debt, and this defect Presidential Government escapes, though at the cost of being likely to maintain that surplus upon inexpedient occasions as well as upon expedient. But in all other respects a Parliamentary Government has in finance an unmixed advantage over the Presidential in the incessant discussion. Though in one single case it produces evil as well as good, in most cases it produces good only. And three of these cases are illustrated by recent American experience.

First, as Mr. Goldwin Smith—no unfavourable judge of anything American—justly said some years since, the capital error made by the United States Government was the 'Legal Tender Act', as it is called, by which it made inconvertible paper notes issued by the Treasury the sole circulating medium of the country. The temptation to do this was very great, because it gave at once a great war fund when it was needed, and with no pain to any one. If the notes of a Government supersede the metallic currency medium of a country to the extent of $80,000,000, this is equivalent to a recent loan of $80,000,000 to the Government for all purposes within the country. Whenever the precious metals are not required, and for domestic purposes in such a case they are not required, notes will buy what the Government want, and it can buy to the extent of its issue. But, like all easy expedients out of a great difficulty, it is accompanied by the greatest evils; if it had not been so, it would have been the regular device in such cases, and the difficulty would have been no difficulty at all; there would have been a known easy way out of it. As is well known, inconvertible paper issued by Government is sure to be issued in great quantities, as the American currency soon was; it is sure to be depreciated as against coin; it is sure to disturb values and to derange markets; it is certain to defraud the lender; it is certain to give the borrower more than he ought to have. In the case of America there was a further evil. Being a new country, she ought in her times of financial want to borrow of old countries; but the old countries were frightened by the probable issue of unlimited inconvertible paper, and they would not lend a shilling. Much more than the mercantile credit of America was thus lost. The great commercial houses in England are the most natural and most effectual conveyers of intelligence from other countries to Europe. If they had been financially interested in giving in a sound report as to the progress of the war, a sound report we should have had. But as the Northern States raised no loans in Lombard Street (and could raise none because of their vicious paper-money), Lombard Street did not care about them, and England was very imperfectly informed of the progress of the civil struggle, and on the whole matter, which was then new and very complex, England had to judge without having her usual materials for judgement, and (since the guidance of the 'city' on political matters is very quietly and imperceptibly given) without knowing she had not those materials.

Of course, this error might have been committed, and perhaps would have been committed, under a Parliamentary Government. But if it had, its effects would ere long have been thoroughly searched into and effectually frustrated. The whole force of the greatest inquiring machine and the greatest discussing machine which the world has ever known would have been directed to this subject. In a year or two the American public would have had it forced upon them in every form till they must have comprehended it. But under the Presidential form of Government, and owing to the inferior power of generating discussion, the information given to the American people has been imperfect in the extreme. And in consequence, after nearly ten years of painful experience they do not now understand how much they have suffered from their inconvertible currency.

But the mode in which the Presidential Government of America managed its taxation during the Civil War is even a more striking example of its defects. Mr. Wells tells us:

'In the outset all direct or internal taxation was

avoided, there having been apparently an apprehension on the part of Congress, that inasmuch as
the people had never been accustomed to it, and as
all machinery for assessment and collection was
wholly wanting, its adoption would create discontent, and thereby interfere with a vigorous prose-
cution of hostilities. Congress, therefore, confined
itself at first to the enactment of measures looking
to an increase of revenue from the increase of
indirect taxes upon imports; and it was not until
four months after the actual outbreak of hostilities
that a direct tax of $20,000,000 per annum was
apportioned among the States, and an income tax
of 3 per cent. on the excess of all incomes over $800
was provided for; the first being made to take effect
practically eight, and the second ten, months after
date of enactment. Such laws, of course, took effect
and became immediately operative in the loyal
States only, and produced but comparatively little
revenue; and although the range of taxation was
soon extended, the whole receipts from all sources
by the Government for the second year of the war,
from excise, income, stamp, and all other internal
taxes, were less than $42,000,000; and that, too,
at a time when the expenditures were in excess
$60,000,000 per month, or at the rate of over
$700,000,000 per annum. And as showing how
novel was this whole subject of direct and internal
taxation to the people, and how completely the
government officials were lacking in all experience in
respect to it, the following incident may be noted.
The Secretary of the Treasury, in his report for
1863, stated that, with a view of determining his
resources, he employed a very competent person,
with the aid of practical men, to estimate the probable amount of revenue to be derived from each
department of internal taxation for the previous

year. The estimate arrived at was $85,000,000, but the actual receipts were only $37,000,000.'

Now, no doubt, this might have happened under a Parliamentary Government. But, then, many members of Parliament, the entire opposition in Parliament, would have been active to unravel the matter. All the principles of finance would have been worked and propounded. The light would have come from above, not from below—it would have come from Parliament to the nation instead of from the nation to Parliament. But exactly the reverse happened in America. Mr. Wells goes on to say:

'The people of the loyal States were, however, more determined and in earnest in respect to this matter of taxation than were their rulers; and before long the popular discontent at the existing state of things was openly manifest. Everywhere the opinion was expressed that taxation in all possible forms should immediately, and to the largest extent, be made effective and imperative; and Congress spurred up, and rightfully relying on public sentiment to sustain their action, at last took up the matter resolutely and in earnest, and devised and inaugurated a system of internal and direct taxation, which for its universality and peculiarities has probably no parallel in anything which has heretofore been recorded in civil history, or is likely to be experienced hereafter. The one necessity of the situation was revenue, and to obtain it speedily and in large amounts through taxation the only principle recognized—if it can be called a principle—was akin to that recommended to the traditional Irishman on his visit to Donnybrook Fair, "Wherever you see a head, hit it". Wherever you find an article, a product, a trade, a profession, or a source of income, tax it! And so an edict went forth to this effect, and the people cheerfully submitted. Incomes under $5,000 were taxed 5 per cent., with an exemption of $600 and house rent actually paid; these exemptions being allowed on this ground, that they represented an amount sufficient at the time to enable a small family to procure the bare necessaries of life, and thus take out from the operation of the law all those who were dependent upon each day's earnings to supply each day's needs. Incomes in excess of $5,000 and not in excess of $10,000 were taxed 2½ per cent. in addition; and incomes over $10,000 5 per cent. additional, without any abeyance or exemptions whatever.'

Now this is all contrary to and worse than what would have happened under a Parliamentary Government. The delay to tax would not have occurred under it: the movement by the country to get taxation would never have been necessary under it. The excessive taxation accordingly imposed would not have been permitted under it. The last point I think I need not labour at length. The evils of a bad tax are quite sure to be pressed upon the ears of Parliament in season and out of season: the few persons who have to pay it are thoroughly certain to make themselves heard. The sort of taxation tried in America, that of taxing everything, and seeing what everything would yield, could not have been tried under a Government delicately and quickly sensitive to public opinion.

I do not apologize for dwelling at length upon these points, for the subject is one of transcendent importance. The practical choice of first-rate nations is between the Presidential Government and the Parliamentary; no State can be first-rate which has not a Government by discussion, and those are the only two existing species of that Government. It is between them that a nation which has to choose

its Government must choose. And nothing therefore can be more important than to compare the
two, and to decide upon the testimony of experience,
and by facts, which of them is the better.

THE POPLARS, WIMBLEDON:
    June 20, 1872.

REPRINTED LITHOGRAPHICALLY IN GREAT BRITAIN
AT THE UNIVERSITY PRESS, OXFORD
BY VIVIAN RIDLER
PRINTER TO THE UNIVERSITY